THE GESTAPO

THE GESTAPO

THE MYTH AND REALITY
OF HITLER'S SECRET POLICE

FRANK MCDONOUGH

Skyhorse Publishing

First published in Great Britain in 2015 by Coronet

Published in the United States by Skyhorse Publishing in 2017

Skyhorse Publishing books may be purchased in bulk at special discounts for sales promotion, corporate gifts, fund-raising, or educational purposes. Special editions can also be created to specifications. For details, contact the Special Sales Department, Skyhorse Publishing, 307 West 36th Street, 11th Floor, New York, NY 10018 or info@skyhorsepublishing.com.

Skyhorse® and Skyhorse Publishing® are registered trademarks of Skyhorse Publishing, Inc.®, a Delaware corporation.

Visit our website at www.skyhorsepublishing.com.

10 9 8 7 6 5 4 3 2 1

Library of Congress Cataloging-in-Publication Data is available on file.

Cover design by Rain Saukas

Print ISBN: 978-1-5107-1465-6
Ebook ISBN: 978-1-5107-1467-0

Printed in the United States of America

For Emily — with love

Contents

Introduction

Paul Schneider was an open-minded Protestant Evangelical preacher. He was born on 29 August 1897 in the small rural Rhineland town of Pferdsfeld. In a sermon on 8 October 1933 he criticised Ernst Röhm, the leader of the Nazi storm troopers, for thinking a Nazi revolution could be achieved without an 'inner spiritual renewal' of the people. His comments were reported to local church authorities. The bishop of the Rhineland area, a member of the pro-Nazi 'German Christian' movement, warned Paul to stop uttering such critical comments against leading Nazis from the pulpit. In a letter to his parents, Schneider wrote: 'For all of my Christian duty of obedience, I do not think that the Evangelical Church will avoid coming into conflict with the National Socialist state.' By February 1934, Paul was judged as 'politically unreliable' by the Protestant church hierarchy. To further constrain him, he was transferred to the role of pastor for two remote rural villages: Dickenschied and Womrath, which had a combined population of fewer than a thousand people. On 11 June 1934, Paul Schneider challenged the local Nazi Party once again. This time he protested against a Nazi storm trooper who said, during a burial service for a deceased Hitler Youth member, that the Nazi martyr Horst Wessel had 'heavenly followers'. Paul's critical response was reported to the Gestapo, and he was placed in 'protective custody' in a local prison. Local parishioners signed a petition pleading for his release. He was freed. During the winter of 1935–1936, Schneider was reported to the Gestapo on no less than twelve different occasions for making anti-Nazi comments. In 1937, the Gestapo banned him from living or even preaching throughout the entire Rhineland area. In open defiance of this 'internal exile' order, Paul returned to his local parish and carried on preaching. On 3 October 1937, he gave yet another critical sermon. This was monitored by a local Gestapo officer. Schneider was arrested and sent to Koblenz prison. On 27 November 1938, he was transferred to the notorious Buchenwald concentration camp. He was placed in solitary confinement. He often loudly recited words from the Bible at the window of his cell in the evenings. Leonhard Steinwender, a Catholic priest, and fellow internee, described Paul as 'an heroic figure to whom the whole camp looked up in respect and admiration. No torture could keep him from appealing again and again to the conscience of the SS guards and the camp commandant.' Paul suffered horrendous maltreatment from SS guards for speaking his mind. Alfred Leikam recalls: 'Schneider was exposed alternatively to severe bodily tortures, humiliations and agonies, and heavy beatings.' Even Karl–Otto Koch, the brutal camp commandant at Buchenwald, realised he could not break the spirit of Paul Schneider. He decided to release him on condition he signed a declaration promising never to return to his local parish or preach again. He refused to sign it. On 18 July 1939, Paul Schneider was killed in the Buchenwald camp infirmary by five lethal injections of the drug strophanthin. His coffin could not be opened or viewed by his heartbroken widow and his six children because his corpse was in such a terrible condition. At his funeral service in Dickenschied, 200 ministers of the local Protestant Confessional Church turned out, in the company of a huge crowd of local parishioners, to pay their respects to this extraordinarily brave individual. Paul Schneider was the first Protestant Evangelical preacher killed for defying the Nazi regime on religious grounds.[1]

This new book examines the vivid and disturbing stories of individuals who were arrested by the Gestapo. It does not attempt to provide a full-blown comprehensive account of the administrative history of the Gestapo, but it does set out to combine a general explanation, underpinned by a considerable number of existing studies, and a fresh interpretation, supported by original sources from German archives, of how the Gestapo operated between 1933 and 1945. It is focused exclusively on what happened inside Germany (*Altreich*) in the Nazi era and not on the territories occupied by Hitler's regime during the Second World War. The central aim of this book is to explore the impact of the Gestapo on German citizens who lived under Hitler's rule. It begins with a detailed examination of how the Gestapo came into being. It then looks at the background and methods of Gestapo officers, providing some very surprising new information. It moves on to explore the key victims of Nazi terror, most notably, religious dissidents, communists, social outsiders, and Jews. It is in these chapters that the tragic human plight of victims takes centre stage. The extent to which the Gestapo was assisted by the public, by the criminal detective police (Kripo), and by the social and welfare agencies is also highlighted. There is also a detailed concluding chapter that explains the fate of Gestapo officers at subsequent post-war trials. Overall, this book provides a very important contribution to the understanding of terror in Nazi society.

In the immediate post-1945 period, historians viewed Nazi Germany as an all-powerful totalitarian dictatorship. During this period, numerous studies appeared. Most were written by historians outside Germany. Hannah Arendt, in her deeply influential book *The Origins of Totalitarianism*, suggested that all totalitarian regimes rely on a secret police to instil fear into the mind of every citizen and to ferociously repress all signs of discontent. She also argued that the key task of all totalitarian secret police forces was not to discover crimes, but to arrest people categorised as 'enemies of the state'. She highlighted that the role of the population was crucial in denouncing opponents.[2] Within this totalitarian framework of analysis, Adolf Hitler was portrayed as the all-powerful 'Master of the Third Reich'. German people were supposedly brainwashed by Nazi propaganda.[3] It was taken for granted that the Gestapo was a huge organisation, with agents everywhere. TV documentaries, novels and films have reinforced this popular view.[4] In reality, any person who accepted and supported the Nazi regime enjoyed enormous individual freedom. Hitler's regime was hugely popular. Once you appreciate this essential fact, you begin to understand the reality of life inside Nazi Germany.

The Gestapo (*Geheime Staatspolizei*) or Secret State Police was the key element in the Nazi terror system, but it must be understood that it began as a police department. It was created in 1933 to deal with the opponents of Hitler's regime. Even today the term Gestapo conjures up feelings of fear and horror. Yet the first general history of the Gestapo by the French historian Jacques Delarue did not appear until 1962.[5] It relied exclusively on the published evidence of the Nuremberg war trials of the late 1940s and placed key Gestapo leaders – Hermann Göring, Heinrich Himmler and Reinhard Heydrich – at the centre of its analysis. Delarue attempted to explain how the Gestapo operated not only in Germany, but throughout Nazi-occupied Europe.[6] It offered by then a familiar portrayal of the Gestapo, as the omnipotent focal point of brutal Nazi terror, and argued that all the German people were under constant surveillance.[7]

This nightmare image of Nazi Germany only began to change during the 1970s as German historians began to look at the Nazi era in more depth, using newly opened German archives. The emphasis shifted away from the traditional 'history from above' (intentionalist) Hitlocentric approach, towards a new 'history from below' (structuralist) approach. The German historian Martin Broszat was central to this radical change of direction. In his 1969 book, *The Hitler State*, he depicted Adolf Hitler as a 'weak dictator' who presided over bitter power struggles between incompatible individuals, within a chaotic system of competing and divisive bureaucratic empires.[8] Broszat then assembled an elite team of historians to work on a major six-volume work entitled *Bayern in der NS-Zeit* (Bavaria in the National Socialist Era). The 'Bavaria project', as it was called, examined resistance to Hitler's rule in everyday life.[9] It concluded that Nazi rule was much less totalitarian in practice than in theory. The public had much greater latitude to criticise and grumble than was previously supposed. The real dynamism of Hitler's Nazi regime came from young radical Nazi bureaucrats who enjoyed huge autonomy. Adolf Hitler often endorsed increasingly radical policies that others had already set in motion. The original totalitarian model was exposed as an imprecise and inconclusive way to examine Nazi Germany.

This 'history from below' approach to the study of Nazi Germany led to a more detailed focus on the relationship between the Gestapo and the German people. The reason for the paucity of work on the Gestapo was due to the limited amount of available sources. Most Gestapo case files were destroyed towards the end of the Second World War either by Allied bombing or by deliberate destruction by the Nazi regime itself. It was only in the Rhineland region that a large number of files remained. The German historian Reinhard Mann looked at a random sample of 825 files out of the 73,000 surviving Gestapo case files held in the Düsseldorf archive. Mann died before his work was fully completed, and his work was never published in an English translation. However, his preliminary findings provided a powerful corrective to the orthodox portrayal of the Gestapo as an all-powerful Orwellian 1984-style 'Thought Police'.[10] He provided the essentials of what has now become known as the 'revisionist interpretation' of the Gestapo.

Mann showed the Gestapo never employed enough staff to spy on everyone. It was a very small under-resourced and over-stretched organisation, with less than 15,000 active officers policing all the political crime of 66 million Germans. Gestapo officers were not the brutal ideologically committed Nazis of popular myth, but career detectives, who joined the police service many years before Hitler came to power. Most Gestapo investigations began with tip-offs from the general public. Yet Mann did not conclude that the Gestapo was an ineffective instrument of terror. On the contrary, he concluded that it targeted its limited resources against groups it defined as outside the 'National Community', especially those who were actively mobilising discontent among the population. There were, however, some key problems with Mann's study. He concentrated, for instance, on private conflicts among 'ordinary Germans', and excluded from his analysis a close examination of key opposition groups, most notably, communists, Jews, foreign workers and a broadly defined group of 'social outsiders'.

It was the American historian Robert Gellately in his book *The Gestapo and German Society*, published in 1990, who made another deeply significant contribution to our understanding of how the Gestapo functioned inside Nazi Germany.[11] Gellately followed Mann's approach of using a random sample of Gestapo files, but he looked at a different region altogether: Würzburg, in Lower Franconia, Bavaria. Gellately examined different groups from Mann too by concentrating on files related to Jews and foreign workers. He revealed that denunciations were crucial in 57 per cent of all the cases he consulted. Gellately's study gave further powerful support to the view that the Gestapo was an under-staffed, reactive organisation that left the vast majority of 'ordinary' Germans alone. He showed more clearly how public support assisted the work of the Gestapo.[12] Mann and Gellately undoubtedly debunked the popular conception of the Gestapo as part of an all-powerful police state imposing its will on a terrified population. The Gestapo, on this view, posed no real threat to law-abiding citizens in Nazi Germany.

Another US-based historian, Eric Johnson, in his detailed book *The Nazi Terror*, published in 1999, offered a powerful and nuanced corrective to the general trend of viewing the Gestapo as little different from a modern over-stretched police force. Johnson focused his research on a random sample of court files from Cologne, and a limited number of Gestapo case files from the Rhineland city of Krefeld, supplemented by interviews with survivors and telling statistical evidence. Johnson's work confirmed the Gestapo was a small organisation reliant on public cooperation. He showed that the Gestapo treated 'good' German citizens with kid gloves. Most Germans did not fear it at all. He differed from Gellately in one important respect by arguing that Gestapo officers were much more proactive and brutal.[13]

My own personal interest in the role of the Gestapo was sparked by my detailed biography of Sophie Scholl, a twenty-one-year-old Munich university student, who was arrested by the Gestapo, on 18 February 1943, for distributing anti-Nazi leaflets, then interrogated and executed four days later in a hastily organised Nazi show trial, presided over by Roland Freisler, known as 'Hitler's hanging judge'.[14] Sophie's interrogator was the calm and professional Gestapo officer Robert Mohr, who acted in the manner of an 'ordinary' detective, not a brutal, ideologically driven Nazi. The book showed the importance of looking at Gestapo investigations in great detail. It also raised two important questions worthy of further investigation. First, were all Gestapo investigations conducted with the efficiency demonstrated in the case of Sophie Scholl? Second, did Gestapo officers always behave as sympathetically as Robert Mohr?

To pursue these important questions in more depth, I decided to examine a wide range of detailed Gestapo case files related to the people who were hunted by the Gestapo in German society between 1933 and 1945. This required a much broader analysis. The largest number of surviving files in Germany is located in the Düsseldorf archive, which houses 73,000. This book is based primarily on these files, but it moves beyond the analysis of the city of Düsseldorf, which Reinhard Mann undertook, to encompass a much broader cross-section of Gestapo cases from the entire North-Westphalia region, which contained 4 million people during the Nazi era. I was given free access to all the surviving files. In the Nazi era, this region was heavily industrialised, with a large Catholic population, a smaller

Protestant contingent, and an average-sized Jewish community in the major cities. The sources from the Düsseldorf archive are supplemented by official documents, court files, eyewitness accounts, extensive memoirs and oral-history interviews. Put together, these sources have allowed me to provide a broad survey of how the Gestapo operated and how its victims were treated.

The book is primarily focused on a broad range of groups targeted by the Gestapo, including communists, religious dissidents, social outsiders and Jews, but it also examines the motives of those who denounced the victims. The major problem with Gestapo files is often not what they record, but what they leave out. It is well known that the Gestapo used what were called 'enhanced interrogation techniques', which often involved severe punishment beatings, but these are not recorded. I have attempted to bring forth evidence from later Gestapo trials and eyewitness accounts to reveal how extensive these brutal practices were.

The key focus of this book is not on the quantity of Gestapo cases, but on their quality. There are thousands of files contained in the Düsseldorf archive that are extremely brief. This book is based on very detailed Gestapo investigations, which often contain hundreds of pages, and involved the interrogation of numerous witnesses.[15] This approach takes the reader into the everyday life of a cross-section of ordinary and extraordinary people who lived during the Nazi era from a wide variety of social backgrounds. We will venture in the pages that follow into the working-class housing estate, the local factory, the street-corner beer hall, the local restaurant, the homes and even the bedrooms of ordinary German citizens. The hidden history of the Third Reich is illuminated here as never before.

Among the many fascinating individual stories examined in the book are: Jehovah's Witnesses who bravely refuse to give up their faith, priests and pastors who would not be silenced, communists who refused to compromise, factory workers who daubed graffiti, young people who formed dissident gangs, work colleagues who denounced co-workers, neighbours who informed on people listening to foreign radio broadcasts, wives who informed on husbands, lovers who denounced each other, and the remarkable story of a German 'Aryan' man and his Jewish fiancée who risked everything for love.

What emerges more clearly in this book than ever before is the high level of autonomy the Gestapo was given to deal with cases, and the often exhaustive amount of time it devoted to them. Most investigations began with a denunciation from an ordinary member of the public. The Gestapo did not just enforce its will, but asked ordinary citizens to police dissident behaviour. What the Gestapo could not predict was that many of these tip-offs turned out to be personally motivated.

Contrary to popular assumption, the Gestapo did not simply arrest and deliver individuals to the gates of concentration camps. Most cases ended up being dismissed, with no charge, or a surprisingly lenient punishment. Gestapo officers tried to ensure that a decision on punishment was agreed before the initial twenty-one-day 'protective custody' order had expired. It was only cases which the Gestapo regarded as serious that were passed on up the chain of command to the public prosecutor, who made the final decision. The harshest forms of treatment were focused on those regarded by the Gestapo as key political, religious, and racial opponents. Releases from custody at the end of investigations were the norm, not the exception. For an organisation often depicted as operating outside the law, I reveal here that it followed very strict legal guidelines.

The autonomy given to Gestapo officers often resulted in diverse, often bizarre, decisions. In the pages that follow, you will frequently be surprised by either the harshness or the leniency shown in each case. Some cases which nominally carry the death penalty are often dismissed, without charge, while other cases that seem very trivial end up with severe treatment. All cases are investigated with customary German thoroughness.

Gestapo officers emerge from this book not as stereotypically evil, but as a widely divergent group, who cannot be easily pigeonholed as 'ordinary men'. During the latter stages of the war, the Gestapo became much more brutal in the way it treated the 'enemies of the state,' and 'enhanced interrogation techniques' were used far more extensively.

It is by drilling down into Gestapo cases in great depth that *The Gestapo* provides a thought-provoking and original doorway into everyday life inside Nazi Germany and offers a graphic portrayal of diverse victims of Nazi terror.

Chapter 1

Becoming the Gestapo

Germany had a long tradition of political espionage. During the 1848 revolution King Ludwig I of Bavaria sanctioned the monitoring of political opponents in local beer halls. When the German Empire was created in 1871, the huge state of Prussia, which covered 60 per cent of German territory, had its own political police (*Politische Polizei*), called Department V, under the leadership of Wilhelm Stieber, who was born in Merseburg in Saxony on 3 May 1818 and came from a solid middle-class background. He qualified as a barrister before joining the police force.[1] He became known as Bismarck's 'master spy' and was instrumental in German domestic and overseas intelligence. Stieber issued the following instructions to agents:

> The agent should be obliged to keep some sort of establishment which he may choose, as long as it is externally in keeping with the commercial or other requirements of the country in which he is employed . . . It must be understood that it is necessary for our agents to inspire confidence in circles where their centre of action lies, and to establish that confidence by outward declaration of an ordinary bourgeois existence.[2]

In his exaggerated and generally unreliable memoirs, Stieber recalls that while carrying out intelligence operations in London he somehow managed to bluff his way into the home of the leading German communist exile Karl Marx and stole membership lists of the Communist League.[3] The primary focus of the Prussian political police inside Germany was the surveillance of anti-government parties and individuals, particularly the communist left.

In 1918, the complex German spy network that Stieber had built up overseas collapsed, but the new democratic Weimar government decided to retain the political police force. In Prussia, it was renamed Department 1A and later simply called Department 1. In 1928, the Prussian Minister of the Interior defined Department 1A as observing, preventing and prosecuting all offences of a political nature.[4] By 1930, it had about a thousand employees operating in each of the forty-four administrative districts of Prussia. The bulk of its officers were drawn from the ordinary criminal police force.[5]

The Prussian political police monitored the activities of communists, but also kept a close watch on the Nazi Party too. A total of 40,000 prosecutions were taken against members of the Nazi Party before 1933 by the Prussian political police.[6] The speeches and writings of all the leading Nazis were routinely monitored. A dedicated Chief Inspectorate of right-wing extremist parties was created as these organisations proliferated during the Weimar period.[7]

The appointment of Franz von Papen as German Chancellor on 20 July 1932 transformed how the Prussian political police dealt with 'enemies of the state'. The drive against communists became the chief focus of attention. Leading Nazi Hermann Göring became the effective commander of the whole Prussian police force, which numbered 50,000 men, and included the political police department. Göring immediately added a special department to deal with the fight against communism. A total of eleven police chiefs who were thought to be sympathetic towards democracy were dismissed.

This development fitted in neatly with the key Nazi objective of seizing control of all the security services. The four key figures in the achievement of this aim were Hermann Göring and Rudolf Diels in Prussia and Heinrich Himmler and Reinhard Heydrich in Bavaria. It was largely through the efforts of these four individuals that the Gestapo was brought into existence. In the end, Himmler and Heydrich would acquire complete control not just of the Gestapo, but of the entire police system of Nazi Germany, but their triumph was by no means inevitable.

Hermann Göring was born in Rosenheim, Bavaria, on 12 January 1893. His family background was solidly upper middle class. His father Heinrich had been a personal friend of German Chancellor Otto von Bismarck, while serving as an officer in the German Army. A military career was mapped out from an early age for young Hermann, but he was a headstrong, stubborn and troublesome teenager. He was expelled from school after several explosive arguments with teachers. His father decided army discipline might tame him. He attended an army cadet school in Karlsruhe and then gained entrance to a military school in Berlin. In October 1914, Göring joined the newly formed German Flying Corps. He became a fearless flying ace, in the elite 'No. 1 Air Squadron', led by the legendary 'Bloody Red Baron', Freiherr von Richthofen. Göring's willingness to undertake dangerous combat missions led to the award of a series of bravery awards, most notably, the Iron Cross, First Class and the *Pour le Mérite* ('The Blue Max'), the highest aviation honour of all. At the end of the First World War, Göring returned to Munich, but found it difficult to find employment. After seeing Adolf Hitler speak in a local beer hall in the autumn of 1922, he joined the Nazi Party. Göring took part in the failed 1923 Munich Beer Hall Putsch, and sustained two bullet wounds during the final bloody showdown with the police on Marienplatz in the city centre. The Putsch had attempted to overthrow the Bavarian state government, but it ended up as a humiliating failure. Instead of gaining power, Hitler, supported by the storm troopers, had gained brief control of a local beer hall before the authorities used the local police to restore order and arrest the conspirators. While recovering in hospital, Göring developed a severe addiction to morphine. This led to a brief period in a psychiatric hospital. By the early 1930s, Göring was

Hitler's chief adviser on internal affairs and leader of the Nazi Party deputies in the Reichstag. In 1932, he was appointed Prussian Minister of the Interior by Franz von Papen and commander of the police.

Göring immediately formed a close working relationship with Rudolf Diels, the head of the Prussian political police. Diels was an experienced civil servant and police administrator. He proved a shrewd and flexible master of bureaucratic office politics. His willingness to do what he was told soon made him an indispensable adviser to Göring. In his self-serving memoirs, Diels glosses over why he moved so swiftly from being a supporter of the democratic Weimar Republic to quickly adapting himself to the Nazi political agenda.

On closer inspection, it's obvious Diels was an unprincipled and duplicitous opportunist. In a curriculum vitae, dating from 1935, he described how he came to be closely involved in the development of the Gestapo in the first place:

> In 1930, I was appointed to the Ministry of the Interior, where I at once became head of the department responsible for combating the communist movement. After June 20 1932, the scope of my authority to combat communism was substantially widened, and I was able, even at that stage, to devote myself to preparations for the overthrow of communism in Germany in very close conjunction with leading members of the NSDAP.[8]

It's not known whether the idea of converting the Prussian political police into the national secret police that became the Gestapo came from Diels or Göring, but Section 1A of the Prussian political police contained the nucleus of officers that did become the Prussian Gestapo. Göring felt existing criminal detectives could be assimilated into the more repressive duties that were shortly to be assigned to them.

Heinrich Himmler, head of the SS (*Schutzstaffel*), Hitler's personal bodyguard, and his young protégé Reinhard Heydrich were also central in the development of the Gestapo. The primary focus of their activities was in Bavaria. Heinrich Himmler was undoubtedly the most important figure in developing the SS and the Gestapo into the fearsome organisations they became within Nazi Germany. Himmler has often been routinely depicted as the quintessential, boring, emotionally cold and calculating Nazi bureaucrat preoccupied with racial theory. This detracts from his immense skill as a manipulator, organiser and highly resourceful political operator. His willingness to seek out loyal, young and highly qualified individuals allowed him to build up a formidable team of efficient and ideologically committed individuals who shared his vision of creating an inter-related police security apparatus. No leading Nazi wrote such convincing reports as Himmler. It was this skill that made him such an indispensable figure among the Nazi elite.

Himmler was born on 7 October 1900 in Munich into a solid middle-class family. His father, a strict disciplinarian, was once a tutor at the court of the Bavarian monarchy. His mother came from a family which made its living as market gardeners. Himmler was brought up as a strict Catholic in the small Bavarian town of Landshut. He attended church regularly, but became progressively antagonistic towards Christian teachings. In 1917, he was called up for the army, but he never saw active service. At the end of the First World War, he was discharged from service in Berlin. He stayed there for two years, moving from one humdrum job to another, including as a salesman for a brush company and a labourer in a glue factory. In 1921, Himmler returned to Landshut. His father bought him a small farm-holding on which he raised chickens. He would kill chickens each day, strangling them with his bare hands. It was around this time that Himmler began reading pamphlets about German nationalism. He became strongly influenced by issues of race and patriotism and wanted to get involved in the drive to overthrow Weimar democracy.

Himmler went to live in Munich, but he did not initially

join the Nazi Party. Instead, he became a member of a group called the 'Empire War Banner' (*Reichskriegsbanner*). It was while he was active in this organisation that he came into close proximity with leading Nazis. He joined the Nazi Party in 1923 and took part in the famous march to the Feldherrnhalle at the end of the bungled Munich Beer Hall Putsch. He completely escaped arrest or punishment.

Himmler rose to prominence within the Nazi Party via his role in Hitler's personal elite bodyguard troop: the SS. On 6 January 1929, he became head of the SS. Himmler was a workaholic with very high standards. He often started work in his office at 8 a.m. and sometimes stayed after midnight. He took meticulous care over all documentation.[9] In 1931, he set up Section 1C of the SS in Munich. Its key objective was to gather intelligence on political opponents, especially communists.

To enhance this organisation, Himmler appointed twenty-seven-year-old Reinhard Heydrich as his chief security officer. Born on 7 March 1904 in Halle in Saxony, this tall, handsome, blond, athletic, hard-working and utterly ruthless individual became Himmler's key protégé. Heydrich came from a middle-class family interested in high culture. His father Richard was a famous opera singer, and fervent German nationalist. His mother Elizabeth was an actress. Reinhard was a gifted pianist and violinist. He was also an excellent fencer, swimmer and athlete. There were several career options open to him, but he decided to enlist in the navy in 1922. In spite of an abrasive manner, he rose to the rank of lieutenant. His good looks always attracted female attention, and he embarked on several love affairs. This eventually embroiled him in a messy scandal. One of his girlfriends, the daughter of a director of the leading chemical company IG Farben, became pregnant, but Heydrich refused to marry her. A naval court of honour decided he had brought the navy into disrepute due to his behaviour and he was forced to resign in April 1931. A promising career seemed over. It was his new girlfriend and later wife Lina von Osten who provided Heydrich with links to leading Nazi Party figures. Lina later recalled that at the time he joined the Nazi Party in 1931 he had never even read Hitler's *Mein Kampf*.[10] He was soon recruited to the SS. He made an indelible impression on Himmler, who viewed Heydrich as the ideal-type elite SS officer: energetic, loyal, ideologically driven, efficient, ruthless, well organised and fearless.

In 1932, Section 1C changed its name to the Security Service (*Sicherheitsdienst des Reichsführers* – SD). The SD was designated as a much more proactive organisation than Section 1C, the latter title borrowed from the German military in which enemy intelligence was the responsibility of 1C officers. The SD would target and track down political and racial enemies and arrest them. Even before 1933, therefore, Himmler and Heydrich wanted to transport the elite racial and ideologically driven principles of the SS into the working practices and activities of a new national secret state police force.

One powerful Nazi figure stood in the way of all their plans and schemes. This was the tough and erratic leader of the storm troopers (*Sturmabteilungen* – SA), Captain Ernst Röhm. Born in Munich on 28 November 1887, Röhm came from a humble background, his father having worked on the railways. He joined the army in 1906 and during the First World War was awarded the Iron Cross First Class. In 1919, he joined the German Workers Party (DAP), which became the Nazi Party in 1920. He was a close comrade and personal friend of Adolf Hitler. Röhm was small, stocky, with a tough-looking face, which seemed even more menacing due to the presence of an unsightly scar on his left cheek.

After the bungled Munich Beer Hall Putsch of 1923, Röhm retreated from an active role in the Nazi Party. Between 1928 and 1930 he became a military adviser to the Bolivian Army, and published an unrepentant memoir called *A Traitor's Story*. In 1930, Hitler sent him a personal letter inviting him to return to Munich to become chief of staff of the reformed storm troopers. Röhm took up this post on 5 January 1931. Hitler wanted the SA to act as a street-fighting force to intimidate political opponents, especially during rallies and election campaigns. He also felt Röhm's invaluable contacts with leading officers in the army would aid the Nazi drive to gain power.

Röhm had ambitious and radical plans of his own. He wanted to create a Nazified secret state police force out of the membership of the SA.[11] Röhm believed that front-line Nazi SA fighters should have primacy over career policemen. Even more controversial was his aim of incorporating the existing army (*Reichswehr*) into the SA. In March 1932, an important meeting was held to discuss the proposed Nazi secret state police force at Röhm's apartment in Goetheplatz in Munich. Those also present were Joseph Goebbels, Nazi propaganda chief, Rudolf Hess, Hitler's secretary, and Heinrich Himmler, the head of the SS and SD. It was agreed that the secret state police of a Nazi regime should be a Nazi organisation, controlled by Himmler's SS, which would work closely in co-operation with the party machine, including the SA. When asked about what type of person would staff this political police force, Himmler said: 'We shall not find them, we shall create them.'[12] This meeting left the SA with an ill-defined role in the security apparatus of a future Nazi state. Not surprisingly, Röhm never felt bound by the decisions reached.[13]

Hitler took a huge political risk in bringing Röhm back to the centre of the Nazi Party leadership. Röhm's uncompromising personality was accompanied by a private life that was the subject of sexual scandal. Röhm made no secret of the fact he was a homosexual, which was then illegal, under Article 175 of the German criminal code. Röhm surrounded himself with a coterie of young gay men.

Newspapers such as the Social Democratic *Münchener Post*, and the left-wing *Welt am Montag*, published a series of incriminating letters in the spring of 1932, from Röhm to his doctor Karl-Günther Heimsoth, in which he confessed to 'homosexual feelings and acts' and described sexual intercourse with women as 'unnatural'.[14] These letters were published as an anti-Nazi political propaganda pamphlet by the Social Democrats during the 1932 presidential election entitled 'The Röhm Case'. It sold 300,000 copies and was widely discussed in the press during the election campaign. But who had leaked these letters to the left-wing press? It was none other than Rudolf Diels, the head of the Prussian political police. Copies of the letters were in the possession of the Berlin public prosecutor's office, which was investigating allegations of Röhm's extensive homosexual activities. These documents were passed to the Munich police, but the case was dropped.

The new 'national coalition' government created on 30 January 1933 contained only three Nazis: Adolf Hitler, the new German Chancellor, Göring, Minister without Portfolio, and Wilhelm Frick, the Minister of the Interior. Frick was born on 12 March 1877 in Alsenz, Bavaria. He held a degree in law and a doctorate. He had led the Munich security police, and participated in the failed 1923 Munich Beer Hall Putsch, receiving a fifteen-month suspended sentence and then dismissed from the police force. He gradually restored his reputation. In January 1930, Frick became State Minister of the Interior for Thuringia and headed the Nazi Party legal department. As a trained lawyer and an experienced government official, Frick had strong claims of his own to control of the police in Nazi Germany. Being conservatively minded Frick wanted to convert the existing independent state police forces into one centralised criminal police force, which would remain a professional state police force. Frick knew it would be no easy task creating a national state police force, due to the existence of the federal system of independently governed states (*Länder*). Each federal state had its own police force, which included a small number of officers who looked after political policing.

There was not even a wholesale nazification of the police in Prussia under Frick. A total of 1,453 police officers who were considered 'suspected enemies' of the Nazi regime were dismissed in the first year of Nazi rule. This was just 7.3 per cent of all officers. Most of these were ordinary policemen at the lowest ranks.[15] Recruitment to the political police and then the Gestapo was based on relevant police experience, and not determined by membership of the Nazi Party, the SS, the SD or the SA. Rudolf Diels later recalled that most of the original Gestapo officers were 'old civil servants, not Nazis' and they tried to 'resist the terror' of the storm troopers. Men such as Diels had great difficulty dealing with SA men in the first year of Nazi rule. The SA tended to view traditional bureaucrats with utter contempt and constantly disregarded orders to operate within any form of regulated state legal process.[16]

It's clear that Göring and Diels supported the brutal crackdown on communists at the outset of Hitler's rule. This had the support of Hitler too, who said: 'The struggle against the communists must not be made dependent on judicial considerations.'[17] In a blunt speech to Prussian police officers on 17 February 1933 Göring said: 'Every bullet that now exists in the barrel of a police pistol is my bullet. If you use it for killing, I am the killer. I have ordered all this, I take it on my conscience. I assume all responsibility.'[18] On 22 February 1933, Göring signed a decree allowing members of the SA to join the auxiliary police. The aim was to use these tough street fighters to crush communists. Within weeks, the number of SA auxiliaries outnumbered the ordinary police by a ratio of seven to one. The result was a wave of terror. The SA mounted brutal raids, rounded up thousands of communists and imprisoned them in what became known as 'wild concentration camps', in which people were held without trial, beaten up, tortured and often killed in abandoned warehouses, barracks, and dilapidated buildings throughout Germany. In retrospect, Göring's decision to use the SA to crush communists was ill advised. It heralded a period of unbridled Nazi terror that proved difficult to contain.

In testimony at the Nuremberg trials, Rudolf Diels described the lawless brutality of the early months of Nazi rule:

> Communists were executed by various party groups, especially the SA . . . The methods applied were as follows: Human beings, who, deprived of their freedom, were subjected to severe bodily mistreatment or killed. These illegal detentions took place in camps, often old military barracks, stormtroop quarters or fortresses. Later on these places became known as concentration camps, such as Oranienburg, near Berlin, Lichtenberg, Papenburg, Dachau in Bavaria, etc. . . . These murders were camouflaged by the expressions: 'Shot while trying to escape' or 'resisting arrest' or similar things.[19]

Diels estimated that around 40,000 people were taken into 'protective custody' during 1933, and 5,000 to 7,000 political opponents were killed in this manner in the first year of power.[20] Official figures reveal that 100,000 prisoners were taken into 'protective custody' during 1933, but most of these were held in the early months. These figures do not include those who were effectively kidnapped by the SA and taken to torture cellars and unregulated concentration camps. The number killed in 1933 is equally hard to estimate accurately, but was most probably nearer to 1,000 than the estimate of up to 7,000 given by Diels.

Heinz Gräfe, a young Berlin law student, witnessed the early violence of the SA in March 1933:

> The state revolt is taking place! Black-white-and-red flags and swastika flags were flown at all the city halls and public build-ings (courts, police and barracks) yesterday and the day before. The SA is armed with machine guns and acts as an auxiliary police force. Under the protection of the state police, they stormed public houses and newspaper presses. In Pirna as well, the SA occupied the local press and bookstore today at noon,

arrested the personnel and drove others out; they destroyed the signs outside and piled all the printing materials in the street and set them on fire.[21]

Werner Schäfer, the camp commandant at Oranienburg concentration camp, claimed Diels had 'very close relations' with the leaders of the SA. According to Schäfer: 'Oranienburg soon became the only camp for political opponents from Berlin and the whole province of Brandenburg . . . Oranienburg did not even have 1,000 internees [at the end of 1933] and . . . Berlin was the centre of political opponents of the NSDAP and therefore had an extraordinarily large proportion of political opponents.'[22]

Schäfer also took issue with Diels' claim that the criminal police and the Gestapo treated political prisoners in a non-violent manner under interrogation in Berlin and that all the brutality during the brutal purge of the communists came from the SA. 'On one occasion', Schäfer recalled, 'the Gestapo in Berlin sent two internees to the camp in a seriously maltreated condition. Next day I went to see . . . my superior, and asked him to protest, together with me, to the Gestapo at Prinz Albrecht Strasse and to demand an explanation, which I intended to make the subject of a report to the Prussian Ministry of the Interior.'[23] After an investigation of this incident, it was accepted that the Gestapo had maltreated the prisoners and should not have sent them to Oranienburg with such injuries.

Hans Frank, a committed Nazi and the Minister of Justice in Munich, argued that the arbitrary arrests, violent interrogations and routine violence of the SA against political opponents needed to cease.[24] On 2 August 1933, Göring disbanded the 'auxiliary police'. Police forces in the other German states dispensed with the violent services of the SA too. Strict regulations were now issued, making it clear that the Gestapo, supported by the police, was the only organisation allowed to place people in 'protective custody'. The SS took control of the concentration camps, and introduced strict regulations concerning activities within them.

If one day can be defined as central to the establishment of the Gestapo then it was undoubtedly 27 February 1933. This was the day when the Reichstag, the German parliament, was set on fire. It occurred in the midst of the final democratic election campaign. When Hitler arrived at the scene of the blaze, he told Diels, 'There will be no mercy now. Anyone who stands in our way will be cut down.'[25] The fire was supposedly started by Marinus van der Lubbe, a Dutch-born, illiterate communist. Whether he acted alone, as he confessed during his lengthy interrogation, or the fire was started as part of a communist plot to undermine Hitler's infant regime or as a pretext for a calculated plan by the Nazis to suppress the communists and set up a dictatorship, has never been fully resolved. It was rumoured that Göring planned the Reichstag fire to press the case for Gestapo repression. In testimony at the Nuremberg war trials, General Franz Halder recalled that Göring had boasted: 'The only one who really knows about the Reichstag is me, because I set it on fire.'[26]

The next day, Hitler's government issued the Reichstag Fire Decree, drafted by Wilhelm Frick, which curtailed 'for the protection of the people and state' all the civil liberties previously offered under the Weimar constitution. All 'enemies of the people' could now be arrested and placed under 'protective custody' (Schutzhaft). This ended the previous right of an arrested person to be released or brought before a court and charged within twenty-four hours. Henceforth, a person could theoretically be held without a charge being brought. There was no legal defence against it. The basic rights enshrined in the Weimar constitution were destroyed. A new category of 'preventive custody' (Vorbeugehaft) was introduced by the civilian police force later in the year to hold 'career criminals' without trial.[27] The existing German legal system continued in the Nazi era, but acting alongside it were the newly created 'Special Courts', set up in 1933 in individual states, which dealt exclusively with 'political crimes'. In July 1934, the 'People's Court' was created to deal with the most serious political cases such as high treason. These courts offered fast-track justice, with many cases being dealt with in a single morning or afternoon.

The Reichstag Fire Decree was important not just in giving the Gestapo the power to use 'protective custody', but also in restricting the independence of the jurisdiction of all the federal German states and allowing central government to make appointments within the legal and police forces all over the country. This was a hugely important development, as it paved the way for the creation of a nationwide political police force.[28]

The Gestapo (*Die Geheime Staatspolizei*)[29] was officially created by the first Gestapo Law, issued by Göring on 26 April 1933. It means Secret State Police. Göring defined its role in the following way: 'Its task is to investigate all political activities in the entire state that pose a danger to the state and to gather and evaluate the results of those enquiries.'[30] It was initially confined to Prussia with the special mission of dealing exclusively with political opponents of the Nazi regime. In carrying out this role, it remained relatively free of internal judicial and government jurisdiction. Regional Gestapo field offices were established throughout Prussia. It was Diels who found the Gestapo its notorious new headquarters: 8 Prinz Albrechtstrasse in Berlin. The Gestapo was based there from May 1933 until 1945. Hermann Göring was nominated as 'Chief of the Secret State Police' and he took sole credit for creating the Gestapo, as he explained in 1934: 'I worked personally on reorganisation and managed to create, by my own efforts, and on my own initiative, the Gestapo. This instrument which strikes terror into the enemies of the state has contributed most powerfully to the fact that a Communist or Marxist danger in Germany and in Prussia is out of the question.'[31]

The day-to-day administration of the Gestapo was assigned

to Rudolf Diels, under the title 'Inspector of the Secret State Police'. The administrative section of the organisation became known as the Gestapa. The SS in Berlin regarded Diels as a conservative bureaucrat and a reactionary. A rumour was spread by Hans Gisevius, Göring's state secretary, that Diels was not pursuing the persecution of communists with enough zeal because he had communist sympathies. The authority of Diels was progressively undermined by such rumours. In October 1933, a renegade SS squad raided the home of Diels in an attempt to discredit him. He was not there at the time of the raid. His wife was locked in a bedroom while the SS searched his house for incriminating evidence. Diel's wife phoned her husband from the bedroom telephone extension. Diels was quickly on the scene, accompanied by a large troop of Gestapo officers, who arrested the SS men. Göring, responding to SS pressure, ordered Diels to be placed under house arrest. Diels, who had by now become paranoid and terrified by all the intrigue swirling around him, resigned and fled to Karlsbad in Czechoslovakia in fear of his life. In fact, Göring only intended to redeploy him, probably outside Berlin, to diffuse the conflict within the infant Gestapo.

He replaced Diels with Paul Hinkler, a loyal Nazi cipher, heavy drinker, with little administrative experience. It was a terrible choice. Officials at Gestapo HQ pointed out to Göring that Hinkler was way out of his depth. He lasted only a month in the job before Göring sent a letter to the exiled Diels, begging him to return. 'I want to get rid of the *Dummkopf* Hinkler today,' Göring wrote. 'I have prepared a decree which gives you independence.'[32] Diels returned and resumed his role at the head of the Gestapo. Göring realised the rumours about his loyalty had been manufactured by his enemies in the SS and SA.

In-fighting within the Gestapo led Frick, the Minister of the Interior, to fear that it was turning into a Nazi organisation outside any form of state regulation. Göring acted quickly to frustrate Frick's efforts to keep the Gestapo within a traditional legal framework by issuing another decree which removed the Gestapo from the control of the Prussian Interior Ministry, and placed it under his personal jurisdiction as Prime Minister of Prussia. On 30 November 1933, the independence of the Gestapo was further strengthened by a second Gestapo Law under which Göring removed the Gestapo from regulation by the Ministry of the Interior.

Parallel to the developments in Prussia, SS leader Himmler and his ambitious protégé Heydrich began the unification of all the other political police forces within the federal states. The process began on 9 March 1933 when Himmler became chief of the Munich police and the political police. Heydrich was appointed head of Department VI of the Munich political police (BPP). Himmler was also responsible for the creation of a new concentration camp at Dachau, on the outskirts of Munich, which was controlled by Theodor Eicke, a dedicated SS man. He used ruthless SS Death-Head Formations to guard the camp. It was Himmler who created the organisational three-way link between the SS, the political police and the concentration camp system. Himmler's model of Nazi terror was subsequently adopted throughout Germany.

Himmler could not initially extend his control over political police forces in the whole of Bavaria. Ernst Röhm's SA had infiltrated the police force in the region after the Nazi seizure of power. Thousands of his street fighters flooded into the newly created Auxiliary Security Police. The local Gauleiter, Adolf Wagner, the leading Nazi Party-appointed official in the area, who was fully aware of the unbridled brutality of the SA, asked Himmler to create a rival Political Auxiliary Police Force, composed of SS men, who would then assume command over the SA auxiliaries. This would allow the SA in the area to be controlled by the SS. Röhm did not raise any objections, as at this stage he still believed the SS was subordinate to the SA. This proved a grave tactical error. Himmler now commanded all the political police forces in Bavaria and the power of the SA was weakened. On 1 April 1933, Himmler was given the title of 'Political Police Commander of Bavaria' and he assumed full command of all the concentration camps. Unlike the chaotic 'wild' camps in Prussia, the Bavarian camps were bought under proper administrative control.

Himmler's rapid take-over of policing in Bavaria led to fears of an SS takeover of the entire state bureaucracy and criminal justice system. The traditional nationalistic conservatives who dominated Bavaria wanted an authoritarian state that ruled through existing legal and administrative organisations, not an SS-run totalitarian police state. In May 1933, two orders were issued by Wagner which severely limited the use of protective custody powers to 'significant suspects'. Wagner argued that with the communist threat now brutally crushed, the authority of the traditional organs of the state should be restored.

Himmler had other ideas. Between September 1933 and January 1934 Himmler's revolution to gain control over all the political police forces of the German states outside of Prussia continued. It started with Hamburg, Lübeck, and Mecklenburg-Schwerin, then came Anhalt, Baden, Bremen, Hessen, Thuringia and Württemberg. In January 1934, Brunswick, Oldenburg and Saxony were under Himmler's jurisdiction. Only the giant state of Prussia and its two small enclaves Lippe and Schaumburg-Lippe remained to be conquered.

There has been much historical speculation about how Himmler gained this remarkable level of control over the German political police outside Prussia in such a short space of time. It was suggested to Wilhelm Frick by the prosecution at the Nuremberg trial that it was he who had brokered these rapid takeovers of the various federal states by Himmler, as he favoured administrative and police centralisation, and had already abolished the last independent powers of German states on 12 November 1933. Frick vehemently denied this. Vastly increased power for Himmler's ideologically driven SS was at odds with

Frick's own desire for a centralised police force recruited on the basis of traditional professional police qualifications. Himmler triumphed over Frick because of a successful PR campaign in which the SS leader went on a tour of all the regional police areas of the federal states and convinced their leaders that the SS was best suited to deal with political and racial enemies. He discovered that this line of argument was more appealing than Frick's attempts to centralise regional administrations and increase bureaucratic interference from central government over the federal states. Himmler's SS also seemed far more acceptable to the Federal States than allowing Röhm and his aggressive local SA men more power over local policing.

Outside Prussia, Himmler's model of a centralised Gestapo was gathering pace. At this stage, Göring showed no sign of handing over the Prussian Gestapo to the ruthlessly ambitious SS chief. Göring favoured a controlled revolution in which the Nazis allied with traditional conservative forces. 'For God's sake,' Göring told Frick, 'if Himmler takes over the police force in Prussia, he will kill us.'[33] Göring was also sympathetic to Frick's idea that protective custody needed tighter regulation. In March 1934, Göring issued a decree that all protective custody orders in Prussia had to be sanctioned by the central Gestapo office in Berlin.

To prevent the increased infiltration of SS men into the Gestapo, Diels issued a directive to police personnel departments which advised that holding a rank in the SS should not carry as much weight in recruitment criteria as police and civil service qualifications and experience. This was a miscalculation. Within a week, due to SS pressure, Diels had to water down his directive. When Frick attempted to regulate protective custody orders outside Prussia in April 1934, Himmler protested and the plan was dropped. These attempts to curb SS power show that the traditional interpretation of Himmler's ultimate triumph over the Gestapo being engineered by Göring is deeply flawed. Neither is there convincing evidence to suggest that Hitler paved the way for Himmler's control of the Gestapo. Göring and Hitler were far more concerned about dealing with the immediate problem of curbing the independence of Röhm to appreciate the implications of giving Himmler even greater control over the German security system.[34]

If Röhm's powerful SA was going to be curbed, Göring reluctantly came to accept SS involvement was a necessary evil. Demands for 'a second Nazi revolution' continued to feature heavily in Röhm's speeches throughout 1933. According to the SA chief, Hitler was flagrantly compromising his Nazi principles in exchange for a collaborationist regime with the conservative right and the army. 'Adolf is disgraceful,' Röhm told one of his close confidantes. 'He is betraying us all. He only frequents reactionaries and takes into his confidence those generals from East Prussia.'[35]

Hitler became increasingly exasperated by Röhm's unsettling talk of a 'second revolution'. 'I am resolved', Hitler said in a blunt speech to SA leaders, 'to repress any attempt that might serve to disturb the existing order. I shall oppose with the greatest energy a second revolutionary wave, for it would result in chaos. Anyone, no matter what his position, who rises against the regular authority of the State will be putting his head into a noose.'[36] In another speech on 6 July 1933, Hitler emphasised that 'revolution is not a permanent state of affairs' and 'must be guided into the safe channel of evolution'.

Hitler brought Röhm into the Cabinet as 'Minister without Portfolio' on 1 December 1933 in the hope this might restrain him. On New Year's Day, Hitler wrote a conciliatory letter to the SA chief:

At the close of the year of the National Socialist Revolution, therefore, I feel compelled to thank you, my dear friend Ernst Röhm, for the imperishable services which you have rendered to the National Socialist movement and the German people and to assure you how very grateful I am to fate that I am able to call such men as you my friends and fellow combatants.

In true friendship and grateful regards[37]

This letter was published in the Nazi Party newspaper *Völkischer Beobachter*, but it did little to ease the tension.

In February 1934, Röhm presented a memorandum to Hitler's Cabinet arguing that the SA should replace the army as the main German security force.[38] General Werner von Blomberg, the Defence Minister, was outraged at any suggestion that the SA should control the professionally trained army. On 28 February, Röhm was summoned to a showdown meeting with Blomberg and Hitler. This was essentially a carpeting. Röhm signed an agreement at the end of the meeting which promised he would make no forcible attempt to replace the army with a new 'People's Army'.

By now, Göring had decided the best way to deal with Röhm was to bring Himmler to Berlin and hand over to him complete control of the Prussian Gestapo. On 1 April 1934, Rudolf Diels was 'redeployed' from his post as head of the Gestapo to the post of District Governor in the Rhineland city of Cologne. This was presented as a promotion to a higher-paid job, but Diels had been sidelined from any further influence over the Gestapo. In his memoirs, Diels recalled that during this period he was suffering from severe physical and mental strain and welcomed his posting to Cologne. It was a good means of escaping.[39] Lina Heydrich recalled there was a great deal of haggling between Himmler and Göring over the plan to bring the SS chief to Berlin to assume control over the Gestapo. The sticking point was Himmler's insistence that his ruthless deputy Heydrich must accompany him. Göring felt Heydrich's arrogant and ruthless personality might cause friction among the conservative bureaucrats who ran the Prussian Gestapo.[40]

On 20 April 1934, Göring appointed Himmler as Inspector of the Gestapo. Reinhard Heydrich, already director of the SD, took control of the Gestapa, the administrative arm of the organisation. Göring retained his now cosmetic job title of 'Chief of the Secret State Police', but Himmler's SS was now in complete charge of the Gestapo, though Göring insisted he be kept informed of all key developments. From this day the Gestapo had jurisdiction throughout Germany. As Wilhelm Frick observed bitterly: 'Himmler now became more and more irreplaceable.'[41]

It was the role Himmler played in the destruction of Röhm that was the key reason why the SS gained total control over policing in Nazi Germany. Reconstructing the motives behind the plot to deal with Röhm is hampered by the fact that all relevant documentation related to the SS, SD and the police has been destroyed. Eyewitness accounts primarily come from those involved and cannot be relied upon uncritically. The only surviving figure directly involved in the plot to deal with Röhm by 1945 was Göring, but he was extremely evasive on the subject under cross-examination at the Nuremberg trial. There was general agreement from eye witnesses that Himmler and Heydrich concocted the rumour that Röhm was planning to overthrow Hitler's regime, and had secured the backing of ex-Chancellor General Kurt von Schleicher and Gregor Strasser, the Nazi radical.[42] Rudolf Diels claimed Heydrich and Himmler were feeding Hitler's mind with equally false rumours that the SA was being infiltrated by communists.[43] In a later interview, Frick commented: 'I am convinced Röhm did not even desire a coup.'[44]

In the account Hitler presented to the Reichstag on 13 July 1934 on the events leading up to the 'Night of the Long Knives', he claimed 'disquieting facts' had emerged in the last days of May to support the idea that Röhm was planning a coup. In the first week of June, Hitler met with Röhm in a final attempt to resolve their differences, thus emphasising that he still hoped to work out some compromise arrangement:

I informed him that I had the impression from countless rumours and numerous declarations of faithful old party and SA leaders that conscienceless elements were preparing a national Bolshevist action that would bring nothing, but untold misfortune to Germany . . . I implored him for the last time to voluntarily abandon this madness and instead to lend his authority to prevent a development that, in any event, could only end in disaster.[45]

Hitler further claimed that instead of following this advice, Röhm made 'preparations to eliminate me personally'. All the evidence suggests this was not true. A neglected aspect of the destruction of Röhm's SA is the role played by the army. It has been shown that General von Reichenau was also involved in concocting fabricated evidence to accuse Röhm of planning a coup.[46]

On 17 June 1934, Vice Chancellor Franz von Papen made a dramatic intervention into the crisis by delivering a sensational speech, with the blessing of President Hindenburg, at Marburg University. He praised Hitler's regime for ending the chaos of the Weimar period, but he warned against a 'second revolution' and then attacked the 'personality cult' surrounding Hitler. 'Great men are not created by propaganda,' von Papen said. 'No organisation, no propaganda, however excellent, can alone maintain confidence in the long run.'[47]

In a speech, on the same day in Gera, Hitler described Papen as 'a pygmy who imagines he can stop, with a few phrases, the gigantic renewal of a people's life'. Due to a Gestapo phone tap it was discovered that Franz von Papen's speech had been written by Dr Edgar Jung, a young conservative lawyer, and a close adviser to the former German Chancellor. Jung believed conservatives could assert control over Hitler's regime and stop it from dominating German life. Four days later, Jung, on the order of Heydrich, was arrested by the Gestapo in Munich, interrogated and transported to the Gestapo HQ in Berlin.

Ernst Röhm only belatedly realised the mortal danger he now

faced. He released a hastily prepared statement in the *Völkischer Beobachter*, on 19 June 1934. It announced that SA members had been ordered to take a month's leave during July, and were strictly forbidden to wear their uniforms during this vacation. He added that he would be departing to Bad Wiessee, a small spa town, south of Munich, for a rest cure, on the advice of his doctor.[48] Röhm hoped this conciliatory statement concerning his activities in the summer period would convince Hitler that the rumour that he was planning a coup was mere speculation.

On 21 June 1934, President Hindenburg held a meeting with Adolf Hitler at his home in Neudeck at which he informed him that either Röhm's power was curbed or martial law would be declared.[49] This was a decisive moment in the crisis. To remain in power, Hitler had to eliminate Röhm and the leadership of the SA. The next day, General von Fritsch, Commander in Chief, placed the army on a state of alert and cancelled all leave. The army stood ready to intervene if the SS could not deal with the SA on its own. On 28 June 1934, Röhm was expelled from the German Officers League. The next day, General von Blomberg declared in an article in the *Völkischer Beobachter* that 'the army stands behind Adolf Hitler'.[50]

That same day, Hitler, guarded by the SS, was in the Hotel Dreesen in the picturesque Rhineland town of Bad Godesberg. He held discussions with Göring, Himmler and Goebbels about how to proceed. It was decided Röhm and his key supporters should be eliminated. The SS and the Gestapo were given the task of drawing up a target list. SS commandos would carry out the killings. It was felt SS men would have the least qualms about acting as executioners, whereas Gestapo officers as former detectives might raise objections to getting involved in arbitrary killing of this type.

Göring, Himmler and Heydrich left for Berlin to direct operations against the SA there. Hitler, accompanied by Goebbels, departed for Bavaria to deal with Röhm and his close SA associates. At 4.30 a.m. on the morning of 30 June 1934, Hitler arrived by plane at Oberwiesenfeld, near Munich. He was later driven, at the head of a convoy of cars full of heavily armed SS bodyguards, towards the Hotel Hanselbauer in Bad Wiessee, where Röhm and his entourage were staying.

When they arrived all was silent. Hitler entered the building and hurried up the stairs. He entered the room of an SA leader called Heines first, and discovered him in bed with an eighteen-year-old homosexual Troop Leader. Both were arrested by SS guards. Hitler then walked into Röhm's bedroom, accompanied by two SS guards, and shouted at him: 'You are under arrest.' The other SA members staying at the hotel were also rounded up and bundled into waiting cars. All those arrested ended up at Munich's notorious Stadelheim Prison.

In Cell number 474, on the next day Röhm was given the opportunity to 'do the decent thing' and kill himself. A prison officer placed a revolver on a table, next to his bed, for this purpose. Ten minutes elapsed. Silence. SS officer Theodor Eicke, commandant of Dachau concentration camp, accompanied by a second SS officer, walked into the cell. They were armed with revolvers. Röhm, sweating profusely, stripped to the waist, stood up, in a defiant stance. The SS officer cold-bloodedly raised his gun and fired several shots into his upper body. Röhm slumped to the floor and died within seconds.[51]

Other old scores were settled in the Munich bloodbath. Gustav von Kahr, former Minister-President of Bavaria, who had betrayed Hitler during the famous Munich Beer Hall Putsch of 1923, was beaten to death by SS guards, using pickaxes near Dachau concentration camp. Some mistakes also occurred during the frenetic wave of SS raids and killings. Dr Willi Schmid, a prominent music critic on a local newspaper, was shot dead in his Munich apartment in front of his wife and children. The SS men who killed him had been looking for a similarly named Willi Schmidt, a well-known local SA leader, but were given the wrong address by a Gestapo officer. Their original target was eventually tracked down and killed too.[52]

While all this had been going on, Göring, Himmler and Heydrich were acting in cool and targeted Chicago gangster style in Berlin. On the morning of 30 June, SS guards rang the doorbell of the home of General Kurt von Schleicher, the former German Chancellor, in the affluent Berlin suburb of Neubabelsberg. When his maid opened the door, SS guards pushed past her, found their target in his living room, and gunned him down in a hail of bullets. His wife, who had tried to protect him, was shot dead too. The maid fled the scene screaming. It was the couple's twelve-year-old daughter who discovered her parents, lying dead in a pool of blood on the living-room carpet, when she came home from school.

The Nazi radical Gregor Strasser, who had given up political activism in the early months of 1933, was running a pharmaceutical company when he was seized from his Berlin home, taken to the Gestapo HQ at Prinz Albrechtstrasse and placed in a large holding room along with a large number of arrested SA leaders. He had never been forgiven by Göring for entering into negotiations with General von Schleicher after the November 1932 elections concerning a possible left-of-centre coalition.

At the Nuremberg trials, Hans Gisevius, a Gestapo official, described what happened to him:

An SS man came to the door [of his cell] and called out Strasser. The man who had formerly been next in importance to Adolf Hitler was to be moved to an individual cell. No one thought anything of it as Strasser walked slowly out of the room. But scarcely a minute later they heard the crack of a pistol. The SS man had shot the unsuspecting Strasser from behind and hit his main artery. A stream of blood had spurted against the wall of his tiny cell. Apparently Strasser did not die at once. A prisoner in the adjoining cell heard him thrashing about on the bed for nearly an hour. No one paid any attention to him. At last, the prisoner heard loud footsteps in the corridor and orders being shouted. The guards clicked their heels, and the prisoner recognised Heydrich's voice saying: 'Isn't he dead yet? Let the swine bleed to death.'[53]

When Hitler returned to Berlin, he was shocked to hear about the horrific circumstances of Gregor Strasser's death, and about how the scope of the purge had broadened to include conservative political figures. Göring told him Gregor Strasser had not been murdered, but had committed suicide while in custody. No investigation of the circumstances of his death was ever carried out. Hitler personally sanctioned the state pension that was awarded to Strasser's widow.

The fate of Franz von Papen also hung in the balance. Himmler and Heydrich had him high up on their hit list. SS guards went to his villa in the Berlin suburbs and placed him under house arrest. It was eventually decided von Papen was too high profile to murder, so they eliminated some of his key advisers, to warn him of the consequences of any further acts of open defiance. A small troop of SS officers stormed into his private office, ransacked it and then gunned down Herbert von Bose, his personal secretary, as he sat at his desk. Erich Klausener, leader of Catholic Action, was also murdered in his office at the Ministry of Communications. The killing of such a prominent religious figure caused protests from the Catholic Church hierarchy. The Gestapo insisted he had committed suicide in a break during questioning. Dr Edgar Jung, who had provided the words for von Papen's Marburg speech, was shot dead by an SS officer on the direct order of Heydrich. His body was then ignominiously dumped in a ditch on the road to the Oranienburg concentration camp. Walter Schotte, author of a book on Franz von Papen's 1932 government which had criticised the Nazi Party, was also shot dead. A suitably terrified Franz von Papen resigned as Vice Chancellor on 3 July. He continued to work for the Nazi regime though, and accepted the role of German Ambassador to Vienna, but his days at the high table of power in Germany were over. Fear and anxiety were now his constant companions.[54]

The bloody 'Night of the Long Knives' was all over by the evening of 1 July 1934. In a radio broadcast the following day, Goebbels claimed the killings were an essential clean-up operation to prevent a coup led by Röhm and Kurt von Schleicher, the former German Chancellor, along with many others who had never accepted Hitler's regime. The 'sexual depravity' of Röhm and his entourage was highlighted too. The Cabinet agreed to a retrospective law, later ratified in the Reichstag, which legalised the murders as 'essential measures of national defence'.[55] The German public were not shocked or unduly concerned by this lawless purge. It led to a sharp fall in membership of the SA from 2.9 million in August 1934 to 1.2 million by April 1938.[56]

President Hindenburg praised Hitler for his 'gallant personal intervention' which had 'rescued the German people from great danger'. He died on 1 August 1934. Hitler amalgamated the posts of Chancellor and President into the title of Leader (Führer). The army agreed to swear the following oath: 'I swear before God to obey without reservation, Adolf Hitler, Führer of the Reich, supreme chief of the *Wehrmacht* and I pledge myself as a courageous soldier always to observe this oath, even at the risk of my life.' Hitler was now the undisputed and unchallenged leader of the Third Reich.

The exact death toll of the purge has never been fully established. All the execution orders were signed by Himmler and Heydrich. Many of those who were killed had no connection with the SA at all. Hitler's Reichstag speech on 13 July gave a total figure of seventy-four dead, including nineteen 'higher SA leaders', and announced that 1,000 others were in custody in prisons and concentration camps. Twelve of those killed had been Reichstag deputies. The *White Book of the Purge*, produced by German dissidents in Paris, claimed that 401 had been killed, but named only 116. The Nuremberg tribunal did not give an exact figure.[57]

The 'Night of the Long Knives' greatly increased the power of the SS and the Gestapo. A few days after the purge, Göring informed Frick that 'in recognition of the special services performed by the Political Police in the past days, the Reich Chancellor has given Reichsführer-SS Himmler and myself a free hand in how the Political Police should be run within the framework of his directives'.[58] It would be unwise, however, to conclude that Himmler's control of the Gestapo and police power in Nazi Germany was complete at this stage. During the latter months of 1935, there were a string of SS murders, which were SA reprisals for the Röhm purge. A total of 150 corpses were found, with a small card pinned to them with the initials 'R.R.', which was an acronym for 'Avengers of Röhm'. These murders were probably carried out by a renegade wing of the SA, but in spite of an extensive investigation by the Gestapo the culprits were never found.[59]

Even more troublesome for Himmler and Heydrich was a conservative counterattack led by Frick at the Ministry of the Interior. On 2 July 1934, Frick complained to Hitler about the involvement of non-police organisations in the 'Night of the Long Knives' and he criticised its generally lawless nature. This was an open attack on Göring, Himmler and Heydrich. Hitler rebuked Frick for this intervention. On 6 July 1934, Göring issued a decree that once more emphasised the Gestapo was an independent part of the administration, under his special juris-diction. On 20 July 1934, Hitler ratified this order and he further emphasised that Himmler was now answerable to him alone.

This did not stop Frick still trying to place further restraints on Himmler. He shifted his line of attack towards the SS-run concentration camps. These were outside of the control of the Ministry of the Interior. It was common knowledge internees were being treated brutally in them. To counteract Frick's criticisms, Himmler introduced a system of graded punishments in all the camps. Frick also requested details about how people arrested under 'protective custody' orders were being treated by Gestapo officers during interrogations. In response, Himmler gave a speech on 11 October 1934 to Gestapo officers during which he said that all cases should be handled with speed, that no law-abiding citizen should fear arrest, and that the German public should be made aware that 'members of the Gestapo are men with human kindness and absolute rightness' who handle those arrested 'courteously and socially'. The Gestapo, according to Himmler, should be regarded as an efficient and rigorous organisation that could distinguish through forensic questioning and the accumulation of evidence who were the real 'enemies of the state' and those who were loyal to the state.[60]

To make the Gestapo an indispensable part of the police system of Nazi Germany, Himmler needed to counter the conservative argument which suggested that with the communists and the SA now crushed, the Gestapo and the concentration camps could be dispensed with. During 1935, Heydrich began to expand the conception of 'enemies of the people' beyond the usual narrow political definition towards what he called a 'camouflaged enemy' that included religious dissidents, and Jews, but was now expanded to incorporate 'racial enemies' such as anti-social and criminal elements.[61]

Dr Werner Best, who became head of the administrative office of the Gestapo (the Gestapa) in the summer of 1934, was a key figure in transforming the Gestapo into a modern and efficient instrument of Nazi terror. He was born in Darmstadt on 10 July 1903. He held a university degree and a PhD. He then trained as a lawyer and served as a judge. He had a tremendous flair for administrative organisation, and proved hugely influential in the development of the Gestapo. He was always coming up with new and often extraordinary administrative ideas. One of his most innovative reforms was to create a centralised file-card system. The huge circular punch-card index system was powered by an electric motor. This allowed its operator speedily to locate the card of an arrested individual.

It was the police national computer of its day. It proved invaluable to Gestapo officers conducting interrogations. Individuals were placed in three categories. Group A1 were classed as 'enemies of the state' and defined as the most dangerous. Their cards had a red mark. Group A2, marked in blue, consisted of individuals who would be arrested in the event of war. Unmarked Group A3 index cards detailed a large miscellaneous group of people deemed 'politically dangerous'. An expanding band of clerical workers was given the task of updating cards and files.[62]

Specialist Gestapo sections were created in local offices. One dealt with political opponents, another concentrated on religious bodies and sects, and there was a dedicated Jewish section. Others dealt with 'protective custody' arrests and other groups defined as 'enemies' of the National Community.[63] All Gestapo officers were encouraged to maintain a 'patriotic duty of silence' and to keep all matters they investigated strictly confidential.[64]

By the end of 1935, Adolf Hitler had come out clearly in favour of giving Himmler supreme power over all police security in Germany. Göring also came to accept that a new Gestapo law was required, which recognised the Gestapo's unique position within the Nazi state. The third and most far-reaching Gestapo Law of 10 February 1936 was drafted by Werner Best and his administrative staff. It decreed that the Gestapo could not be subjected to any judicial or administrative tribunal. The mission of the Gestapo was to inquire into anyone who put the state at risk, to execute the will of a single leader and to preserve the German people from all attempts at destruction by internal and external enemies.[65] The law also stipulated that the Gestapo officers were the grand inquisitors, and that the Gestapo office would administer the state concentration camps. In practice, a specialised section of the SS continued to run the camps. The role of the Gestapo office was to assign arrested individuals to specific camps. The concentration camps were still deemed independent of state supervision by the new 'fundamental law'.

In a decree, signed by Hitler, dated 17 June 1936, Himmler became 'Chief of the German Police' with the aim of defending the German people 'against all attempts of destruction by enemies within and outside the country'.[66] Within days, the German police was split into two divisions, controlled by Himmler: (i) The Main Office of ORPO (*Ordnungspolizei* – Order Police), which included the municipal, rural and local police forces and was led by Karl Daluege, a committed SS officer, who had previously served as commander of Prussian police forces; (ii) The Main Office of SIPO (*Sicherheitspolizei* – security police), which was led by Reinhard Heydrich. This consisted of the Gestapo, now led by Heinrich Müller, a non-Nazi career policeman. The chief role of the Gestapo was to fight against 'political enemies'. Kripo (*Kriminalpolizei*), the detective wing of the plain-clothes criminal police force, was led by Arthur Nebe, also a career policeman. Its key role was to act against 'criminal' elements that were a threat to the community due to their 'physical and moral degeneracy'. The Gestapo and Kripo retained separate administrative organisations, but worked very closely together. The Gestapa, the administrative centre of the Gestapo, remained under the control of Dr Werner Best. The Gestapo, which had been confined to Prussia in 1933, was now the 'Secret State Police' for the whole of Germany.

Heinrich Himmler gloried in his triumph over policing in Nazi Germany by depicting his haughty conservative enemies as misguided in their belief that a return to 'normality' could be achieved by emptying the concentration camps and dissolving the Gestapo. The only concession Frick achieved in this protracted and ultimately futile struggle was to prevent Himmler becoming a Cabinet Minister. Himmler was given the title of 'State Secretary' and was supposedly subordinate to Frick, within the Ministry of the Interior. Frick asked Himmler to report to him personally on police matters at monthly meetings, but Himmler never even bothered to turn up to any of them. Himmler was no longer 'subordinate' to anyone in the Third Reich, except Hitler.

The extent of Frick's defeat was explained by Hans Lammers, head of Hitler's Reich Chancellery, at the Nuremberg trial. 'Tell Herr Frick', Hitler told Lammers, 'that he should not restrict Himmler as the chief of the German police too much; with him the police is in good hands. He should allow him as free rein as possible.'[67] By 1937, Frick had given up reporting directly to Hitler on police matters at all.

On 27 September 1939, the Gestapo, Orpo, Kripo and the SD were all merged into one single centralised security authority for the whole of Nazi Germany: The Reich Security Main Office (RSHA). All the regional police authorities were subordinated to the jurisdiction of this all-powerful office.

Heinrich Himmler's policing revolution inside Nazi Germany between 1933 and 1939 was now complete.

Chapter 2

Gestapo Men and Methods

Nazi propaganda liked to give the impression that Gestapo officers were everywhere. Nothing could be further from the truth. In reality, the Gestapo was a very small organisation. In 1933, it had just 1,000 employees, rising to 6,500 in 1937 and 15,000 in 1939. A peak of 32,000 employees, including a team of administrators, was reached at the end of 1944.[1] Gestapo offices in the localities were severely under-staffed. In Düsseldorf, with a population of 500,000, there were 126 Gestapo officers in 1937. Essen, with a population of 650,000, had 43. Duisburg, with 400,000 inhabitants, had 28.[2] In 1942, Cologne with 750,000 inhabitants had a mere 69 officers.[3] In small rural towns there was usually no Gestapo personnel at all. The number of active full-time Gestapo officers in Hitler's Germany never exceeded 16,000.[4]

The Gestapo did employ spies, but little information has survived on how many there were or how much they were paid. Walter Weyrauch, acting for the US allied occupying power, found index cards on 1,200 Gestapo informers operating in Frankfurt am Main. Many had been in opposition groups and agreed to act as double agents in return for early release from concentration camps or prisons. A number of Catholic priests were recruited.[5] Surviving files from Düsseldorf list 300 Gestapo informers, all with a communist background. Information from informers was used most successfully against communist resistance groups. However, the Gestapo completely failed to spot in advance the Valkyrie bomb plot against Hitler led by Claus von Stauffenberg and his co-conspirators on 20 July 1944.

From 27 September 1939 the head office of the Gestapo was

located in Office 4 (Amt IV) of the Reich Main Security Office (RSHA) in Berlin. This office employed 1,500 officers and was divided into six sections: IVA: Enemies of Nazi Germany – this dealt with Marxists, communists, reactionaries, liberals, counter sabotage and general security; IVB: focused on the political activities of the Catholic and Protestant Churches, religious sects, Jews and Freemasons; IVC: specialised in processing Protective Custody orders; IVD: concentrated entirely on the Nazi-occupied territories; IVE: examined espionage at home and abroad; IVF: Border Police – was concerned with passports, identity papers, and the policing of foreigners, especially the huge number of foreign workers in Germany during the war-time period.[6]

The leadership of the Gestapo at the Berlin HQ consisted of three types. First: experienced former criminal policemen, who had mostly never been members of the Nazi Party before 1933. Second: young, university-educated career-minded administrators. Third: members of the SD, who came to the Gestapo via the Nazi Party SS machinery.[7]

The director of the Gestapo between 1936 and 1945 was Heinrich Müller. Born in Munich in 1900, he was the son of a policeman from a traditional Catholic working-class family. He left school with no qualifications. His school reports describe him as 'average' in all the subjects he studied. He had a broad working–class Munich accent which he never tried to lose. He served an apprenticeship as a metal fitter in the Bavarian Aircraft Company, but he decided not to continue working in this growing industry. In 1918, he joined the police force and was assigned to its small political police department. It was the generous occupational police pension scheme that appealed to him. He was only thirty-six years old when he became the head of the Gestapo for the whole of Nazi Germany. Müller was an adaptable streetwise individual. He worked for the Bavarian monarchy, the democratic Weimar government and the Nazi regime.

He was not only a scrupulous bureaucrat, but was also very good at tracking down major political opponents. He discovered that British intelligence was behind the assassination of Reinhard Heydrich in 1942.[8] He broke the infamous 'Red Orchestra' socialist spy ring. Rudolf Hess claimed at the Nuremberg war trials that Müller was 'politically uncommitted' and most probably remained a 'conservative nationalist' all his life.[9] A confidential personnel report from 1937 observed: 'His sphere of activity [in the Weimar period] was to supervise and deal with the left wing movement. It must be admitted he fought against it hard. But it is equally clear that, if it had been his task to do so, Müller would have acted against the right in the same way.'[10] He was not a member of the Nazi Party until 1939, and only joined for career reasons.[11] Müller rose to the top of the Gestapo not because of any ideological affinity to Nazism, but due to his administrative skills; particularly, his ability to track down communist resistance groups. He set the same high standards of bureaucratic efficiency for all his staff. His signature appears on numerous Gestapo documents, usually endorsing or amending the decisions of others. He often lunched at the Adlon Hotel, near the Brandenburg Gate in Berlin, with Heydrich, who greatly valued him, and other leading Gestapo figures.

All the other section heads of the Gestapo at the Berlin HQ also began their careers in the ordinary criminal police during the democratic Weimar Republic. In Section IVA, which concentrated on communist opposition, the backgrounds of all the leading figures were very similar. They were all born between 1894 and 1903. They joined the police before 1933. Most were university-educated graduates from a middle-class background. These young men employed methods of investigation that were identical to practices of the criminal detective police. Only one of them, Horst Kopkow, had ever been an active member of the Nazi Party before 1933.[12]

The head of Section IVA between 1940 and 1942 was Josef

Vogt, who was born in 1897. He studied economics at university. In 1925, he joined the police force. Between 1929 and 1933, he worked in the homicide department of the criminal detective police department. In May 1933, he joined the Nazi Party. He personally volunteered to join the Gestapo. It was his energetic role in countering communist resistance that caught the eye of his superiors and marked him out for fast-track promotion.[13]

His deputy, Kurt Lindow, born in 1903, replaced him in 1942. He studied law and economics at university. In 1928 he joined the criminal detective police. In 1933, he joined the Gestapo and worked on several high-profile cases involving high treason. He was essentially an effective organiser and a reliable administrator.

Another key figure in Section IVA was Rudolf Braschwitz, born in 1900. He studied dentistry at the University of Breslau, but decided not to pursue a career as a dentist and joined the police force instead. By 1928, he was working for the Prussian political police, leading a protection squad guarding world-famous German Foreign Minister Gustav Stresemann, who had received several bomb threats from right-wing groups. In 1933, Braschwitz became the leader of a group dedicated to combating communism. He only joined the Nazi Party on 1 May 1933.[14]

Another expert on communism in section IVA was Reinhold Heller, born in 1885. He went to university to study law, but he failed his degree.[15] In 1919, he joined the political police. By 1931, he was heading a department dedicated to fighting the communist threat. He joined the Nazi Party on 1 May 1933. He played a key role in the investigation of the Reichstag fire, at the age of forty-eight. Men of Heller's age were viewed by Himmler and Heydrich as steeped in the democratic Weimar tradition of policing. It was Heller's invaluable administrative experience, his adaptability and his expertise in dealing with communist resistance that allowed him to retain a leading role within the Gestapo.

Section IVB dealt with the Christian churches, religious sects such as Jehovah's Witnesses, and the Jews. There was a sub-section within this department that concentrated on the evacuation of Jews during the period of the Holocaust. It was headed by one of the most infamous Gestapo officials of all: Adolf Eichmann, who was born in 1906 in Solingen in the Rhineland, but was brought up in Linz, Austria, a city where Hitler had also lived during his teenage years. Eichmann's father Adolf was the owner of a profitable mining company. The family were devout Protestants, but his childhood outside the family home was an unhappy one. A withdrawn child, he was ill suited to teenage rough and tumble. His school mates nicknamed him 'the little Jew' (*der kleine Jude*), due to his dark complexion. He left school without any qualifications. During the 1920s his father used his extensive business contacts to get him jobs in the electrical industry and then as an oil salesman. His father's business went bankrupt during the depression. In 1932, Eichmann joined the Austrian Nazi Party.[16] The turning point in his career came in 1933 when he went to Germany as a protégé of Ernst Kaltenbrunner, a leading figure in the SD. He worked at the infamous Dachau concentration camp before emerging as a key adviser within the SD on Jewish affairs. Eichmann's hard-working, unquestioning bureaucratic skills came to the notice of Heinrich Himmler. For two years between 1938 and 1940 Eichmann organised the deportation of Austrian Jews to Poland and repeated this process for Czech Jews in Prague. This led to his promotion to lead the Jewish section at the Berlin HQ of the Gestapo. Eichmann organised the entire transportation of all Europe's Jews to the death camps during the Holocaust.[17] Eichmann, who lacked a university degree and a police background, was not the usual type of Gestapo bureaucratic official who could aspire to a high position.

The biggest department in the Berlin Gestapo HQ was IVC2, which dealt with protective custody orders. All its key figures had been criminal police officers before 1933. By 1944, it employed eleven inspectors and forty-four filing clerks and typists. It was headed by Emil Berndorff, born in 1892. He had studied law and political science at the University of Berlin. In 1920, he gained a doctorate in law before joining the criminal police. He worked on several high-profile murder cases in the homicide department during the Weimar period. He joined a newly created secretive Nazi Party organisation for police officers in August 1932. He then became a specialist in processing protective custody orders. He also helped develop instructions for Gestapo 'enhanced interrogation' techniques, which allowed the use of beatings and torture.[18]

Section IVD concentrated on policing in the Nazi-occupied territories. All the key figures in this department were very young. In 1939, none of them was over the age of forty. They all possessed university degrees, and half of them had gone on to gain doctorates. They all came from the SD and had joined the Gestapo between 1937 and 1938. All the employees in this section were active in the *Einsatzgruppen* mobile killing squads that operated in Poland and especially in the Soviet Union during the Second World War. These young, politically committed Nazis were being groomed for a prominent role in the post-war Nazi era.

The SD had a separate Domestic Office (III) within the Berlin HQ. It specialised in domestic intelligence and assessed public opinion. It was headed by the young Nazi high-flyer Otto Ohlendorf, born in 1907. He studied law and economics at university before gaining a doctorate in law from the University of Pavia. In 1925, he became a Nazi Party member, and joined the SS a year later. He then carved out a very successful academic career as an economic expert at the Kiel Institute of World Economy. In 1936, he was appointed as economic adviser to the SD. In 1939, Ohlendorf was head-hunted by Heydrich to lead Office III at the Berlin HQ. When he took up his post, he was just thirty-two years old. The rapid promotion of such young, highly educated individuals was not unusual in Nazi

Germany. In many ways the over-promotion of young people gave the regime its energetic radicalism. In the summer of 1941, Ohlendorf became the head of Einsatzgruppen D, the mobile killing unit in the Soviet Union: which was responsible for the mass killing of thousands of Jews. He could switch between being an academic, an effective desk-bound bureaucrat and a mass killer in an SS uniform without ever being troubled by the small matter of the morality of what he was doing. Ohlendorf created a group within SD Office III in the Berlin HQ which secretly observed public opinion in public places inside Nazi Germany. This section was headed by Dr Hans Rößner, born in 1910, who had studied German and history at the University of Leipzig before gaining a doctorate. He joined the Nazi Party in 1933. He then became a member of the SD.[19]

The Gestapo had fifty-four regional offices within the federal states. The leading commanders in these regional offices were also career-minded individuals, with backgrounds very similar to those at the Berlin HQ. They were all young, middle class and university educated. They usually held a law degree and often a doctorate. Very few came from the local community in which they were employed. Many had passed a special security police training school course in Berlin. These regional heads wielded enormous decision-making power over the local Gestapo offices they ran. They decided which cases were investigated, and picked the Gestapo officer best suited to conduct them.

Regional Gestapo heads of department tended to be enthusiastic and ideologically committed Nazis. A typical example is Dr Emanuel Schäfer, born in 1900 and head of the Cologne Gestapo. He was a protégé of Reinhard Heydrich. His father owned a hotel. He gained a law degree from the University of Breslau and then a doctorate on civil law. He joined the Potsdam criminal police in 1926. In 1928, he became the head of the homicide department of the Breslau police department. In February 1933, he took charge of the political police in Breslau.

He joined the Nazi Party on 1 May 1933, then the SS and SD. In May 1934, he was appointed head of the Gestapo in the city of Oppeln. In his annual staff appraisals, he is described as holding a 'very solid National Socialist world view'. In October 1940, he became the head of the Cologne Gestapo. He organised the deportation of Jews from Cologne to the death camps that began in October 1941. Everyone who knew him mentioned his deep passion for National Socialism.[20]

For young, ambitious, ideologically driven, university graduates such as Emanuel Schäfer the sky was the limit in the Gestapo. Without these attributes, the reverse was invariably true. Ludwig Jung, born in 1910, head of the Krefeld Gestapo, is a prime example. His father owned a butcher's shop. He failed to complete his law degree at the University of Giessen, but as the only Gestapo officer in the Krefeld office who had ever attended a university, he still maintained a noticeable career edge over his academically challenged colleagues. His passionate support for National Socialism clearly helped him too. He joined the Nazi Party in 1930. Being a member before Hitler came to power nearly always helped at job interviews. After attending a specialist police leadership training course in Berlin in March 1938 Jung was appointed head of the Krefeld Gestapo, aged just twenty-eight years old. However, he moved no further up the promotion ladder in the Gestapo. His failure to finish his degree and his lower-middle-class background both counted against him.[21]

In 1938, 95 per cent of Gestapo regional directors had completed their school-leaving certificate (*Abitur*).[22] A total of 87 per cent held university law degrees and nearly half of them had been awarded doctorates. The high ranks of the Gestapo resembled an academic university senior common room more than a police department. All of them were under forty. A police background was becoming much less important in the Gestapo promotion stakes by the late 1930s. The key university qualification to gain graduate entry to the Gestapo was a law degree. It became normal for graduate entrants to gain rapid promotions over the heads of older, experienced, but less academically qualified police detectives.[23] Dr Werner Best, head of personnel at the Gestapo HQ, believed the hard-working requirements of a law degree suited the investigative work of the Gestapo, which was why he proactively encouraged the appointment of law graduates to the highest positions within the Gestapo from 1936 onwards.

Ordinary Gestapo officers were very different from their highly educated leaders. Rank-and-file Gestapo officers were divided into two ranks: Criminal Assistant (*Kriminalassistent*) and Criminal Secretary (*Kriminalsekretär*). Most came from a solid working-class or lower-middle-class background. They had nearly all left school at sixteen without any formal qualifications. Hardly any possessed a university degree and few rank-and-file Gestapo officers rose up the promotion ladder. It has been estimated that 50 per cent of the old pre-1933 career policemen who joined the Gestapo were still in post in 1945.[24] In 1939, only 3,000 Gestapo officers had an additional SS rank.

At subsequent war trials, Gestapo officers defined themselves as ordinary career policemen who conducted themselves during investigations no differently from criminal detectives. All the Gestapo officers who testified at the Nuremberg trials claimed the personnel of the Gestapo in 1933 consisted of members of the existing police force.[25] They were, according to their own testimony, professional and efficient police officers who took orders from their superiors, and rarely took any initiatives of their own.[26] They pragmatically adjusted to new circumstances and joined the Nazi Party primarily to keep their jobs. During post-war denazification investigations, conducted by Allied occupation officials, the vast majority of former Gestapo officers were classed as 'ordinary men' and 'Denazified' as 'Exonerated' of being responsible for 'crimes against humanity'. Most retained their generous occupational pensions.

Historian Eric Johnson examined the backgrounds of the nineteen Gestapo officers who served in Krefeld between 1937 and 1945. He found all had served as police officers in the Weimar police force. None were Nazi Party members. They all came from a working-class or lower-middle-class background, left school at sixteen with no qualifications, and none possessed a university degree. Most joined the Nazi Party for purely career reasons. They were all very good at the clerical tasks associated with the job though. Their reports displayed an impressive grasp of grammar and spelling. In subsequent trials, Gestapo officers in Krefeld stressed they had all been dragooned into the Gestapo and forced into the Nazi Party, but they remained essentially decent and professional 'ordinary men'.[27]

Robert Gellately looked into the background of the twenty-two Gestapo officials in Würzburg. All were career policemen. Before 1937, virtually all of them had not joined the Nazi Party. It was only the head of department, Joseph Gerum, born in 1888, who was a Nazi. He became head of the Würzburg Gestapo in April 1934. He had joined the Nazi Party in 1920, and participated in the famous Munich Beer Hall Putsch, for which he was given a fifteen-month prison sentence. He was also a very experienced policeman who had been in the force since 1917. In 1933, he joined the political police in Munich before being parachuted in to lead the Würzburg office.[28]

The term 'ordinary' can be stretched too far in relation to Gestapo officers. The German police in the Weimar period had to deal with an unprecedented wave of street violence enacted by Nazis and communists. Most criminal detectives who joined the Gestapo were already schooled in tough policing, and were not averse to brutality either. They had dealt frequently with murders, rapists and serious gangsters on a daily basis before the Nazis came to power. They were skilled in the art of detailed questioning too.

By the late 1930s the Gestapo continued to recruit individuals from lower-middle-class and working-class backgrounds, but there were some noticeable changes. Most new recruits were under thirty. Very few had any previous police experience at all. The key job criteria of a Gestapo officer became: proof of a German blood-line, good general education but no specific educational qualifications, physical fitness, and shorthand and typing skills. Membership of the Nazi Party or one of its sub-organisations was now deemed 'desirable', but still not essential.[29] This influx of young, inexperienced officers undoubtedly changed the ethos of the Gestapo. It was hard to train newcomers in established professional investigative police techniques. The 'old school' professional policemen of the Weimar era were retiring year by year. During the war-time period, more brutal interrogation methods increased among these ideologically committed young Gestapo officers.

On appointment, every Gestapo officer was issued with a detailed instruction manual on how to conduct themselves in tracking down, arresting and interrogating individuals. It advised Gestapo officers not to carry identification papers and to wear only 'plain clothes, including personal underwear', when going to arrest an individual.[30] Detailed instructions were given on such matters as how to use a compass, prepare maps for an intelligence report, conduct surveillance operations, mount raids, and how to compile all the necessary reports and to collect evidence linked to an investigation.

Detailed guidelines on how a Gestapo officer should deal with those arrested were also spelled out. Each prisoner had to be interrogated by either a Gestapo officer or a Criminal Detective from Kripo, depending on the nature of the charge. It stressed that a state lawyer and an investigating judge should be appointed at the outset of each case. The chief task of each Gestapo officer was to collect and secure all the evidence, question witnesses, keep a detailed record of all interrogations and investigate every detail fully. It was advised in the Gestapo manual that 'all applicable investigative techniques will be used' during the course of the investigation.[31] In subsequent chapters, we will see how Gestapo officers dealt with individual cases in detail.

The assumption that Gestapo officers arrested individuals, interrogated them brutally, then sent them to a concentration camp, is a myth. Each case was dealt with exhaustively before any decision on punishment was decided upon. Most of those arrested ended up within the traditional justice system, and were charged with a specific crime that was dealt with by the courts. Sending individuals to a concentration camp was always a last resort, especially for an ordinary German citizen who was not linked to the selected target opposition groups. Many of those arrested were released without any charge.

In the early years of Nazi rule, the concentration camp system was very small when compared to the traditional prison system. By the summer of 1935, only 4,000 prisoners were left in the SS-run Nazi concentration camps.[32] Numbers did grow rapidly in the late 1930s, but this was due to a widening of the definition of an 'enemy of the state' from a 'political' to a 'racial' opponent. On 1 September 1939, the SS held 21,400 prisoners in the following six key concentration camps: Dachau, Sachsenhausen, Buchenwald, Mauthausen, Flossenbürg and Ravensbrück. These camps, as we shall see in more detail later, became dumping grounds for these newly defined 'asocial' racial enemies.

In comparison, 120,000 prisoners were detained in traditional German prisons before the Second World War. Most inmates in prisons served traditional criminal sentences, but political and religious opponents often ended up in prison too. A system of close co-operation developed between the Gestapo on the one hand and prison officials on the other. Political prisoners who served sentences in prisons often found it difficult to escape the clutches of the Gestapo. Prison governors, mostly old-school conservative bureaucrats, would compile a report on any political or religious opponent due for release. This was invariably passed on to the Gestapo. In some cases, a prisoner might be released, if given a glowing report by the governor, but was then immediately taken back into 'protective custody' by the Gestapo at the prison gates. A typical case concerned a communist activist called Max. He was sentenced to twenty-seven months in prison in June 1934 for playing a leading role in a communist underground movement. While in prison, he had behaved impeccably. However, three months before his release, the prison governor informed the Gestapo:

> He did not attract any special attention in the institution. But in view of his past life, I cannot believe that he has changed his mind and I believe that he has, just like most leading communists, only kept out of trouble now through cunning calculation. In my view, it is absolutely essential that this active, leading communist is taken into protective custody after his sentence.[33]

There was an established manner in which every case was dealt with by Gestapo officers. A case usually began with a denouncement from the public, which arrived in the post, by telephone call or in person. Less often, cases started via surveillance operations, tip-offs from Gestapo informers or from information sent by local Nazi block leaders. Gestapo policy was to investigate every public denunciation, no matter how trivial. All these allegations were then examined by the head of the local Gestapo department, and his key administrative personnel. The head of department would decide which officer was best suited to take over a case. As each Gestapo office had specialists in all the key areas of opposition activity, the allocation of cases was a pretty straightforward task.

The Gestapo officer appointed to lead the investigation would then gather information on the case, organise the arrest of an individual and conduct the associated interrogations. The accused person could be arrested after the issue of a 'Temporary Arrest Order', which allowed the accused person to be held for ten days before any charge needed to be brought. Before a 'Protective

Custody' order was granted a charge needed to be brought against the accused. The interrogation statement was examined by the head of department and the final decision over a 'protective custody' order needed to be endorsed by the appointed prosecutor and was often passed to the department in the Berlin HQ that dealt with protective custody orders.[34]

Every arrested person who entered a Gestapo office was fingerprinted and photographed. They were mostly kept in custody while the investigation was conducted. Each Gestapo case file was ascribed to a single accused individual, even when a number of other people were involved. The information in each personal case file was recorded on a uniform official Gestapo document. The vast majority of these files are typed. Three mug shot photos of the accused appear on the front page. The first pages include personal details, including name, date and place of birth, home address, marital status, religion, previous convictions, military service record, details of previous time served in prison or concentration camp. The bulk of each file contains the interrogation statement of the accused, and the interrogations of all the other witnesses involved in the case. All letters related to the case are included. Many Gestapo files run into several hundred pages. Each file was clearly compiled on the assumption it might end up in court.

The key part of all Gestapo investigations was the interrogation. The accused person was asked to answer a series of questions. The Gestapo often used the denunciation statement and witness statements to frame these questions. The aim was to get the accused to confess. Documentary evidence such as letters and diaries was often produced and highlighted during the interrogation. The major source of information determining guilt or innocence in the vast majority of Gestapo cases proved to be the interrogation protocol. As each case progressed, the investigating officer would often consult with the departmental head. Once the investigation was concluded the lead Gestapo officer would then compile a full written report on the case and recommend what course of action should be taken. Final decisions were always taken by heads of department, heads of regional Gestapo officers, state prosecutors and, more rarely, by the Berlin HQ. Files are often marked with a number of stamps and signatures from all these individuals and departments. The decision on whether a person was sent to a concentration camp or if the case went to a court was decided by the head of department, who consulted with the regional head of the Gestapo office, and the public prosecutor. This hierarchical and clearly defined bureaucratic framework shows Gestapo officers did not wield the arbitrary power often ascribed to them. Most departmental heads endorsed the decisions arrived at by the Gestapo officer who carried out the investigation. It was only higher authorities who revised or changed decisions, but this was extremely rare.[35]

Torture was undoubtedly used by certain Gestapo officers to extract confessions during investigations. Torture beyond prescribed punishments was never officially sanctioned in any of the surviving written Gestapo documents. The Justice Ministry frequently sent warnings to Gestapo officers pointing out the severe criminal penalties that would be imposed if prisoners were ill-treated while in custody.[36] The extent of torture is also notoriously difficult to estimate. It was much less common inside Nazi Germany than in the occupied territories. It was most commonly used during the early months of Nazi rule when the SA acted as auxiliary police and set up 'wild concentration camps'.

It did unquestionably continue during the Nazi period, especially against communists and other key targeted groups. Some individuals committed suicide during long periods of Gestapo interrogation. The cause of death in these cases is often recorded as 'suicide', but may have been the result of periods of torture that went too far. There is no way of establishing the true cause of death from the surviving documentation. In subsequent war trials, and denazification investigations, nearly all Gestapo officers denied ever using torture at all, especially inside Nazi Germany. Witnesses at post-war trials told a different tale.

The most common officially sanctioned punishment was a bamboo cane. Up to twenty-five strokes to the buttocks, with a doctor present, were administered by Gestapo officers using this method. Jan Valtin, a communist activist, recalled that he was whipped so hard on the back that his shirt was soaked with blood by the end.[37] Other 'unofficial' torture methods reported by survivors include water torture. This involved plunging a person into a bath full of cold water until almost asphyxiated. Exhaustion exercises and sleep deprivation were also mentioned. Electrical currents were seemingly wired to hands, the anus and the penis of male prisoners. The testicles of male prisoners were often crushed with a press, similar to a garlic press, to extract information. Many prisoners were hung by their hands for varying periods of time until they confessed. Fingers were sometimes burned with matches.[38]

These extreme measures were exclusively reserved for 'social outsiders' and key political prisoners, particularly communists. Each time a confession was not forthcoming, the torture was stepped up. Maria Grimme, a prisoner, observed Mildred Harnack (born 1902 as Mildred Fish in Milwaukee, Wisconsin, USA), a member of the socialist 'Red Orchestra' opposition, being brought into a cell in Berlin after she had undergone an 'enhanced' Gestapo interrogation in October 1942:

> Someone was carried into the waiting room on a stretcher, hardly breathing. The stretcher was placed so that the person's head was right next to me. I looked over and was startled by the expression in the person's eyes ... shortly thereafter two Gestapo officers came in, pulled this individual up by the arms and said, 'So Frau Harnack, feeling better?' Frau Harnack was then taken out [for further interrogation], some time later she was brought back again on the stretcher. Although she complained of being cold, none of the prisoners dared to give her a blanket from those on

hand. After a while she tried to fetch one of the blankets herself, but collapsed.[39]

The criminal detective policemen in Kripo tended to look down on these brutal Gestapo techniques. They did not enjoy involvement in the 'political' work of the Gestapo. Detectives in Kripo saw themselves as using forensic and scientific techniques and physical evidence to prove the guilt of an accused person. Their work was subject to the close scrutiny of the traditional court system and defence lawyers. Kripo officers felt the Gestapo method of focusing the entire investigation on the interrogation was not designed to find the truth, based on independent evidence, but to settle cases quickly.[40]

It is clear that the majority of Gestapo officers were career policemen, with right-wing leanings, not brutal Nazi fanatics. Gestapo officers of this type remained in post during the entire Nazi era. The Gestapo leadership in Berlin and in the regions was very different. Here young, radical and dynamic university-educated individuals were intent on changing the 'old school' police values inherited from the Weimar era, and moulding them into ideologically and racially driven prerogatives that turned a blind eye to the 'rule of law'. There was no overnight revolution in the personnel of the Gestapo, but a very gradual transition in which the 'ordinary' Gestapo officers of the Weimar period were challenged to conform to new racially directed types of policing, led by high-flying university-educated graduates, who were a million miles away from the bully-boy thugs who had been storm troopers during Hitler's rise to power.

Chapter 3

Policing Religious Faith

In *Mein Kampf* Adolf Hitler bitterly criticised the Christian churches for their failure to recognise the importance of the Jewish Question. Point 24 of the Nazi Party programme offered the following ambiguous promise on religious matters:

> We demand freedom for all religious denominations in the State so far as they are not a danger to it and do not militate against the customs and morality of the German race. The Party as such stands for positive Christianity, but does not bind itself in the matter of creed to any particular denomination. It fights the spirit of Jewish materialism *inside* and *outside* our ranks and is convinced that our nation can achieve permanent health from within only on the principle: 'Common welfare comes before individual welfare.'[1]

In reality, the Nazi regime was determined to limit the influence of the Christian religion over the German people. The 1939 census shows this was an uphill task. A total of 95 per cent of those who lived within the original 1933 German borders registered themselves as members of the two Christian churches, with only 1.5 per cent listing themselves as 'atheists'.[2] This helps to explain why so few Gestapo cases against clerics began with a denouncement from a member of the public.[3]

On coming to power, Hitler promised in public 'to protect Christianity as the basis of our whole morality', but said in private: 'Neither of the denominations – Catholic or Protestant – has any future left. At least not for the Germans . . . One is either a Christian or a German. You can't be both.'[4] In a diary entry, dated 29 December 1939, Joseph Goebbels offered the following observation on Hitler's religious outlook: 'The Führer is deeply religious, though completely anti-Christian. He views Christianity as a symptom of decay. Rightly so. It is a branch of the Jewish race. This can be seen in the similarity of their religious rites.'[5]

In a major speech to Reichstag deputies on 23 March 1933, Hitler made a soothingly calculated promise to the Christian churches:

> National government sees in both the Christian denominations the most important factor for the maintenance of our society. It will observe the agreements drawn up between the Churches and the provinces; their rights will not be touched ... The Government will treat all other denominations with objective and impartial justice . . . The National Government will allow and confirm to the Christian denominations the enjoyment of their due influence in schools and the state. And it will be concerned for the sincere cooperation between Church and State.[6]

To ease the anxiety of Catholics, Hitler opened up negotiations with the Vatican to secure a Concordat, which, in principle, would allow the Catholic Church independence to run its own affairs in return for a promise to withdraw completely from political affairs. On 20 July 1933, a Concordat between Germany and the Vatican was duly signed in a lavish ceremony at the Vatican in Rome by Vice Chancellor Franz von Papen, on behalf of the German government, and Monsignor Eugenio Pacelli for the Roman Catholic Church.[7]

These moderate public demonstrations of toleration towards religious affairs hid a very different private agenda. The Christian churches had to accept the conformity demanded by the Nazi regime or face incrementally escalating persecution. The Gestapo, under orders from Heydrich, was instructed to draw up plans to deal with any sign of religious dissent. Heydrich's hatred of the churches 'bordered on the pathological'.[8] Heinrich Himmler also spoke in private with utter contempt for the Christian clergy, but often gave the impression in public that his SS men were believers in God:

> We object to being called atheists, because as a society we are not bound to this or that denomination, nor as individuals. But we do take it upon ourselves to draw a sharp and clear line between church and denominated society on the one side, and political or ideological soldierliness on the other and we will attack any overlap very sharply. At the same time, despite some very bad experiences and well-justified cause for exasperation which our [SS] people have had in the past in this area, we still teach our men to respect anything which is holy to our fellow citizens, from education to upbringing, which will be esteemed by us in word and deed.[9]

During the Nazi era, priests, nuns and monks were arrested, Catholic schools, youth organisations and schools closed down, and church property seized, without any compensation being awarded. Catholic priests were depicted as agents of reaction and systematically persecuted. No fewer than 447 German-born priests spent some time in the Dachau concentration camp.[10] A sizeable number of priests were imprisoned in all the other Nazi concentration camps and some were maltreated and executed. The persecution of Catholics in Germany was not a uniquely Nazi-linked phenomenon. Otto von Bismarck's notorious 'Cultural Struggle' (*Kulturkampf*) between 1871 and 1878 had ruthlessly attempted to reduce the power and influence of the Catholic Church and its clergy in Prussia.[11]

The Gestapo led the Nazi drive to weaken the influence of Christianity over the hearts and minds of the German people, but its officers avoided interfering with religious services, as this circular letter to Bavarian Gestapo officers from 6 May 1935 made clear:

In recent months it has become clear that the clergy of both the Christian denominations are more openly and more actively working against the State. In order to overcome this, it is necessary for each detachment to pay particular attention to the activities of the clergy. But it is strictly ordered that there should be no interference under any circumstances in the services of the church. Immediate reports should be made on any important matter.[12]

The Protestant Evangelical Church represented about 40 million Germans, numbering 66 per cent of the population. It was organised into 28 federated regional Lutheran and Calvinist churches. They had traditionally enjoyed considerable autonomy. Protestant pastors were wedded to the Lutheran idea of deep loyalty towards the state. Most had been pretty antagonistic towards the democratic Weimar Republic. In 1933, a total of 40 per cent of all Evangelical clerics were members of the Nazi Party. It was hardly surprising, therefore, that a group of pro-Nazi religious zealots called the 'German Christians' – made up of 3,000 of the 17,000 Protestant pastors – came to prominence shortly after Hitler became Chancellor on 30 January 1933. The 'German Christians' demanded a centrally controlled and 'Nazified' Reich Church, with all 'Non-Aryan' clergymen dismissed.[13] Their bold rallying slogan was: 'One People. One Reich. One Faith'. In church elections held on 23 July 1933, this group polled 75 per cent and took control in many areas throughout Germany. Ludwig Müller, a fervent Nazi, was named bishop of the new 'Evangelical Reich Church'. German Christians wanted to build a Nazified version of Christianity which downplayed the Jewish aspects of the Old Testament and to purge the internationalist aspects from the New Testament of the Bible. What is more, they viewed the cross as a Jewish symbol, and the crucifix as a defeatist sign.

For many members of the Evangelical clergy these proposals were far too radical. A strong opposition to the German Christians was mounted by Martin Niemöller, who was born in 1892. He was an unlikely rebel. He was a dedicated conservative nationalist during the Weimar period. In 1931, he was appointed pastor for the Dahlem district of Berlin. He welcomed Hitler's appointment as Chancellor. In his best-selling autobiography *From U-boat to Pulpit*, published in 1933, he described his own personal odyssey from a patriotic submarine commander during the First World War to a career as a leading Protestant clergyman afterwards. In the conclusion, Niemöller made clear that he did not oppose Hitler's regime on ideological grounds at all. His opposition to the 'German Christians' was purely theological. He firmly believed the content of church services and the words of the Bible were sacrosanct.

Meetings opposing the plans of the 'German Christians' began occurring all over Germany. A synod in Barmen, in May 1934, inspired by the ideas of Professor Karl Barth, a leading Protestant theologian, defended the 'central truths of Christianity' and totally rejected the 'false doctrines' of the 'German Christians'.[14] An Evangelical organisation to defend the independence of the Church from ideological penetration followed on 11 September 1933 with the formation of the Pastors' Emergency League. This became known as the 'Confessing Church' (*Bekennende Kirche*). A total of 9,000 Protestant Evangelical pastors joined. They were mostly university-educated members of the middle classes. Only 5 per cent of them were members of the Nazi Party. By November 1934, the 'Confessing Church' claimed to be the only 'legitimate Protestant Church in Germany'.[15] This dissident behaviour scuppered the plans of the 'German Christians'. Reichsbischof Ludwig Müller, obviously out of his depth, was sidelined by Hitler, who decided Nazifying Christianity was politically unworkable in the short term and it was never implemented during the Nazi era. In 1935, a new Ministry of Church Affairs was created, under the control of the Nazi lawyer Dr Hanns Kerrl, who aimed to win the loyalty of the Protestant churches towards the Nazi regime and break the resistance of dissident rebels in the 'Confessing Church'.

By 1937, the Gestapo had created a specialised section called 'IV-B' to deal with 'Political Churches, Sects and Jews'. It contained three former Catholic priests and one ex-Protestant Evangelical minister. The inside knowledge of these men enabled the Gestapo to devise a co-ordinated plan to intimidate and repress dissident clergymen.

Enke Hansse (born in 1896) was a pastor of the 'Confessing Church' who lived in Cologne.[16] He was forty-one years old when Gestapo agents began to secretly observe his religious services. On 30 September 1937, he gave a sermon at a church service in the North Rhineland city of Wuppertal. It was attended by a large congregation, estimated between 1,300 and 1,500 people. Enke said the untold misery and hardship imposed on local clerics due to bans and imprisonments imposed by the Nazi regime had led to 'Children no longer being taught in a Christian manner', and to clerics being confronted on a daily basis with 'the mockery of the word of God'. Another pastor, called Hamburg, also spoke critically against Nazi religious persecution during the service by declaring that the leadership of the Protestant church was in the hands of men who were distant figures. He also reminded the congregation that a wave of Gestapo imprisonments in Brandenburg and Saxony were now occurring. The Gestapo noted down these critical comments, but decided not to arrest either pastor

It was two years later when Enke was finally arrested by the Gestapo. This occurred because an accusation was made against him by a member of the public. It alleged Enke had acted as the chief invigilator of an examination organised by the 'Confessing Church', which took place on 2 October 1939, in full knowledge that such an examination had no official jurisdiction. During his interrogation, Enke told the Gestapo he had fought for his country in the 'Great War' between 1914 and 1918, admitted he was active in the 'Confessing Church', but denied ever being present at the exam, as he claimed he had already resigned from the examination committee before the exam took place. On 27 April 1940, the Gestapo dropped the case due to 'lack of evidence'.[17]

This case was not atypical. The Gestapo often proceeded with great caution before arresting clerics from the 'Confessing Church'. It was extremely rare for such cases to proceed to trial. Fair trials were the norm for Protestant clergymen, not the exception. Most judges were old-school conservatives, not Nazis. The case of the most high-profile member of the 'Confessing Church', Martin Niemöller, illustrates the point well. After four years of his public opposition to Nazi religious policy, the Gestapo finally decided to arrest Niemöller on 27 June 1937 as he ended yet another critical sermon in the Dahlem parish in Berlin. He was held under 'protective custody' in Moabit prison in Berlin, and then placed in solitary confinement at the notorious Sachsenhausen concentration camp.

The chief prosecutor's office spent seven months preparing what they thought was a watertight case against the rebel pastor. Prior to Niemöller's high-profile trial, which attracted international media attention, the Propaganda Ministry under Goebbels orchestrated an unseemly character assassination against him in the press. Niemöller was accused of being a 'traitor' on the grounds he was admired in 'Jewish dominated' democratic countries. On 2 March 1938 the three presiding judges in the 'Special Court' delivered a surprising verdict of not guilty, and recommended Niemöller should be released, having already endured ample punishment.

This verdict outraged Adolf Hitler, who personally ordered Niemöller to be rearrested. In 1939, Niemöller's wife Pauline wrote a personal letter to Hitler, pleading for his release. Hitler stated in a reply that if her husband was freed he would once again become the centre of an opposition circle whose activities endangered the unity of the German people.[18] Niemöller's arrest severely weakened the rebellion within the 'Confessing Church', though it did not extinguish it completely. By the end of 1938, the majority of Protestant pastors had sworn a voluntary oath of allegiance to Hitler.

In spite of enduring solitary confinement in Sachsenhausen and Dachau, Niemöller survived Hitler's regime, but he always felt deep remorse in the post-war era that he'd not spoken out more vociferously in opposition to all those who were persecuted by the Nazi regime, especially the Jews. These feelings were most memorably and eloquently expressed in his statement (now regarded as a poem) on Gestapo persecution of opponents called 'First They Came':

First they came for the Socialists, and I did not speak out—
Because I was not a Socialist.

Then they came for the Trade Unionists, and I did not speak
out—
Because I was not a Trade Unionist.

Then they came for the Jews, and I did not speak out— .
Because I was not a Jew.

Then they came for me—and there was no one left to speak
out for me.[19]

Of all the groups mentioned in 'First They Came' it was the Jews who received the least support from the Protestant Church. Few pastors spoke out against the escalating Nazi policy of anti-Semitism. The only direct assistance offered to Jews was confined to a small number of brave and dedicated Protestant churchmen. A Berlin pastor of the 'Confessing Church', Heinrich Grüber, set up a relief agency to help Jews emigrate, most of whom had converted to Christianity. He saw his role as that of a 'Good Samaritan'. Grüber was arrested by the Gestapo on 19 December 1940, and spent three years in 'protective custody' in the concentration camps at Sachsenhausen and Dachau. He endured severe beatings. One ended with him losing all his teeth.[20]

It was only in 1943 that members of the 'Confessing Church' began to speak out openly about the forcible transportation of Jews to Poland. On 12 March 1943, Bishop Theophil Wurm of Württemberg wrote a letter to the Nazi Church Ministry concerning the treatment of Jews:

> The measures taken against the Jews, in particular, so far as they do not take place in the scope of the laws at present in force, have for a long time been depressing many circles in our nation, particularly the Christian ones. In the present difficult circumstances, the question automatically arises in many minds whether our nation has not made itself guilty of bereaving men of their homes, their occupations and their lives without the sentence of a civil or military court . . . The Christian Churches have exercised great restraint in this respect. They cannot, however, be silent when lately even Jews living in mixed marriages with German Christians some even themselves members of Christian Churches have been torn from their homes and occupations to be transported to the East.[21]

Helmut Hesse (born 1916) was another Protestant pastor who refused to remain silent on Nazi persecution of the Jews. He came from Bremen and lived in Wuppertal when he came under investigation by the Gestapo.[22] The members of the deeply religious Hesse family were already well known to the Gestapo as long-standing critics of the religious policy of the Nazi regime. The family contained a number of Protestant pastors, including Helmut's father Hermann, his two brothers, and his brother-in-law. All served time in 'protective custody' for uttering words of dissent during church services in the Nazi era.[23]

On 24 May 1943 a Gestapo informer spied on a sermon given by Hesse in a church in the Elberfeld area of Wuppertal. Helmut read out a chapter of the Bible to the congregation which contained the lines: 'And you, Lord, side with the Jews, bring together the chased people of Israel. We beg you, Lord, that you may save these good people, and we beg you for the evil people, that you may change their hearts.' On 7 June 1943 another Gestapo officer observed a service in Wuppertal at which Helmut said the 'Confessing Church' in its struggle with the Nazi state was fighting the 'hidden powers of darkness'. He also mentioned that a growing number of clerics were being sent to concentration camps and prisons for their religious convictions. Finally, he expressed his deep alarm over the escalating persecution of the Jewish population.

This prompted the Gestapo to arrest Helmut on 8 June 1943 for 'publicly siding with the plight of Jews in public'. A letter was seized by the Gestapo in which Helmut had expressed pro-Jewish sentiments to Bavarian Bishop Hans Meiser:

We, as fellow Christians, must not endure any longer that the church in Germany remains silent about the persecution of Jews. The church bears responsibility right now as even so called privileged Jews are deported. Every 'non-Aryan' in Germany today is in danger of being murdered and therefore the church has to take sides: whether to act as priests and Levites or as Samaritans? This is a question of charity. The Jewish question is an evangelical one, not a political question. The [Confessing] church has to support the Jews and to resist any 'Christian Anti Semitism' within its own community . . . The church has to resist any attempt, to eliminate the Jews whatever the cost and must regard this attempt as an attack on the church and Christ. This resistance is necessary as a testimony against the violation of the Ten Commandments. In public, in sermons and speeches the bishops have to bear witness, to instruct the conscience of the Jews, the Christian communities, as well as the persecutors.

In the last week of June 1943, Helmut Hesse was interrogated twice by the Gestapo. He denied being fundamentally anti-Nazi. He joined the SA in March 1934, he said, and had only left it in October 1935 because he couldn't combine academic theological training to qualify as a pastor with service in the storm troopers. He went on to say he was ordained on 11 April 1943 and assigned to a church in Oberkassel near Bonn. Under further questioning, he admitted he had offered prayers for imprisoned clerics and for the Jews because he believed it was a duty of the Church to pray for every human being. His prayers for the Jews, he said, were designed to aid their conversion to Christianity, because an apostle had once said that Christ will only return to earth if all Jews become Christians. He concluded by saying his speech was directed to the congregation within the context of a church service and was not intended as a public statement on Nazi anti-Semitic policy.

The Gestapo officer noted in his summary of the case, dated 29 June 1943, that Hesse was a radical follower of the 'Confessing Church' and that his pro-Jewish statement had been made in public before a large audience. He also pointed out that further enquiries by the Gestapo into Helmut's private life had revealed that he had been conducting a love affair with the wife of a fellow pastor, who was away serving as an officer in the *Wehrmacht* on the Eastern Front. It was further reported that Helmut had been in contact with the exiled Professor Karl Barth in Basel, Switzerland, a high-profile figure in the 'Confessing Church'.

The Gestapo concluded that Helmut Hesse was a dangerous opponent. He was sent to Dachau concentration camp. On 24 November 1943 he died there of what was officially recorded as 'heart failure', but it's far more likely his life was ended by a lethal injection administered in the deadly camp infirmary. At just twenty-seven years of age, Helmut Hesse became the youngest martyr of the 'Confessing Church'.[24]

It was negative comments on the worsening military situation on the Eastern Front in 1943 that brought married Protestant Pastor Wilhelm Kenath (born 1896) to the attention of the Gestapo. He was born in the picturesque town of Sigmaringen in the south German state of Baden-Württemberg.[25] In May 1943, Wilhelm was living in the small Lower Rhineland village of Gahlen when he said some words at the graveside of a deceased local parishioner in Bruckhausen. Wilhelm highlighted the misery of the dead *Wehrmacht* soldiers at Stalingrad, bemoaned the fact so few field chaplains were present to comfort soldiers during the battle and claimed German people had completely 'abandoned God'. Several mourners were not pleased about these comments and reported them to the local police, who passed them on to the Gestapo. 'Such statements are insulting and intolerable to every German man or woman,' the local constable noted in his report on the matter. 'All the sacrifices in battle were desecrated.' It was further recorded that Gerhard Berger, the son-in-law of the deceased, had told the town mayor of Bruckhausen on 24 May 1943 about the unpatriotic comments of the Protestant pastor. A local teacher, in further evidence, said the speech at the graveside was unwelcome and had demoralised those present by questioning the courage of the brave soldiers who were fighting in the war on the Eastern Front. The Gestapo interrogated Wilhelm, who admitted to all the allegations that had been made against him. On 21 October 1943, he was fined 2,000 Reichsmarks by a Nazi 'Special Court' for making 'subversive comments' about the war effort, but he luckily escaped a prison sentence.[26]

The Catholic population, which numbered 20 million and made up 33 per cent of the German population during the Nazi era, was regarded by the Nazi regime with far more suspicion than the Protestant community. Before 1933, Catholic industrial areas in Berlin, the Rhineland and Bavaria had been most resistant to the electoral appeal of the Nazi Party. In contrast, Nazi voting strength was at its strongest in rural Protestant areas in north and east Germany. Reinhard Heydrich felt Catholics owed their allegiance to Rome and were therefore 'racially suspect'. Under the terms of the Concordat the religious freedom of the Catholic Church was seemingly guaranteed. Catholic bishops thought Hitler would abide by its terms. This proved a fatal miscalculation. The Concordat was never rescinded by the Nazi regime, but priests, nuns and monks were defamed, harassed and arrested, monasteries were dissolved, church property and bank accounts were seized, youth groups banned, and Catholic schools closed down.

On 2 July 1933, instructions were issued to officers of the Bavarian political police on how to deal with cases involving Catholic priests:

1. Members of the clergy may be taken into protective custody as a matter of principle, only if (a) the established facts make it certain that a criminal charge will be instituted, or (b) custody appears absolutely essential to protect the priest's safety.
2. In all cases, the records of proceedings are to be submitted, as a matter of course, to the Political Police Commander before any further action is taken. In the absence of facts justifying a prosecution, members of the clergy may be taken into protective custody without prior reference to the Political Police Commander only if this appears absolutely essential for the maintenance of public safety and security.[27]

Joseph Broch (born 1907) in Genhülsen near Münchengladbach was a Catholic chaplain and part-time teacher in the small rural town of Monschau in the North Rhineland area.[28] On 24 April 1934, he was reported to the Gestapo by a local Hitler Youth member who had attended one of his religious education classes during which Joseph had apparently told the boys not to join any organisation that did not allow them time off to attend church services.

The Gestapo conducted a very detailed investigation into the allegations against Joseph by extensively interviewing a number of boys who recounted what had happened. Hubert Hösener, a nineteen-year-old local Hitler Youth leader, denied Broch had ever recommended to the boys that they should only attend Catholic religious and youth organisations. Josef Roden claimed

Broch had once given another sermon in which he had attacked the Nazi Party and the Hitler Youth, and claimed education should remain the sole responsibility of the Catholic Church. Another boy recalled that Broch said during a sermon: 'There is a lack of the right guidance for the youth today.' Another witness heard Broch speak about the 'heresies of Nazism' and ridiculed the SA. Yet another boy reported that Broch had allowed prohibited hiking songs to be sung during a camping trip.[29]

On 1 May 1934, yet another witness came forward, who reported that Broch was seemingly in the habit of leading a delegation of Catholic youth scouts, accompanied by SA men, whenever a storm trooper was released from a local prison. On one occasion Broch was apparently among a group that cheered an SA man as he left prison, sang a song of support to him and even handed him a bunch of flowers. Afterwards, Broch supposedly took the whole group to a local beer hall and bought them a round of drinks. The Catholic Chaplain had done all this for an ulterior motive, his denouncer claimed, as during the drinking session he advised all those present to join a Catholic workers' group when they got a job and not the Nazi-sponsored German Labour Front (DAF).

The Gestapo put all these accusations to Broch during his lengthy interrogation. He categorically denied them all one by one. He only lectured on religious topics once a week. He never said it was a sin to miss a religious service when it clashed with a Hitler Youth meeting. He never met SA men when they left prison or went to beer hall drinking sessions with them either. He had never criticised the SA or the Nazi regime in any of his classes or sermons. All the lectures he gave to the boys were completely voluntary. He never told any of the boys to place their duties towards the Hitler Youth below their obligations to the Catholic Church.

Broch told the Gestapo that his account of events was true and the version put forward by the boys was a fabrication. The Gestapo rejected all of the allegations made by the youths, except the one that alleged Broch had ridiculed the SA during a religious education class. For that alone, he served one week in prison. This was a short, sharp Gestapo warning to stop him being critical of the Nazi Party in future. His treatment by the Gestapo clearly angered him. On 2 May 1934, one day after his release, Broch sent an angry letter to the local Gestapo office in Aachen, requesting that all the individuals who had 'falsely' denounced him should be arrested. The Gestapo did not even reply, and the case was closed.[30]

In July 1934, Heydrich issued an order to all Gestapo officers, which prohibited Catholic youth organisations from participating in any public activities not of a purely religious nature. Catholic church events increasingly took place within church buildings. Sporting events, marches and camping trips were banned. The wearing of uniforms and insignia of Catholic youth groups were expressly forbidden. Yet attempts to remove crucifixes from school buildings met with very strong public opposition. In Oldenburg, in north Germany, in 1936, there was such strong opposition to the crucifix policy that it was abandoned.

Persecution of priests increasingly became a central focus of Nazi harassment of the Catholic Church. A third of all the 25,500 German priests in Hitler's Germany were subject to some form of badgering from the Gestapo in the Nazi era, ranging from monitoring church services to interrogations, trials, bullying, imprisonment, torture, beatings and, in some cases, execution.[31] The Gestapo drew up lists of priests regarded as disloyal and singled them out for extensive harassment.[32] The SS weekly newspaper *Das Schwarze Korps* (The Black Corps) carried repeated anti-Catholic propaganda, and highlighted allegations of sexual abuse. In 1937, all priests and Catholic theological students were banned from joining the Nazi Party. An inventory taken of the number of priests who left in Dachau on 15 March 1945 gives an indication of how widespread Nazi provocation of the Catholic clergy was throughout Nazi-occupied Europe. Of the 1,493 left in the camp, 261 were

German, 791 Polish, 122 French, 64 Austrian, 38 Dutch, 34 Belgian and 29 Italian.[33]

At the centre of the attempt to undermine the credibility of the Catholic Church with local parishioners were charges of currency smuggling and sexual abuse. Joseph Goebbels, of the Propaganda Ministry, portrayed the Catholic Church as a hotbed of homosexuals and child abusers in numerous public speeches. In May 1936, 200 Franciscan monks were charged with the sexual abuse of children. Nuns were charged with running brothels. The Gestapo urged the public to come forward to report historic complaints of sex abuse. A newspaper report in April 1937 claimed that 1,000 Catholic priests and monks were awaiting trial for sexual abuse.[34] It's clear many of these cases were false. In some cases children were even offered sweets by the Gestapo to make false sexual abuse allegations against priests.[35] If a case was true, it received maximum publicity. In March 1937, an assistant Catholic priest from Münchengladbach was reported to the Nazi Party by a rector of a Catholic church for sexually molesting several young boys between 1931 and 1933. The case was reported to the Gestapo, which undertook an extensive investigation. Six boys, all under fourteen, were questioned. All claimed they had been touched inappropriately by the cleric on several occasions. The Gestapo decided to send the priest for a trial. The lurid details were reported daily in the local press. The Catholic cleric was sentenced to twenty-one months in prison. Upon his release, he continued to sexually abuse children. He was arrested and convicted once again. After a further eighteen-month sentence he was transferred to Dachau concentration camp and he died there of pneumonia on 19 January 1943.[36]

Dissident priests who could not be denounced or proven to be sexually corrupt were silenced in other ways. In July 1935, Göring in his capacity as Prime Minister of Prussia issued a directive designed to deal with what he called 'political Catholicism':

It has to be fundamentally understood that all priests who are employed in the public service – as for instance in giving religious instruction in public [state] schools – will be expected not merely to avoid any possible negative attitude towards Nazism in their teaching, but also like all other members of the public service to commit themselves positively on Nazism's behalf and thus stand without hesitation in Nazism's service.[37]

There were some priests who steadfastly refused to comply with such gagging orders. Rupert Mayer, born in Stuttgart on 23 January 1876, was the first Catholic priest to be awarded the Iron Cross First Class in the First World War. In 1916 he was badly wounded in Romania, and lost his left leg. He wore a heavy wooden leg for the rest of his life. After the war, he studied theology, became a priest and joined the highly disciplined Jesuit order. He worked tirelessly on behalf of the poor throughout the Munich area, establishing the Sisters of the Holy Family Congregation, which assisted many families in dire poverty. In 1923, Rupert attended a meeting which discussed the question: 'Can a Catholic be a National Socialist?' The keynote speaker was Adolf Hitler. Mayer told the audience: 'A German Catholic can never be a National Socialist.'

For the remainder of his life Rupert Mayer maintained this view. By May 1937, his bulging Gestapo file notes seventy-seven reports of 'insubordination' towards the National Socialist regime.[38] By then he was one of the most popular and charismatic Catholic priests in the Munich area. His services attracted huge numbers. He gained a reputation for defending the Catholic Church against Nazi attacks. The Gestapo banned him from speaking at public meetings. On 5 June 1937, he was placed in 'protective custody' under the 'Law against Treacherous Attacks on State and Party'. At his high-profile trial in July 1937, Mayer said he would go on defending the Catholic Church because the Concordat entitled him to do so. The three presiding judges accepted that Rupert Mayer was a man of 'great intellect and heart', but they decided his sermons and speeches made him a 'risk to the stability of the state'. He was sentenced to five months' imprisonment at Landsberg fortress, ironically the very same prison where Hitler had served his sentence for 'high treason' in 1924, after the bungled Munich Beer Hall coup.[39] There was a public demonstration against the prison term imposed on Mayer inside the court. After his release, the gagging order on him was never lifted. When war broke out in September 1939, he was taken back into 'protective custody' once more and placed in solitary confinement at Sachsenhausen. A year later, he was moved to a remote Benedictine monastery in Ettal, and ordered never to venture outside it. Rupert survived the war, but suffered a fatal heart attack while conducting a Catholic mass on 1 November 1945.[40]

The imprisonment of high-profile dissidents like Rupert Mayer was part of the intensification of attacks on the Catholic Church, which had followed the widely publicised papal encyclical *With Burning Anxiety*, issued by Pope Pius XI on 14 March 1937. It had charged the National Socialist government with persistent evasions and violations of the Concordat. It was smuggled into Germany and read out by priests at every Catholic Church service on 21 March 1937. The Pope claimed the Nazi regime was carrying out a 'religious war' against Christian doctrines that must be resisted. He also criticised the 'neo-paganism' spreading in Nazi Germany.[41] Hitler was deeply outraged by the intervention of the Pope into German religious matters. Gestapo officers raided Catholic churches throughout the country and seized all copies of the encyclical they could find. The German Foreign Ministry protested to the Vatican against 'this interference in the domestic affairs of Germany'.[42] In his Christmas address in Rome in 1937, the Pope once more highlighted the issue of the harsh treatment of the Catholic Church in Hitler's Germany:

In Germany there exists in truth a religious persecution. For a considerable time efforts have been made [by the Nazi regime] to make people believe there was no persecution. But it is known there is such a persecution and that it is a heavy one. Indeed, seldom has there been a persecution, so harsh, so terrifying, so grievous, and lamentable in its far-reaching effects. It is a persecution that spares neither force, nor oppression, nor threats, nor subterfuge of intrigue and the falsification of false facts.[43]

The public speeches of many cardinals and bishops often contained references to the general intimidation of the Catholic Church by the Nazi regime. Cardinal Bertram was a pensive, cautious and intransigent critic in Breslau, who repeatedly submitted petitions and complaints to the Nazi regime outlining numerous contraventions of the Concordat. These were all completely ignored by the Nazi regime. In March 1936 Bishop Clemens Galen of Münster gave an outspoken speech at Xanten that pulled no punches:

See how the Holy Church, the Pope, bishops, priests . . . see how the loyal children of the Church are insulted, reviled and derided publicly and with impunity. How many Catholic priests and laymen have been attacked and insulted in the papers and at public meetings, driven out of their professions and positions and imprisoned and ill-treated without judicial sentences being passed. There are graves in German soil in which are laid the ashes of those that the Catholic people regard as martyrs for the Faith.[44]

A special conference of Gestapo personnel was held in Berlin in July 1937 entitled 'Next Objectives in the Campaign against Denominated Opponents'. It proposed a proactive plan to deal with church opposition. A system of intelligence contacts – 'V-Men' (*V-Männer*) – would be assigned to deal exclusively with the dissident clergy. They would report on the content of sermons within churches and identify all religious opponents. Information received would then be analysed by Gestapo office heads to determine whether or not a cleric should be arrested. The publications of the church would be systematically monitored, restricted and, when necessary, banned.[45] Clergymen who travelled abroad on church business would be kept under the closest surveillance. In November 1938, Monsignor Ehrenfried, the Bishop of Würzburg, was held up at the Italian frontier for hours on a visit to Rome. His luggage was rifled through, and all his documents were photocopied before being returned to him.[46] Catholic church property was also extensively seized without compensation. In April 1940, it was reported that property worth 30 million Reichsmarks was confiscated from the Catholic Church in Wiesbaden alone. The Catholic bishops, supported by the Vatican, protested against these property seizures. In the summer of 1941, they were halted on the personal order of Adolf Hitler.[47]

By 1939, the political power of the Catholic Church in Hitler's Germany had been progressively undermined, but the loyalty of the overwhelming majority of Catholics to their faith survived. Indeed, church attendance in Catholic churches increased during the war-time period. As leading Nazi Rudolf Hess put it: 'A religion which has influenced, indeed dominated, the life of the people for two thousand years cannot be overcome by external measures and certainly not through superficial ridicule.'[48] The leaders of the Catholic Church emphasised they fully supported the German war effort. In September 1939, Catholic bishops issued the following statement outlining their attitude to the coming struggle: 'In this decisive hour we encourage and admonish our Catholic soldiers in obedience to the Führer to do their duty and to be ready to sacrifice their whole existence. We appeal to the faithful to join in ardent prayer that God's providence may lead to blessed success for the Fatherland and people.'[49]

Catholic priests began tailoring the funeral services of the war dead to the needs of patriotic parishioners, as this secret Gestapo report made clear:

The Catholic Church is developing an extraordinary fantasy [atmosphere] in which funerals are arranged, so say reports from the Catholic areas – unanimously. Consequently, it is exercising a deep and lasting influence on the relatives [of the dead] and the local population. The focus of these events in honour of the dead are memorial services or masses for the dead soldier:

1. The memorial sarcophagus [*Tumba*] is decked in black and decorated with flowers. Numerous candles burn at its side, a steel helmet and crossed side arms lie on it.
2. Or, instead of this, a symbolic soldier's grave is set up in the church and is richly covered with flowers, a birch cross, a steel helmet or an Iron Cross.
3. The cultish proceedings make special use of choirs and orchestral pieces, processions of children and poetry readings.
4. Occasionally, a side altar is transformed into an altar for the fallen soldier. Under flowers and burning candles, pictures of the fallen, together with their names and their military decorations are set up. Relatives and the population [in general] can bury themselves in the memory of the fallen at any hour of the day.[50]

In spite of these public displays of affinity towards the fate of German soldiers, priests were still regarded as untrustworthy by the Nazi regime. Many Catholic churches in large cities were closed, if they were a long way from air-raid shelters. The state gradually reduced its state subsidy to the Catholic Church. In a lengthy Gestapo report, submitted to Hitler in October 1939, Heydrich warned that clerics still needed to be closely monitored, as they would probably engage in passive resistance, and he further warned that anyone engaging in subversion or making defeatist comments would be dealt with in the very harshest manner.[51]

Catholic priest Carl Lampert (born 1894) in Göfis, Austria, had already spent several periods in 'protective custody' before his arrest by the Gestapo in Stettin in February 1943, for making critical comments in a number of sermons about Hitler's conduct of the war. Carl endured several months of brutal pre-trial interrogations. In three Nazi show trials he was falsely accused, along with two other priests, of passing on military secrets to the Allies. The presiding judge at the third trial, which was held at Torgau military prison on 24 July 1944, thought all the allegations had been fabricated by the Gestapo. The night before the judge would have been obliged to pass a death sentence on the three priests he shot himself. This did not prevent the death sentences being imposed. In a farewell letter to his brother, Carl wrote: 'Now the hour has come, the so terrible hour for you and all my loved ones, but the hour of release for me. I am approaching the final destination on my road to Calvary. Darkness has descended, but "day" is dawning. In You, O Lord, I trust.' Carl Lampert was executed on 13 November 1944.[52]

The biggest challenge to the Nazi regime by the Catholic Church during the Second World War was directed against the Nazi policy of euthanasia, established in August 1939 under the notorious T4 programme. Thousands of mentally ill and physically handicapped adults and children were killed in a number of German mental hospitals.[53] Catholic bishop Clemens Graf von Galen gave a powerful sermon in St Lambert's Church in Münster in which he delivered a strong defence of the sanctity of human life:

I have been assured that the Reich Interior Ministry and the office of the Reich Doctors' Leader, Dr Conti, make no bones about the fact that in reality a large number of mentally ill people in Germany have been deliberately killed and more will be killed in the future.

For what reason?

These unfortunate patients must die ... because, in the opinion of some department, on the testimony of some commission, they have become 'worthless life' because according to this testimony they are 'unproductive national comrades'. The argument goes: they can no longer produce commodities, they are like an old machine that no longer works, they are like an old horse which has become incurably lame, they are like a cow which no longer gives milk . . . If you establish and apply the principle that you can kill 'unproductive' fellow human beings then woe betide us all when we become old and frail![54]

Copies of the sermon were distributed throughout the country. Hitler considered having Galen hanged for delivering such an open public attack on a policy he had personally ordered.[55] The Gestapo attempted to confiscate all the copies of the sermon. Galen's outspoken beliefs were opposed by nurses (*Reichspflegerinnen*) who were employed in the hospitals carrying out the killings. Many Catholic priests gave the last rites to those selected for death. A Catholic nurse who participated in the T4 programme later recalled:

We endeavoured to make the final journey of the selected patients as easy as possible. In this connection it occurs to me that one female patient was strongly Catholic and on the last day she asked if she could be given the last rites by a Catholic priest before [being killed]. I can still remember clearly and can say with absolute certainty that the Catholic priest was informed before the killing and that the patient, who at least on this day was perfectly rational, was given the last rites by the priest.[56]

An elderly pensioner called Seline Winter (born 1873) was brought in for questioning by the Gestapo after being accused of distributing Bishop Galen's sermon. Seline was living in the North Rhineland city of Krefeld at the time of her arrest.[57] Her background was regarded by the Gestapo as somewhat eccentric. She had regularly attended services of the Protestant Evangelical Church, but then left it. She was a member of the obscure pro-monarchist 'Luise League' (*Luisenbund*) which regarded Louise von Mecklenburg-Strelitz, a former Queen of Prussia during the Napoleonic era, as a saintly figure. This cultish little group admired this former Prussian monarch for her outstanding beauty, deep patriotism and her 'feminine outlook'.[58]

At the time of her arrest, Seline was also a member of a non-denominational, atheistic, neo-paganist sect called 'God Believers'. It was a pro-Nazi alternative to the Christian churches, approved of by SS leader Heinrich Himmler and some other leading Nazis, though not by Hitler.[59] On 15 December 1941 Seline was reported to the Gestapo in Krefeld by one of her own relatives to whom she had given a copy of Bishop Galen's sermon.

A Gestapo report on the case on 17 December 1941 claimed a man called Hans Forst had made copies of Galen's sermon and had given one to Seline Winters. Forst was a former police inspector in Kassel. In 1933 he was put in charge of a hastily assembled 'wild' concentration camp in the poor Berlin working-class area of Lichtenberg. A year later he was suspended from this post due to accusations of the severe maltreatment of prisoners in the camp and he served a year in a concentration camp for these offences. After his release he worked as an insurance agent. He then applied to join the SS, but was turned down due to his previous conviction. During his Gestapo interrogation, Forst claimed he was also a member of the 'God Believers', but claimed there was no political motive at all behind his decision to give Seline a copy of Galen's text.

On 16 December 1941, Seline Winters was interrogated by the Gestapo. She claimed her desire to see the sermon grew out of mere curiosity. She claimed she was given a copy by a friend, but contradicted Forst by saying she asked him to copy it for her. She refused to give the Gestapo the name of the friend who had handed it to her. Far from being in agreement with the censorious words of Bishop Galen, Seline told the Gestapo she fully approved of the Nazi euthanasia policy. Finally realising Seline was an avid supporter of the Nazi regime, the Gestapo released her without charge.[60]

After Bishop von Galen's outburst on euthanasia the Nazi regime decided to scale down its repression against the Catholic Church. Hitler feared such public conflicts might lead to the regime becoming unpopular during war-time. In September 1941, the following set of instructions was issued to Gestapo officers on how to deal with church matters in future to ensure:

1. The avoidance of all major operations and measures against the churches and their institutions.
2. The cancellation of further measures against monasteries, including disguised measures in this matter.
3. In individual cases action may be taken but the Reich Security Main Office is to be informed. Particularly important cases must be left for the Führer's decision.
4. The main thing is that we see that the Church does not win back any of its former positions. We must limit ourselves to seeing that we maintain positions already captured.
5. The main stress should [now] be put on intelligence work. Any material of significance which might be of future importance is to be collected carefully . . . The network of agents is to be carefully maintained and extended by recruiting new contact men. Particular attention should be paid to the connections between church circles and government offices.[61]

The Nazi regime was acutely aware that weakening the hold of the Christian churches over the German people was a long-term project. Smaller religious sects proved much easier to intimidate, as they had few powerful public figures willing to defend them. One religious group singled out for extremely brutal persecution by the Gestapo was the Jehovah's Witnesses, created in 1879 by US businessman Charles Russell.[62] In Gestapo files they are called either the 'International Bible Students Association' or the 'Earnest Bible Students'.[63] They were the first religious denomination to be officially banned in Hitler's Germany. Some historians have viewed them as the 'forgotten victims' of Nazi religious persecution. The 25,000 German Jehovah's Witnesses were primarily drawn from the hard-working sections of the working classes. The Gestapo viewed them as dangerously and fanatically independent. It's been estimated that 85 per cent of Jehovah's Witnesses had never voted for any political party. The remainder were mostly former KPD or SPD voters. Martin Broszat called their resistance 'futile martyrdom'.[64] Their stubborn adherence to Old Testament prophecies and pacifism led the Nazis to believe their religious beliefs were a mask to hide underlying sympathy towards communism. It needs to be appreciated that the Jehovah's Witnesses did not oppose the Nazi system on ideological or political grounds but to preserve their own religious practices. Many chose death in preference to renouncing their religious faith. Only weeks after coming to power, a Nazi official wrote:

> The danger to the State from these Jehovah's Witnesses is not to be underestimated, since the members of this sect on the grounds of their unbelievably strong fanaticism are completely hostile to the law and order of the State. Not only do they refuse to give the German greeting [Hitler salute], to participate in any National Socialist or State functions or to do military service, but they put out propaganda against joining the army, and attempt, despite prohibition, to distribute their publications.[65]

In December 1933, Heydrich ordered that anyone discovered being a follower of the Witnesses should be taken into 'protective custody' by the Gestapo. In 1935, the organisation was officially banned. This did not stop Jehovah's Witnesses holding meetings, engaging in door-to-door preaching and distributing publications such as 'The Watch Tower' and the 'Golden Age'. Denouncements by the public played a minor role in Gestapo persecution of Jehovah's Witnesses. Most cases began via surveillance information collected by the Gestapo.[66] During the era of the Third Reich, 10,000 Witnesses were imprisoned and estimates of those killed in Nazi custody range from 950 to 1,200.[67] In concentration camps, they wore a purple triangle on their uniforms, refused to stand to attention during the daily roll call, went on hunger strikes, and refused to serve in the army or undertake military-related work in factories.[68] A report from Sachsenhausen concentration camp noted: 'The behaviour of the "Earnest Bible Students" is truly amazing. These people display an unshakable disposition of opposition.'[69]

A Gestapo head of department, in August 1937, advised officers how to handle cases involving Jehovah's Witnesses:

1. If a Witness is acquitted during a penal procedure or if his imprisonment is declared served by the protective custody he should not be brought to court [again] but placed instead in protective custody.
2. If the authorities responsible for carrying out the sentence announce an imminent release of a [Jehovah's] Witness [from prison], I must be consulted immediately on measures to be taken by the State Police [Gestapo] concerning his transfer to a concentration camp as soon as his term has been completed.
3. If the transfer to a concentration camp is not possible after the completion of their jail sentences the [Jehovah's] Witness must be held in a police cell.[70]

Wilhelm Gerres (born 1901) worked in a variety of jobs including as a van driver and a locksmith. He was married and lived in Rheydt, which was an independent city in the Nazi era, though it merged with Münchengladbach in 1975.[71] On 13 December 1936, the Gestapo placed Wilhelm in 'protective custody' for being an active member of the Jehovah's Witnesses, under the terms of a Prussian decree dating from 1933 which had prohibited membership of the organisation. The Gestapo discovered books and pamphlets after searching Wilhelm's house. His father, also a member of the Witnesses, sent a letter to the Gestapo on 12 January 1937 pleading for his son to be freed. The Gestapo let Wilhelm out, but only after he had signed the standard declaration, which all Witnesses were required to sign before they were released:

1. I have come to know that the International Bible Students Association [Jehovah's Witnesses] disseminated fake doctrines and under the guise of religion promotes aims dangerous to the state.
2. Therefore, I have completely left this organization and I have freed myself entirely from the teachings of this section.
3. I herewith give the assurance that never again will I participate in the activities of the International Bible Students Association. Should any persons come to me with the teachings of the Bible students or in any way shows their association with them, I will immediately report them [to the police]. Should any Bible student literature be sent to me, I will immediately take it to the nearest police station.
4. In the future I will respect the laws of the state, and especially in the event of war I will defend the Fatherland, weapon in hand, and I will completely join myself to the racial community of the [German] people.
5. I am informed that I will again be immediately taken into protective custody should I act contrary to the declaration given today.[72]

Wilhelm did not keep to the bargain he had made with the Gestapo. He was arrested again. On 12 February 1937, he was sentenced to three months in prison. The local newspaper reported the details of the case. It was reported that Wilhelm was an active 'missionary' of the Jehovah's Witnesses, and had distributed leaflets for the organisation every Sunday, even though he knew full well it was an 'illegal organization'. The newspaper also claimed the local Witnesses were secretly collecting money for the communist underground resistance, though no mention of any such link was ever mentioned in his Gestapo file.[73]

Wilhelm was released again, but he still refused to compromise his religious principles. During another Gestapo interrogation on 26 June 1939 Wilhelm said that he had been a Protestant until 1924 before joining the Jehovah's Witnesses. He didn't regret any of his actions. He would stick to his religious convictions no matter what punishments were imposed upon him. All he promised was not to distribute the leaflets of the organisation in public any more. The Gestapo recommended that he should be sent to trial this time. In July 1937, a 'Special Court' sentenced him to a year in prison, but he was not released until June 1939. In spite of all this punishment, Wilhelm, almost fanatically, still refused to abandon his faith. On 14 July 1939, he found himself back in 'protective custody', but this time he did not go to court or prison, but to a local concentration camp.

Members of Wilhelm's family wrote several pleading letters to the Gestapo trying to get him released. In a letter from the Düsseldorf Gestapo office to colleagues in Münchengladbach, dated 14 July 1939, the family was described as 'faultless', but Wilhelm was depicted as having a 'primitive and pig-headed mentality' and was prone to being easily misled. The Düsseldorf office approved 'a tentative release', but the Münchengladbach Gestapo office took a much harsher view of the case and suggested as a repeat offender he should now be sent to Buchenwald concentration camp, which had established a dedicated 'Punishment Company' (*Strafkommando*) to deal specifically with Jehovah's Witnesses. If they refused to denounce their faith they were given harsh forced labour in stone quarries, put on starvation rations, prohibited from sending or receiving letters and forced to endure physically draining fitness drills involving rolling on the floor, hopping on one leg and running extreme distances.[74] By December

1937, 10 per cent of all the prisoners in Buchenwald were Jehovah's Witnesses.

There was clearly a major difference of opinion between the Gestapo office in Düsseldorf and the local Münchengladbach office over how to deal with Wilhelm's case. On 4 August 1939, the Gestapo in Düsseldorf noted that a release of Wilhelm was not possible at the moment, but gave no reasons. Wilhelm was transferred to Buchenwald camp, but his Gestapo file gives no indication of his ultimate fate.[75]

The peak year for the persecution of Jehovah's Witnesses by the Gestapo was 1937. It was during that year that an 'open letter' entitled 'To the People of Germany who believe in the Bible and Love Jesus' was widely circulated. It's been estimated that approximately 100,000 copies of the letter were distributed.[76] The letter complained about the ban imposed on the Witnesses for defending their 'spiritual freedom' and it itemised detailed allegations about how believers had been defamed, slandered, persecuted, intimidated and subjected to 'treatment reminiscent of the Inquisition' in prisons and concentration camps.[77]

Heinrich Winten (born 1905) in Orken, a Rhineland town close to the city of Münchengladbach, was one of hundreds of Jehovah's Witnesses who were arrested during 1937 for distributing the open letter. He was married and listed his occupation as a 'pattern maker'.[78] On 25 October 1937, Heinrich was among ten people arrested by the Gestapo under suspicion of having been active members of the Jehovah's Witnesses. During his interrogation he freely admitted that he had distributed forty copies of the open letter in the local area. His wife Elizabeth was then brought in for questioning. She admitted to being a Jehovah's Witness too, but she denied having distributed any copies of the open letter. She claimed a neighbour had offered to sell the couple a magazine, published by the Earnest Bible Students Association, but they refused, as they considered it was much too dangerous to be in possession of such material.

On 23 December 1937 a 'Special Court' in Düsseldorf sentenced Heinrich Winten to eighteen months in prison. His three young children were taken into care, as the court ruled that Elizabeth, his second wife, who acted as stepmother to the youngsters, had no legal right to custody of the children.[79]

Many other children of Jehovah's Witnesses were taken into care. Paul Schlemann (born 1882) was a district judge in Oberhausen, an industrial city in the Ruhr, who presided over a guardianship court that issued child care orders.[80] Paul was reported to the Gestapo because he had refused to grant a care order for two children whose parents were Jehovah's Witnesses. In his judgment on 19 February 1942, Paul had said: 'Everything is all right with the Mokr family, except for the religious beliefs of the parents, and therefore one cannot deprive parents of child custody for that reason alone. There will always be some people, who are not interested in National Socialism, even fight it, but they are too few to be a potential danger.' The Youth Welfare officer disagreed, and told the judge: 'Public enemies could not be allowed to educate their children.' It was decided on 20 July 1942 that Schlemann should no longer be allowed to preside in child custody cases ever again.[81]

Within concentration camps Jehovah's Witnesses, as we have already seen, were frequently subjected to brutal and inhumane punishments. Eugen Kogon observed one such incident at Dachau concentration camp one Christmas Eve during the war-time period:

A large [Christmas] tree was put up and decorated with electric candles and other forms of decoration. The camp's 45,000 prisoners, including 200 Jehovah's Witnesses, hoped they would enjoy a few days' peace. But what happened? At eight o'clock on Christmas Eve when all the prisoners were in their barracks, the camp sirens suddenly began to wail; the prisoners were to march out into the courtyard as fast as possible. One could hear the SS band playing. In marched five companies of fully equipped SS troops. The Camp Commandant, accompanied by SS officers, delivered a short speech that they wanted to celebrate Christmas with them in their own particular way. He then pulled out a list of names from his briefcase and for almost an hour read the names of those who had been recommended for punishment in the last few weeks. The [punishment] block was brought out and the first prisoner strapped down to it. Afterwards two SS men equipped with a steel whip took their places to the right and to the left of the block and began to beat the prisoner while the band played 'Silent Night'; all the prisoners were expected to sing along. At the same time the prisoner being given twenty-five strokes was forced to count these out in a loud voice.[82]

Women were also subjected to equally appalling punishments. A twenty-seven-year-old Jehovah's Witness described her treatment by a Gestapo officer during an interrogation in Krefeld:

When I did not give him the required information, he delivered a powerful slap on the face. He then called two other Gestapo officers on the telephone, who led me to the cellar. Soon Dihr showed up there. At the order of Dihr, both of the officers stretched me out across a table standing nearby. After pulling up [my] dress, both of the officers beat me on my behind with a stick or something like that. After many blows, the officers stopped for a while and Dihr questioned me again. When I continued not to provide a satisfactory answer I was beaten anew until I said I would testify. I was then brought back upstairs where Dihr continued my interrogation. I confessed, which was to having worked illegally against the Hitler government, because I preferred to receive a death sentence than be tortured to death. Because of the abuse [I suffered] I was not able to walk for several days.[83]

Ilsa Unterdorfer, who was held in the women's concentration camp in Lichtenburg, later recalled how Jehovah's Witnesses were treated there:

Everything was done to force them to sign a declaration renouncing their faith. One day Sister Elizabeth Lange who came from Chemnitz was called before the [camp] director. She refused to sign the statement which earned her a lockup in the dungeon of this old castle. The [punishment] cells were black holes with a narrow window with bars. The bed was stone and most of the time she was forced to lie down on that cold hard bed without even a straw mattress. Sister Lange spent six months in that hole.[84]

The Nazi attempt to weaken and undermine Christian belief in Germany proved counter-productive. The Christian churches defended their organisational autonomy and spiritual independence successfully. The Jehovah's Witnesses preferred martyrdom to compromise. Nazi ideology was never integrated into the religious practices of the churches at all. Germany remained as much a predominantly Christian church-going society in 1945 as it had been in 1933. During the Second World War, praying to God comforted most Germans – especially those who had lost loved ones in the war – far more than Hitler's increasingly rare speeches. It is, perhaps, no surprise to find that devoted Catholic Claus von Stauffenberg visited the Rosenkranzkirche (church of the rosary) in Berlin on the evening before his assassination attempt and that his last outcry before he was executed on 20 July 1944 was: 'Long live Holy Germany.' 'Es lebe das heilige Deutschland!'

Chapter 4

Hunting the Communists

A young communist activist named Walter Husemann wrote the following letter to his father on the day of his execution on 13 May 1943:

> Be strong! I am dying as I lived; as a fighter in the class war! It is easy to call yourself a communist as long as you don't have to shed any blood for it. You only show whether you really are one when the hour comes when you have to prove yourself. I am one, father.[1]

Communists such as this were the most systematically persecuted political group in Nazi Germany. It was difficult to remain a dedicated communist and avoid denouncement to the Gestapo. Most communist activists spent some time in a Nazi concentration camp or a prison cell for their political beliefs between 1933 and 1945. They were often subjected to torture, beatings and psychological intimidation.[2] In 1933, alone, 60,000 communists were arrested and approximately 2,000 were killed.[3]

Before 1933 Germany had the largest Communist Party outside of the Soviet Union. Established in 1919, the German Communist Party (KPD) was the passionate voice of the revolutionary sections of the German industrial working class. It was led by Ernst Thälmann, a blunt and charismatic 'man of the people'. In January 1933, there were 360,000 official KPD members, with an average age of thirty, thus emphasising its very strong appeal to young Germans in the big industrial cities. White collar workers, professionals and civil servants made up only 10 per cent of members.[4] In 1929, only 17 per cent of the KPD membership were women even though the party strongly advocated women's rights.[5] Women rarely appear in court files involving communist resistance groups. In a study of 355 communist court cases involving those who opposed Nazism between 1933 and 1935 in the North-Westphalia region, just 4 per cent involved women.[6]

The typical KPD member was a young, male, semi-skilled or unskilled worker, living in a tight-knit working-class district of a large industrial city.[7] It was in the 'red citadel' solidly working-class neighbourhoods in Berlin, Stuttgart, Hamburg, Cologne, Düsseldorf and Münchengladbach that KPD membership was at its strongest. In the November 1932 election, the last democratic election before Hitler came to power, the KPD polled 37.7 per cent in key industrial areas. Communist activists saw themselves as tough, self-sacrificing, uncompromising soldiers in the fight against fascism.[8] The KPD had a paramilitary section called the Red Front Fighters League.[9] This was closely allied to the Revolutionary Trade Union Opposition.[10] In working-class areas, there were numerous KPD-sponsored sports clubs, bands, choirs, community centres and social clubs. The party also produced a wide range of literature, including, books, newspapers, periodicals, leaflets and posters.

The leadership of the KPD was in close contact with the Soviet regime and the Comintern, the international body set up to spread communist ideas. It has often been alleged that the KPD was a mere 'puppet' or 'cipher' of Stalin's regime, and drew substantial financial support from the USSR. Yet the official accounts of the KPD show no direct finance from the Soviet Union. The party was exclusively funded from membership subscriptions, donations and income generated from the sales of party newspapers and periodicals.[11]

It needs to be understood that the working class in Germany became bitterly divided shortly after the end of the First World War. This happened because the Social Democratic Party (SPD), the most popular Weimar working-class political party, collaborated with right-wing Free Corps renegades and the army to suppress the revolutionary 'Spartacist Revolt' of 1919, led by the iconic communists Dr Karl Liebknecht and Rosa Luxemburg, who were both brutally murdered in Berlin. This event earned the SPD the communist nickname of 'social fascists', and produced a devastating split within the working class. This disunity on the left greatly assisted Hitler's rise to power. The moderate SPD leadership was viewed by KPD activists as consisting of 'reformers and compromisers' with the existing state. SPD leaders and rank-and-file members were bitterly anti-communist, viewing KPD members as pro-Stalinist intolerant and sectarian fanatics. There was little common ground between them.

A defiant communist leaflet, produced on the day Adolf Hitler took office, described his regime as 'an open fascist dictatorship' and called for mass strikes.[12] KPD activists contemptuously believed Hitler's coalition government would soon split apart. On 7 February 1933, KPD leader Ernst Thälmann gave a rabble-rousing speech in which he argued that only a revolution could overthrow Hitler's regime, but he doubted this would happen. This proved a very accurate prediction of what followed.

The Reichstag fire on 27 February 1933 offered Hitler's regime an ideal pretext to launch a brutal wave of unprecedented violence against the Communist Party. On the night of the blaze, 10,000 communists were arrested. Communist newspapers were closed down, and demonstrations and meetings were banned. The makeshift 'wild' SA concentration camps became the chief forum for anti-communist violence. The Gestapo, the criminal police, the courts, and the local authorities all co-operated in this orgy of terror. The high priority given to crushing communism by Hitler's regime can be gauged from the surviving Gestapo files, which reveal that over 80 per cent of those taken into 'protective custody' in 1933 were communists.

The KPD was not officially banned, but it could not openly campaign in the last supposedly democratic election on 5

March 1933. Two days before the polling day, the KPD leader Ernst Thälmann was taken into 'protective custody'. He was kept in solitary confinement, repeatedly interrogated and often beaten. He was kept in various prisons and concentration camps until being shot dead, on Hitler's orders, on 18 August 1944 in Buchenwald concentration camp. In spite of the violent blitz against the communists that preceded the election, the KPD gained 4,847,939 votes, in the March election, which was 12.3 per cent of overall votes cast. The KPD was entitled to 81 Reichstag deputies, but they were prohibited from ever taking up their seats.[13] Given the extraordinarily violent circumstances surrounding the election campaign, the KPD voting performance was remarkable, and showed the residual loyalty it enjoyed in working-class areas in the early phase of Hitler's rule.

Though officially banned on 14 July 1933, the KPD defiantly urged the working class to continue resisting the Nazi regime. The written word was the key weapon in the communist struggle with the Nazis, as an arms struggle or terrorism was ruled out. Newspapers, periodicals and especially leaflets were at the heart of KPD underground propaganda. Many leaflets had print runs of in excess of 10,000 copies. The communist daily newspaper, Rote Fahne (Red Flag), continued to be published illegally between 1933 and 1935. On 13 October 1933, the distribution of 'treasonable literature' was made a crime punishable by death, life or fifteen years in prison.

In 1934, the Gestapo seized a staggering 1,238,202 communist leaflets, and a further 1,670,300 in 1935. This shows how proactive the Gestapo was in pursuing communists. According to surviving KPD records, 2 million copies of newspapers were produced in 1935. Most illegal KPD literature was produced outside Germany and then smuggled into the country. Some KPD publications were often bizarre, including one seized by the Gestapo in 1934, entitled: 70 Approved Recipes, all no doubt prepared with suitable non-Nazi ingredients.[14] In retrospect, the communist obsession with producing and distributing anti-Nazi leaflets was self-defeating, as those who received them usually passed them on to the Gestapo.[15]

In June 1933, a KPD circular letter continued to strike a decidedly optimistic tone:

> The heroic struggle of our party against the Hitler dictatorship is already bearing fruit. We have succeeded – in spite of the bloody fascist terror and the striking down of tens of thousands of our finest comrades – in pulling the party together . . . Now in the different conditions of fascist dictatorship our truly Bolshevik cadres are growing into courageous, resolute class system leaders of the masses.[16]

The same month this letter was distributed numerous working-class communities were being subjected to lightning raids by the Gestapo. In the Berlin suburb of Köpenick, seventy communists were killed in what the Nazi regime claimed was the suppression of an armed uprising. In July 1933, six communists were sentenced to death for killing two SA men during a street battle in Cologne four months earlier. The executions of those convicted of the murders were carried out using a hand-held axe.[17] The Gestapo was able to round up communists even more systematically after KPD headquarters were raided and membership lists confiscated.

It's clear that the Gestapo was also assisted in hunting communists by informers who had infiltrated the KPD resistance groups, as Jakob Zorn, a leading party activist, later recalled:

> At first we conducted our resistance relatively openly. We didn't pay proper attention to the rules of conspiracy, which you have to follow if you are up against such a brutal enemy. I think that is the reason why we suffered such heavy losses. Hordes of informers infiltrated the party waverers, people who had let themselves be bought off, the sort of people you always get.

Behind almost every court case in Cologne there was an informer, who had belonged to the labour movement.[18]

In just six short months in 1933 the largest and most well-organised working class of any of the major industrial nations in Europe had been dramatically weakened. Hannah Galm, a deeply committed communist, observed the changes Nazi rule had brought to her own home town:

> I could not recognize the town. Offenbach under the Swastika! Swastika flags everywhere. The Marktplatz was astonishing. We went down into the workers' district where our [communist] votes had come from. Swastika flags in every window. That was hard to take. It was a deep disappointment. Where on earth had they got all the flags from? Well we know, of course. There was a lot of despair involved. Of course there was. We could not understand how this had happened.[19]

The aim of the brutal wave of Nazi terror was not only to crush key KPD functionaries, but also to warn the working-class community of the mortal danger it now faced if it continued to assist communists. On 2 February 1934, John Schehr, a member of the KPD Politburo, was murdered by the Gestapo in his cell, leaving Franz Dahlem as the only member of the KPD leadership still at large. The remaining key figures, with the exception of the imprisoned Ernst Thälmann, had already fled into exile. A number of countries became havens for exiled German communists during the Nazi era, most notably, France, Holland, Belgium, and especially the communist Soviet Union.

The USSR was viewed as a model communist system by members of the KPD.[20] According to Article 22 of the Soviet Constitution of 1925, political asylum was granted to anyone forced to leave their own country due to 'revolutionary activity'. In practice, visas were only issued to active and trusted communists.[21] It has been estimated that 3,000 members of the KPD lived in exile in the Soviet Union after Hitler came to power. Many leading German exiles stayed at the luxurious Hotel Lux in Moscow, which also contained the office of the Comintern. Stalin's Russia did not prove the safe haven German communists had idealistically supposed. Of the sixty-eight leading KPD figures who fled Hitler's Germany and went to live in the Soviet Union, forty-eight were killed. Overall, 70 per cent of German communist exiles were killed in Stalin's brutal political purges. The Stalinist regime had deemed them too wedded to ideas of internationalism enshrined in the Comintern or portrayed them as favourable to the ideas of Leon Trotsky. It is a great irony to note that Stalin was responsible for more of the deaths of the leading figures in the KPD than Hitler.[22]

Only a small minority of German communist exiles ever returned to Germany alive. Returnees faced administrative harassment, and came under the scrutiny of the Gestapo. Luise Vögler (born 1904) was one German exile who returned. She had lived in the Soviet Union since 1931, with her husband Karl, a locksmith, who had been an active member of the KPD during the Weimar era.[23] In 1937, Luise, a dressmaker by occupation, was living in a hostel in Düsseldorf for repatriated Germans when the Gestapo began to investigate her life in exile in the USSR. Luise came from an affluent Austrian middle-class family, but they had ostracised her after she married a German communist and moved to the Soviet Union. In 1936, the couple applied for Soviet citizenship, but the Russian authorities turned them down. Luise offered no explanation to the Gestapo as to why the citizenship requests of the couple were rejected. Upon their return to Germany, Karl was immediately defined by the Gestapo as an 'enemy of the state' and placed under 'protective custody' in a local concentration camp. He was never released.

The Gestapo questioned several other German exiles about the activities of the Vöglers in the USSR. In January 1938, Josef Solmitz and his wife both offered damning evidence against the couple. They said they were active communists during the time they lived in the Soviet Union. Luise had written two anti-Nazi articles that were published in Soviet newspapers. One gave details of her four-week vacation to Hitler's Germany in 1936. The working class, she wrote in the article, were starving and her former homeland was depicted as 'one big concentration camp'. In August 1938, Aloisia Karn, who also knew the couple when they lived in Woroschilowgrad in the Ukraine, during their period of exile, was questioned by Gestapo officers in Vienna.[24] The couple, she said, were 'committed communists' during all the time she knew them in Russia. The Foreign Organisation branch of the Nazi Party (*Auslandsorganisation NSDAP-AO*) also confirmed the couple had written anti-Nazi articles which appeared in the Soviet press.

Luise Vögler was interrogated by the Gestapo on four separate occasions. She admitted her husband Karl had been an active member of the KPD in Germany before the couple left. Karl's prime loyalty was to the Soviet cause against Nazi Germany. She did not deny her own sympathy towards communism and the USSR either. She confirmed that she did visit Mannheim for a four-week period in the summer of 1936. The sale of a property the couple owned in the city was the chief purpose of this visit. She gained the impression on her trip that unemployment remained very high in Hitler's Germany, in spite of all the Nazi propaganda. She denied ever writing anti-Nazi articles in the Soviet press. Luise said the evidence of the Solmitz couple should be discounted. She pointed out that Mrs Solmitz was not only Jewish, but also envious of the new dresses she had brought back from her trip to Germany. Luise claimed Mrs Solmitz had looked at her, while she was wearing one of the new dresses, and said: 'You are a fine example of how the German economy thrives.' All the accusations made by the Solmitz couple were driven by personal malice, she added. The Gestapo decided to accept Luise's version of events. In August 1938, it was decided no further action would be taken against

Luise, but she was advised not to work for companies connected with the armaments industry.

This was not the end of the story. In August 1941, a representative of the Nazi-supporting 'German Women's Work' (*Deutsches Frauenwerk*) organisation sent an unsolicited letter to the Gestapo concerning Luise. It explained that she was still living in Düsseldorf, together with her nine-year-old daughter, and still working as a dressmaker, with a hugely affluent clientele. Luise Vögler is described in the letter as 'intelligent, well educated and guarded'. But set against this was an allegation that she was 'behaving as a communist', though no specific details of what this meant were offered. It was also emphasised in the letter that Luise had formed a close friendship with a 'Mrs Sellicht', the Russian wife of another German returnee from the Soviet Union, whose husband was also being held in 'protective custody' as a suspected communist activist. The letter writer urged the Gestapo to monitor these two women very closely on the grounds they were 'obviously communist sympathisers'.

In September 1941, the Gestapo replied. It noted that Luise and Mrs Sellicht had both been placed under close surveillance by Gestapo officers and Nazi Party officials for the previous six months, but no evidence of any communist activities had turned up. Luise, the letter went on, had been in close contact with the local leader of the Nazi Party, who had supported a petition to gain the release of her husband, who was still detained in a Nazi concentration camp.[25]

It is difficult to know whether Luise remained a communist activist. She was undoubtedly a supporter of Stalin's regime, while she lived in the USSR. Historians who have examined why German exiles returned to the Soviet Union have emphasised that fear of Stalin's purges or disillusionment with the Soviet Union were two of the key motivating factors.[26] Yet the Vöglers only returned because their request for Soviet citizenship was unexpectedly rejected. The fact that so much time was devoted to monitoring Luise's personal life suggests the Gestapo felt there was a real possibility she might be involved in Soviet espionage or communist resistance activities and they clearly felt they might discover a possible Soviet spy ring if they left her at large.

Proven active communist resisters were not treated as leniently as Luise Vögler. Eva Maria Buch's fate is far more typical. Eva (born 1921) in Berlin was studying foreign languages at Humboldt University when she became involved with the famous group of socialist resisters called the Schulze-Boysen-Harnack group, which had associations within the Air Ministry, the universities and the civil service, and were suspected of passing on intelligence secrets to the Soviet Union.[27] The Gestapo called the group 'The Red Orchestra'. On 10 October 1942, Eva was arrested by the Gestapo, after it was discovered she'd written and translated a leaflet calling on French foreign slave labourers to agitate against the Nazi regime. When a Gestapo officer told her, during her interrogation, that she would be treated more leniently if she named other collaborators in the group, she replied: 'That would make me as low and depraved as you want me to appear.' The judge said, in his summing-up of the case, that Eva had shown the 'cunning of a Catholic and the subversiveness of a communist'. She was sentenced to death. On the day of her execution, she wrote the following words, in a farewell letter to her parents: 'I am sorry that I could not spare you this most terrible grief. But it's good it turned out the way it did. There was such an accursed conflict within me; living through the last few months brought the answer. Now all is calm and peace.'[28]

Brave communist activists such as Eva Buch appear frequently in Gestapo files. The memoirs of Rudolf Goguel, the leader of the communist trade union for white collar workers, offers a good insight into the problems faced by those who engaged in active clandestine communist underground activity. He claimed that in the aftermath of the 'Night of the Long Knives' the

KPD tried to appeal to discontented members of the SA in Düsseldorf. The results were catastrophic. KPD activists were denounced one by one by the SA members they had foolishly befriended. By October 1935, of the 422 key KPD functionaries when Hitler came to power, 219 were in custody, 125 had fled into exile, 24 had been killed and 42 had left the party; the remaining 12 were still at large.[29] It's been estimated that only 10 per cent of the original 360,000 members of the KPD in 1933 continued to be actively involved in communist underground activity by 1935.

A Gestapo report from October 1935 praised the bravery of those communists who continued what now seemed a hopeless underground struggle:

> During the various discoveries of KPD groups which have taken place in recent months, there has repeatedly been occasion to note the self-sacrificing readiness of all the supporters of the illegal KPD who were willing to fill any gap which occurred in their ranks and to take the place of comrades who were arrested, without letting themselves be deterred by the high prison sentences. This readiness to make sacrifices for the communist idea goes so far that convinced communists again and again sacrifice their lives to avoid having to betray their comrades.[30]

In some working-class areas solidarity with the communist cause was not easily extinguished. On 24 March 1937, Adam Schäfer, a well-known KPD activist, was shot dead in a barracks in the Dachau concentration camp by an SS guard, who claimed he had been attacked by him. The bullet-riddled corpse of Schäfer was released to his grieving family for burial. On 29 March, Schäfer's funeral took place in a working-class district of Wiesbaden. A huge crowd, estimated at 800, turned out to pay their last respects to this local communist hero. A Gestapo officer was sent to observe the burial incognito. In his report, he claimed 75 per cent of those present were former well-known members of the KPD. A local KPD activist laid a huge wreath on the grave in a symbolic gesture of working-class solidarity with a fallen comrade. This man was soon taken into 'protective custody' by the Gestapo.[31]

How widespread such open public demonstrations of communist resistance in working-class areas is very difficult to calculate. Some KPD activists felt the situation for communists changed dramatically in the late 1930s. Jakob Zorn, a leading KPD functionary, who had been arrested in 1934, then released in 1937, painted a very gloomy picture of communist resistance during the late 1930s. 'I could see how much the resistance had shrunk,' he observed. 'The number of victims was enormous. It was not, therefore, the same revival as 1933–1934, which had been huge, massive. The losses which the party [KPD] had suffered, which anti fascism as a whole had suffered, had kept the resistance comparatively small.'[32] The figures of Gestapo arrests of communists indicate a sharp decrease in communist resistance activity. In 1936, 11,678 communists were arrested. In 1937, this had reduced to 8,068 and then dropped further to 3,800 in 1938.[33] In the city of Dresden, KPD records from January 1936 indicated there were only seventy-five active members left in the city.[34] A similar pattern emerged elsewhere. The underground SOPADE reports, compiled by underground SPD activists, revealed that most of the working class had reluctantly accepted the Nazi regime as a 'fact of life' by the late 1930s, as this report from July 1938 illustrates:

The general mood in Germany is characterised by political indifference. The great mass of the people is completely dulled and does not want to hear anything about politics . . . The most shocking thing is the ignorance in wide circles about what is actually going on. They are completely convinced that there are no longer concentration camps; they simply do not want to believe that the Nazis treat their opponents with ruthless brutality.

They do not want to believe it because that would be too terrible for them and they prefer to shut their eyes to it.[35]

In the face of growing working-class apathy, communist dissident behaviour became more individualistic. The Gestapo increasingly relied on the public to denounce a dwindling number of pro-communist trouble makers. Karoline Krupp (born 1905) in the working-class industrial city of Essen in the Ruhr doggedly remained a committed communist during the Nazi era. She lived with her husband Erich in a ground-floor apartment of a very large house in Essen that was divided into several apartments.[36] On 14 April 1937, she was arrested because her neighbour Karl Muth, an unemployed shoemaker, reported to the Gestapo that Karoline was repeatedly making pro-communist comments and even used a Soviet Red Flag as a tablecloth for her dining table. When Karoline heard her neighbour Karl listening to a speech by Adolf Hitler being broadcast by German national radio during the 1936 Olympic Games she ran upstairs to his apartment on the second floor, banged on the door and shouted loudly: 'Turn off that rubbish.' When she heard another neighbour complaining about not having enough money to buy butter she said to her scornfully: 'You're to blame for your own hardship because you voted for Hitler in the first place.'

The Gestapo investigation soon revealed there were simmering tensions among nearly all the tenants in the apartment-house. Karl Muth told the Gestapo he'd known the Krupp family since 1930. He then admitted the real reason he'd denounced Karoline in the first place was because she and her husband Erich often bullied him and engaged in frequent arguments and disputes with him, and with many other residents. Maria Graf, who had acted as a mother's helper to Karoline, told the Gestapo that the story about the Red Flag on the dining room table was true. Karoline had seemingly been a long-standing supporter of the KPD before Hitler came to power. Maria remembered seeing Karoline carrying a Red Flag at KPD rallies many times during the Weimar period. An elderly resident called Rosa Barr claimed it was common knowledge Karoline had been a member of the KPD, and asserted that Karoline had once told her she only enrolled her children in Hitler Youth organisations to give the impression she was now loyal towards the Nazi regime. Hermann Gablon, who also lived in the apartment-house, said he'd never witnessed arguments between Karoline and other residents, but his daughter had told him about them. He believed that all the allegations made against Karoline concerning her continuing loyalty towards the communist cause were true. The caretaker of the building confirmed that Karoline was a disruptive influence and pointed out that she was often involved in arguments with residents in the communal laundry room.

The Gestapo undertook a lengthy interrogation of Karoline. She denied all the allegations of her accusers. She pointed out that as her husband was an official in the German Labour Front, and her children were members of the Hitler Youth, this proved she was a loyal member of the National Community. 'These accusations are nothing less than a disreputable act of revenge,' she added. Under further questioning, she admitted to once being a member of the socialist SPD, but not the KPD.

The Gestapo officer noted in his report that Karoline was a 'dishonest woman' who only admitted to anything when she was faced with 'irrefutable proof'. The Nazi Party leader for the district of Essen was asked to provide a report on the political reliability of the Krupp family. He described Karoline as 'quarrelsome' and 'politically unreliable'. It was also verified that neither Karoline nor Erich had ever been members of the KPD, but they had been active in the socialist SPD during the Weimar periods. At the end of this lengthy investigation, the Gestapo officer in charge of the case concluded that Karoline's communist sympathies were quite apparent. He was satisfied the allegations made against her were not motivated by revenge, but expressed genuine and broad concerns within the apartment-house about Karoline's political loyalty to the National Community. No evidence was ever produced which showed that Karoline was still active within the communist underground, but she was charged by the Gestapo with 'preparing high treason' and sent for trial in the 'Special Court' in Dortmund, and sentenced to a short spell in prison.[37] The Gestapo decided to show Karoline that the Nazi regime had zero tolerance towards proven dissident communist attitudes.

Another communist sympathiser, Peter Penk (born 1915), lived in the west Rhineland industrial city of Münchengladbach.[38] He was a Catholic, as were most of the residents of the city.[39] The KPD had its largest number of supporters in an area surrounding local cotton and textile factories. Peter worked in one of these as a cotton spinner. On 2 May 1937, the window of a local shop, owned by Buray Kuzment, a Jew from Poland, was smashed. The shop owner claimed three people carried out this attack. He identified two of them in a local pub: Michael Dorf and Arnold Siegler. The Gestapo arrested both of them. They denied any involvement, but named Peter Penk as the wrongdoer. Other witnesses soon came forward. They all described Peter as a well-known local communist activist and nuisance. The Gestapo decided not to see the incident as motivated by anti-Semitism. Instead, the Gestapo officer leading the investigation claimed it was a well-known communist ploy to attack Jewish shops and pin the blame on local Nazi storm troopers. 'The public is easily inclined to burden the [Nazi] movement with such [anti-Semitic] crimes', he noted in his report of the incident. This statement was not backed up by any specific examples concerning attacks by communists on Jewish shops.

The Gestapo brought Peter Penk in for questioning. He denied having any sympathy with communist doctrines. He was a good National Socialist, he said, and a member of the Hitler Youth from 1931 to 1933. He only left because he lost his job, and couldn't afford the necessary HJ uniform and equipment. The

Gestapo officer asked Peter to explain how the shop window came to be smashed in the first place. He said he'd been in a beer hall during that whole day and had drunk about twenty beers in all. He was walking home, very drunk, had lost his footing, then accidentally fell against the window. When he got up, he kicked the window, in pure frustration, and then went home to sleep off his heavy binge-drinking session.

The Gestapo found Peter's story totally 'unreliable'. His previous record was examined. He'd been convicted seven times before for criminal offences, most notably, theft and smuggling. His reputation as a loyal supporter of the National Community, was, according to the Gestapo report, 'considerably damaged' by his succession of minor criminal offences. No evidence of any politically motivated offences ever came to light during the investigation.

The Gestapo asked Michael Dorf, who had been drinking with Peter on the day of the incident, to give his version of events. Peter wasn't as completely drunk as he claimed when he left the beer hall, Dorf said. Other discrepancies in Peter's story soon began to emerge. He had never been a member of the Hitler Youth, nor was he a firm supporter of National Socialism as he suggested during his interrogation. The Gestapo decided a short sharp shock might be the answer. Peter was not brought before a criminal court, for breaking the window, but detained in 'protective custody' for seven days. On the day of his release, Peter signed a declaration in which he promised not to make any statements or undertake any actions against the Nazi government in the future.

It was a promise Peter could not keep. On 18 October 1938, eighteen months after the window-smashing incident, Peter was reported to the Gestapo again. A local waitress said he had not only given a lengthy pro-communist rant in a packed beer hall in Münchengladbach, but had screamed 'Heil Moskau' (Hail Moscow) too. Three days later, he was arrested by the Gestapo, and held in 'protective custody' for sixteen days in a Düsseldorf prison cell, while the incident was investigated fully.

The Gestapo questioned a number of people. The first witness interrogated was Gertrud Engel, the daughter of the landlady of the beer hall. She had made the original allegation. She was acting as a waitress in the bar on the day in question. Peter ordered and drank several beers, but he then refused to pay the bill. A heated quarrel ensued during which Peter called Gertrud's mother 'an old harridan'. He then launched into a long ranting speech aimed at all the other customers near the bar, attacking Hitler's 'aggressive' foreign policy and the 'corrupt' annual Nazi 'Winter Relief' (*Winterhilfswerk*) programme, which used public donations to finance help for old-aged pensioners and poor people in rural areas.

Peter Schoemann, a local chimney sweep, corroborated Gertrud's story. Peter, he said, was a well-known committed communist supporter. During his anti-Nazi speech, Peter asked all the other customers in the pub if they would join him in 'taking up arms against Hitler'. When they all replied, 'no way', Peter called them 'idiots and cowards'. He then called Schoemann a 'scoundrel' and slapped him in the face, before telling another group of drinkers, near the bar: 'If you all say "Heil Hitler", you are all arseholes and cowards. I say *Heil Muskau* and the most important thing is that we [the communists] are marching on.'

A forty-one-year-old storekeeper called Wilhelm Herson told the Gestapo that Peter also claimed during his extended drunken rant that capitalists and Nazi leaders lived a high life on the proceeds of the payroll deductions of the workers. Herson countered by saying that as a veteran who had fought for Germany in the First World War, he would 'march within a moment, if Hitler calls the nation to arms'. Peter called Wilhelm an 'idiot'.

In a lengthy Gestapo interrogation, Peter was asked to explain his actions in the beer hall. He was completely drunk that day, he said, and couldn't remember what had happened at all. He'd lost his job in 1932, at the height of the depression, but then joined the Nazi Labour Service organisation, and secured a job as a cotton spinner. There was no reason for him to blame Hitler's government, he claimed, and he denied ever having sympathised with the KPD.

The Gestapo concluded that the witnesses in the case were telling the truth and Peter was lying. In spite of this, and possibly due to the fact he had already spent almost three weeks in prison, Peter was released, pending a final decision by the public prosecutor on what action should ultimately be taken in the case. Peter's downward spiral continued. On 13 December 1938, he was arrested yet again. This time the charge was a criminal one. He'd been driving a car, while drunk, and hit a pedestrian, causing him 'bodily injury'.[40] On 9 January 1939, the Gestapo office in Münchengladbach told HQ in Düsseldorf that the case concerning the allegations in the pub was being dropped. The senior prosecutor had, however, made an arrangement with the local military authorities for Peter to be immediately enlisted to serve in the German army.[41]

There was clear evidence of Peter Penk holding strong pro-communist opinions, but his criminal activities, including theft, vandalism, drink-driving, assault and smuggling, were equally serious. The Gestapo had treated him with remarkable leniency. On top of all this, he was a serious problem drinker and local troublemaker. The final decision of the public pros-ecutor was to forcibly conscript him into the German army. Given Peter's anti-authoritarian personality, it's difficult to imagine that the rigid discipline of army life would have ended his conflict with the Nazi system. Peter's ultimate fate is unknown.

By 1937, as military rearmament intensified, communist worker resistance moved into factories and building sites. Instances of absenteeism, slow working and sabotage became a constant problem within armament factories.[42] In June 1936, 262 workers engaged in a seventeen-minute stoppage at the Rüsselsheim Opel Works in protest over a wage cut. This led to the arrest by the Gestapo of all its rebel leaders. There were similar strikes during this period in Berlin, Dortmund and Hamburg.[43] An intelligence report from 1937 produced by the Düsseldorf Gestapo raised worries about the growth of this worker discontent:

After factory meetings at which speakers of the Labour Front had spoken, some of whom were in fact rather clumsy in their statements, the mood of discontent among the workers was apparent in subsequent discussions. In one fairly large factory the speaker from the Labour Front greeted the workers with the German [Nazi salute], but in reply the workers only mumbled. When the speaker ended the factory parade with the German salute, it was returned loudly and clearly, but they [the workers] made it clear that they had only used the German salute because it brought the factory parade to an end. The shifting about of workers within the various factories, necessitated by the shortage of raw materials, creates more fertile soil for the subversion of the workers by the KPD.[44]

It's clear that many KPD activists were determined to undermine the rearmament programme. One such person was Anton Kendricks (born 1887), an unskilled building labourer from Münchengladbach and a committed communist. He lived in Viersen, a town that was about eight kilometres outside the city of his birth. Anton was Catholic by religion. His marital status is listed in his Gestapo file as 'divorced'.[45] In the summer and autumn of 1938, he worked for the Züblin construction company on military fortifications on the western frontier of Germany.[46]

Ludwig Esslinger was the foreman of the site, which employed about a hundred and forty workers. They lived in makeshift barracks adjacent to the site. The work was back-breaking, the hours long, and the pay poor. Rumblings of discontent about conditions on the site soon emerged among a small minority of discontented workers. Trouble came to a head one Friday afternoon in the autumn of 1938 when three workers (named

Feder, Bloedel and Glanzer) left the site, without permission, and headed to a local beer hall. When they returned from their unauthorised drinking session, the foreman told them their pay would be docked for the day. On hearing this, all three became angry and very aggressive. They threatened to beat up Esslinger and said they wouldn't work any more if he carried out his threat not to pay them.

The site manager reported the matter to the Gestapo. A number of workers on the site were interrogated. Emil Schuler told the Gestapo that Anton, who was not even involved in the drinking incident, was the real ringleader of all the worker discontent on the site. He'd reportedly been grumbling to workers about long hours and low wages for weeks, and had started a whispering campaign designed to undermine the management. The same story was corroborated by another worker named Kurt Dorner, who claimed Kendricks beat him up for refusing to join the walkout. All four workers leading the discontent were active communists, he added. Another worker called Wilhelm Gelling claimed the ringleaders were constantly bullying and inciting all the workers on the site. During night shifts they persistently distracted workers from concentrating on their important rearmament work. Wilhelm had also heard Glanzer say while listening to a radio speech by Adolf Hitler, 'The Führer can kiss my ass.'

On 28 October 1938, the Gestapo interrogated Anton Kendricks, who admitted that all the allegations made by his co-workers, including violent bullying, were true, but he denied supporting the KPD. Feder was questioned on the same day and denied expressing any communist opinions. On the next day, Glanzer was interrogated. He admitted serving a two-day prison sentence in 1931 for distributing communist leaflets. He said he'd never been a member of the KPD, but acknowledged that he had been 'an active sympathiser' with the Communist Party until 1936, though he was no longer the strong 'militant supporter' he'd been before 1933. He too admitted the bullying allegations, but claimed Feder and Kendricks were the ringleaders of worker discontent on the site.

On 29 October 1938, the final report of the Gestapo noted that Kendricks had been a militant member of the KPD since 1927. It concluded that all three leaders of worker disruption on the site were most probably in contact with a local communist underground group, but this link could not be fully verified. Kendricks and Glanzer were put in prison until January 1939, and Feder until March 1939. Bloedel, who had been involved in the original afternoon drinking session, escaped punishment altogether.

It's fascinating to glimpse how a group of committed communists attempted to incite worker discontent on a project that was related to national defence. The sentences they received were very lenient. The pressure used to gain worker support on the building site was not persuasion, but threats of bullying and violence. The case reached the Gestapo because the tiny rebellious group of workers, under the influence of alcohol, threatened to attack the foreman. Once the matter was reported to the site manager, he acted quickly and brought in the Gestapo. The silent majority of workers, now free of any worker intimidation, felt able to denounce the protesters to the Gestapo.[47]

In many cases, it was often difficult for the Gestapo to differentiate between 'dissident' behaviour and genuine communist resistance. The Gestapo investigation into Heinz Wasschermann (born 1921) and a group of factory apprentices is a prime example. Heinz came from Essen and was an apprentice silk weaver.[48] He was accused of being the ringleader of a group of young workers who had written anti-Nazi slogans on the toilet doors of two factories in Essen. The case began when a factory manager at the Gehr silk-making factory in Essen informed the local Labour Front that 'communist writings' had been discovered in the toilets. The slogans 'Shoot Hitler', 'Hang Göring', 'Long live Thälmann' (the imprisoned KPD leader) and 'Hail Moscow' had been found scrawled on several toilet doors in the Gehr factory. On 16 December 1937, a drawing of an Native American Indian looking at a red star symbol of the Soviet Union above the slogan 'A look at the future' was also discovered in the toilets. All this information was passed on to the Gestapo on 5 January 1938.

The Gestapo linked this case to a similar wave of anti-Nazi graffiti that was discovered in 1937 at a nearby factory, owned by the Colsmann Company. The slogan 'The Russians will come to Germany' and other similar pro-Soviet comments were found on several toilet doors. The factory manager suggested that 'labour peace in our factory is seriously disturbed by such slandering'. Due to the fact that so many workers used the toilets it became impossible for the Gestapo to determine who the real culprits were and the case was dropped.

Hans Zindel, the Labour Front shop-floor leader at the Gehr factory, told the Gestapo that the writer of the pro-communist slogans might be Rudolf Keelmann, as he noticed he never gave the Nazi salute and was generally regarded as unsympathetic to the Nazis by his co-workers. Keelmann was interrogated by the Gestapo. He denied ever having been a member of the KPD. He had discovered the drawing of the Native American Indian in the toilet, been angered by it, and then reported it to the foreman at the factory immediately. Another worker called Wilhelm Frenz said it was true that Keelmann had discovered the graffiti in the toilet, but Frenz believed Keelmann was a pro-communist 'grumbler and moaner' and cast doubt over his claim that he was outraged about the graffiti.

The Gestapo interrogated many workers in the factory to try and find out who was responsible. Heinz Dresden, a pro-Nazi member of the Hitler Youth, denied he'd written anything on the toilet doors. Hermann Stein, another Hitler Youth member, admitted that in October 1937 he'd written his name on the toilet door, but denied writing any of the other slogans found in the toilets. He claimed Heinz Wasschermann had drawn the image of the Native American Indian and written the words 'A look at the future' underneath it. He also claimed Wasschermann had drawn an image of a gallows on another toilet door above the words 'Russia Today'. This was clearly an anti-Soviet slogan, and a clear reference to Stalin's brutal purges. It could not be seen as anti-Nazi.

Hans Zindel, the DAF factory representative, told the Gestapo that the writing on the toilet doors was just a 'juvenile prank', and not evidence of major communist resistance activity in the factory. He thought Keelmann had probably egged on the other young apprentices to write the graffiti, but he doubted he had the artistic ability to draw the figure of the Native American Indian. Hans Gudland, a fifteen-year-old apprentice, admitted he'd drawn the outlines of 'Red Indian' heads on several toilet doors, but had written no slogans below them. Another young apprentice, Friedrich Wolf, said he'd seen the head of a Native American Indian on the door (obviously drawn by Gudland), and noticed that the Soviet red star and the slogan were added a few days later. Heinz Wasschermann underwent two Gestapo interrogations. He denied drawing the Native American Indian figure, but admitted he had written the slogan underneath it. He denied it was a pro-communist statement. In a second round of questioning he admitted to drawing the head of the Native American Indian too.

All the suspected apprentices were arrested on 12 January 1938 and imprisoned in Elberfeld, as the Gestapo continued to exhaustively interrogate other witnesses. The Gestapo discovered in subsequent interrogations that all the boys had agreed not to betray each other. Samples of handwriting were taken from each of them and compared to the graffiti on the toilet doors. The Gestapo concluded, by checking the handwriting on the door against handwriting of all the workers, that Gustav Feelich had definitely written the graffiti. During his belated interrogation, Feelich admitted that he was indeed the writer of all the graffiti, except the image of the Native American Indian.

He assured the Gestapo that he had done it as a juvenile prank, and not for political motives.

In the concluding Gestapo report, dated 8 January 1938, though eight suspects are mentioned, it is just three – Gustav Feelich, Friedrich Walles, another person who had not been previously questioned, and Heinz Wasschermann – who are cited as the main perpetrators. A criminal case against all three was begun. The Gestapo decided to look into the background of their parents. It was noted that the fathers of Walles and Feelich were both unemployed members of the working class, and in receipt of state welfare benefits. There was, however, no hint of any involvement with communism within any of the families of those accused. It was noted, favourably, that the mother of Walles was a member of the Nazi Women's organisation 'NS-Frauenschaft'.

After this huge investigation, which took up an enormous amount of the time of all the Gestapo officers involved, for what was a very trivial matter, all three boys were released from prison within days of their arrest, and the case against them was dropped by the public prosecutor on 18 March 1938.[49]

The signing of the Nazi–Soviet Pact on 23 August 1939 was a key watershed for anti-Nazi communist resistance in Germany. Two days later, the KPD leadership issued a formal statement that placed a positive spin on this unexpected turn of events:

> The German working people and especially the German worker must support the peace policy of the Soviet Union, must place themselves at the side of all peoples who are oppressed and threatened by the Nazis and must take up the fight as never before to ensure peace pacts in the spirit of the pact that has just been completed between the Soviet Union and Germany are made with Poland and Romania, with France and England and with all the peoples who find themselves threatened by Hitler's policy of aggression.[50]

In spite of this unfathomable ideological U-turn by Stalin, sympathy among communists for the Soviet Union remained very powerful. The case of Erich Weiss (born 1900) in Remscheid, a city in the south of the industrial Ruhr, is a prime example. Erich was a married Catholic. He listed his occupation as 'vermin exterminator'.[51] He was unquestionably a committed supporter of the KPD, and had been since the Weimar period. His Gestapo file lists four previous convictions, including illegally owning guns and 'making preparations for high treason'. Between August and September 1933, he was held in 'protective custody', and then sentenced to nine months' imprisonment for buying weapons for communist resistance groups. Weiss was released early due to a general Nazi amnesty for political prisoners that came into effect in December 1933.

After his release, Erich Weiss completely disappears from Gestapo records until he made a tragic error. This happened on 31 August 1939, the day before the German invasion of Poland, which began the Second World War. Erich's car was rapidly running out of petrol on his journey home. He stopped at a local filling station only to discover that no petrol was available. A well-meaning young man offered to use a hand pump to siphon some petrol from his own car into Erich's petrol tank. The two men then started chatting about the current international crisis. Erich told the young man that if he was forced to join the German army he wouldn't be willing to shoot at foreign enemies. 'Germany will lose the war,' he added. 'Stalin will come to Berlin to play the *Internationale* and that will be a good laugh.'

A man called 'Herr Thumann' overheard this conversation, noted down the licence number of Erich's car, and then reported the incident to the Gestapo. Weiss was arrested, but he denied ever having made the defeatist comments he was accused of. The Gestapo did not believe him. He was charged with 'preparing high treason' and held in 'protective custody' for six months. On 1 March 1940, the Higher Regional Court of the city of Hamm, in the northeastern area of the Ruhr, sentenced Erich Weiss to three years in prison as a communist activist. The seemingly innocuous overheard conversation at a petrol station was the chief evidence used to secure this conviction. Erich was not released until 1942, and on 1 December 1942 he was once again placed in 'protective custody' on suspicion of continued communist sympathies. In January 1943, Erich was sent to the infamous Dachau concentration camp.[52] His ultimate fate is not known. On the surface, Erich's unguarded comments at the petrol station might seem quite trivial, but his past record of serious underground communist activity meant the Gestapo took him out of circulation for the entire war-time period.

Another communist, Aloys Vock (born 1891), who came from Duisburg, an industrial city in the western part of the Ruhr, within easy commuting distance of Düsseldorf, the capital city of North-Rhine Westphalia, was treated far more leniently by the Gestapo. He listed his religion as Catholic, marital status as 'divorced' and occupation as 'sailor'. He was involved in inland navigation work on the Rhine.[53] Aloys was a committed supporter of the KPD before 1933. He'd been arrested by the Gestapo in May 1933 on suspicion of working with the KPD resistance against Hitler's regime, but the charges were dropped due to 'lack of evidence'. On 5 October 1939, he was arrested by the Gestapo again, because a group of Nazi Party members had overheard him making derogatory comments about Adolf Hitler in a beer hall in Ruhrort, a working-class dockland area of Duisburg. 'Hitler is on the ropes,' he reportedly told fellow drinkers, and was 'clutching the treaty with Russia'.

The Gestapo now undertook a detailed investigation into the political reliability of Aloys Vock. Several witnesses were questioned. Three members of the Nazi Party gave evidence concerning the views expressed by Aloys in a beer hall on the night before Germany attacked Poland on 1 September 1939. A speech by Adolf Hitler was being broadcast on national radio in the beer hall. Within ear-shot of other drinkers, Aloys was heard openly praising Soviet leader Joseph Stalin as the most able world statesman. 'I would never go to the front line,' he continued. 'I would prefer to shoot myself in the brain.'

A local Nazi leader reported that Aloys Vock was employed as a river pilot, and was respected by his colleagues, who were seemingly 'under his spell'. Others depicted him as a 'trouble-making communist', frequently urging colleagues to agitate for better pay and conditions. The local Labour Front (DAF) branch claimed Aloys and a colleague named as 'Franz' had lobbied Belgian and Dutch sailors to oppose the introduction of fixed weekly wage rates, which had ended generous overtime payments. Ten other foreign workers had allegedly joined this agitation.

Armed with this evidence, the Gestapo interrogated Aloys Vock. He denied ever being a member of the KPD, but was willing to admit he attended rallies of the party in the Weimar period, and those of the SPD too, 'out of boredom'. He categorically denied refusing to accept the new fixed wage regulations in his job or that he was some sort of underground trade union agitator or communist resister. As for the conversations in the beer hall, Aloys claimed his views had been distorted by those who had denounced him. What he had really said was not that the Nazi–Soviet Pact was a victory for Stalin, but that it was of 'great advantage' to Germany.

A month later, the Gestapo released Aloys Vock without ever charging him.[54] They were clearly worried about the pro-Soviet comments Aloys had made in the beer hall, and the additional allegations that he might be acting as an unofficial shop steward, but in the end they decided he did not represent a serious threat to the National Community, even though his continued affinity with the communist cause was firmly established.

The outbreak of the Second World War led to a resurgence of German patriotism that affected even some of those who had previously opposed the regime. This was felt even within working-class communities that had previously been resistant to the appeal of National Socialism. The case of Wilhelm Struck (born 1905) in Mörsch, a small town in the upper Rhine valley, provides a typical example. He was married, listed his occupation as 'painter', and claimed he was not affiliated to any religion.[55]

Wilhelm had fought with selfless bravery for the communist cause for years. His wife Anna was a committed communist too. In the autumn of 1932 Wilhelm became a KPD official in the Hamburg-Altona area. He was already an active member of 'Red Front Fighters' (*Rotfrontkämpferbund*-RFB), a paramilitary association that was closely allied to the KPD. It had been heavily involved in bitter street fights with the Nazis in the years before Hitler came to power. Erich Honecker, who later became the leader of the post-war East German communist regime (DDR), was a member of the organisation, which was even banned by the SPD-led Weimar government in 1929.

Members of the RFB were among the first people arrested in the anti-communist raids of the SA and the Gestapo in the early months of Hitler's rule. Wilhelm Struck was placed in 'protective custody' from 27 April to 5 May 1933. He was charged, tried and sentenced for 'preparing high treason'. The judge deemed him 'dishonoured' as a citizen. This ruling prohibited him from ever serving in the German army. Wilhelm was sent to Rendsburg prison, located in the state of Schleswig-Holstein, to serve his sentence. He was released on 5 May 1935. The Gestapo regarded him as an 'enemy of the state' and continued to monitor him very closely. Reports continued to appear in his file updating his location and his activities.

On 7 March 1938, the Düsseldorf branch of the Gestapo received a request from the Hamburg office asking for Wilhelm to be brought in for questioning as it was felt he was still involved in underground communist activity. On 24 March 1939, he was interrogated. Wilhelm freely admitted that his main task in the KPD before 1933 was to distribute leaflets to the rank-and-file of the police force, to gather information about policemen and to develop close connections with them. Communist infiltration into the police force in the Weimar era was strong, he said. He even gave the names of individual policemen who had provided the KPD with information. After this interrogation, no charges were brought against him. On 3 November 1939 the Gestapo office in Osnabrück informed colleagues in Düsseldorf that Wilhelm was now working in an armaments factory in the city. There were no concerns that he was actively involved in resistance activities.

On 12 December 1940, this long-standing and seemingly dedicated communist suddenly and inexplicably applied to join the German army. There is no explanation as to why he wanted to fight for Hitler in the *Wehrmacht*. At that time, the Nazi–Soviet Pact was still in force, and Germany's sole enemy in the Second World War was Britain. In his application to join the army Wilhelm writes: 'Today I support the Führer and National Socialism strongly. I want to get my honour back by serving in the army.'

The National Socialist administration for the district of Krefeld refused to accept his application. His sudden conversion to the Nazi cause was regarded with deep suspicion. On 15 August 1941, nine months later, the Gestapo office in Krefeld reported that Wilhelm was now living in Krefeld. He'd divorced his pro-communist first wife Anna, and was now married to a woman who owned a local fruit and vegetable shop. Wilhelm worked in the shop. The local employment office brought him in for an interview. He was offered a job as a painter, but he turned this down. It was noted that Wilhelm was paying thirty Reichsmarks per month in maintenance payments for the two children from his first marriage. These payments were being subsidised by state welfare payments. It's clear that the local employment office regarded Wilhelm as a 'slacker'. He was warned that unless he took up regular full-time paid work very soon he would be punished. A person defined as 'work-shy' could be sent to a concentration camp.

In March 1942, Wilhelm again asked if he could join the army. Once more the Gestapo office in Düsseldorf refused to support his application. On 19 February 1943, just days after the catastrophic German defeat at Stalingrad, there was a belated change of mind and Wilhelm's request to fight for Germany was finally granted. He was enlisted in an army unit that was destined to fight, not against the USSR, but in North Africa against the Western Allies.[56]

This case further illustrates the complexity of the experience of communists under Hitler's regime. Here was an individual whose views seemingly underwent a radical transformation from a fanatical dedication to the KPD to support for National Socialism, and a surprising desire to join the army. What brought about his disillusionment with communism is unclear, but his divorce from Anna, his first wife, who was a committed communist, and his marriage to a local pro-Nazi greengrocer, may have been contributory factors. It was only after the shock defeat at Stalingrad that he was finally allowed to join the army. His ultimate fate is not known.

It was in the period after the invasion of the Soviet Union on 22 June 1941 that communist resistance revived. The number of anti-communist leaflets grew from a mere 62 in January 1941 to 10,277 by October 1941. A number of small, but dedicated underground communist groups now resurfaced. Some former comrades, who had obviously been lying low, returned to the fold. Married locksmith Friedrich Grossmann (born 1899) was one of them. He was born in Metz, in the Lorraine region, which was part of France at the time of his birth. He claimed to be 'unaffiliated to any religion'.[57] On 25 January 1943, Friedrich was living in the industrial city of Wuppertal, in the Ruhr, when he was arrested by the Gestapo on suspicion of 'preparing high treason'. According to six witnesses, some of them his own relatives, he'd been active in reconstructing the illegal Communist Party in Wuppertal, had taken part in distributing leaflets, and had even held communist meetings in his own flat. The Gestapo searched his apartment, but could find no evidence of any communist literature.

During his interrogation Friedrich told the Gestapo he had originally been a member of the SPD, but joined the KPD in 1923, and then served in the paramilitary 'Red Front' (RFB). He was part of a group that killed a policeman during the Weimar era, for which he had been sentenced to eleven years for 'high treason'. He was released after serving four years. He then left the KPD after falling out with a local leader, and joined *Rote Hilfe* (Red Aid), a solidarity branch of the KPD, which provided support to former political prisoners. He continued to vote for the KPD until it was officially banned in 1933. Afterwards, he claimed, he had ceased being active in the party and retreated into political apathy.

After the invasion of the Soviet Union he had a chance meeting with an old KPD comrade.[58] They started to meet up regularly, together with their wives, but never talked about politics. His old friend then tried to recruit him for illegal KPD underground tasks and he agreed. In the clubhouse of his choral society, he met Erich Lossner, another ex-KPD member, who gave him three underground communist leaflets. When he returned home, he burned the leaflets on his kitchen stove. He soon regained his confidence, however, and joined a communist underground group led by Alois Kape and which included the former KPD-deputy Hugo Paul.

The Gestapo held Friedrich Grossmann in 'protective custody' for five months and then released him. His lenient treatment was probably due to the fact he provided the Gestapo during his interrogation with the names of other key members of the communist underground.[59]

A far bigger problem for the Gestapo during the war-time period was the growing collaboration between communists and the huge groups of foreign labourers that flooded into Germany and were used as slave labourers in the armaments factories. Gestapo officers were given instructions on how to deal with foreign workers by Reinhard Heydrich on 8 March 1940. The following activities were all to be treated harshly: insubordination at work, industrial sabotage, any sexual relations between Germans and foreigners, and any social contact in bars and restaurants. Foreign workers, just like Jews, were given identification badges which they were required to wear in public. Poles, for example, were given a purple badge, with a 'P' on it.[60] By August 1944, 6 million foreign workers and a further 2.5 million POWs were working in cities and in the countryside. This 'new proletariat' consisted of 2 million Soviet workers, 2.5 million Red Army POWs, 1.7 million Poles, 300,000 Czechs, 270,000 Dutch and 200,000 Belgian workers.[61]

Between May and August 1942, 79,821 foreign workers were arrested, and 4,962 of these cases involved 'improper' sexual relations with Germans. The Gestapo became overloaded with cases involving German fraternising with foreign workers. Sexual relations between a foreign worker and a German carried a death sentence. The number of German males who abused foreign female workers in factories and labour camps is incalculable. Many women and girls were reluctant to report sexual abuse, as they feared they would be placed in a concentration camp.

German women who engaged in sexual relations with foreign workers while their husbands were away at war faced severe forms of public humiliation. Nazi propaganda placed strong emphasis on the need for an 'Aryan' soldier's wife to set a good moral example while her husband was away at war. The case of Dora von Cabitz, a farm worker from Oschatz, who was accused of having sex with more than one Polish worker, provides a typical and graphic example.[62] The local Nazi Party organised her punishment. A report by the SD recorded what happened to her:

Already in the morning word had spread that a German woman was going in a pillory. From 9 o'clock onwards the scene in the city was already changing and until roughly 11.00 innumerable people gathered in front of Oschatz town centre: they wanted to see this dishonourable German woman. At 11, on the stroke of the hour, von Cabitz appeared, with head shaven bald, greeted by spontaneous derisive calls from the assembled crowd of people and was placed in a caged pillory. On the front of the pillory hung a sign which bore the following words:

I have been a dishonourable woman in that I sought and had relations with Poles. By doing that, I excluded myself from the community of the people.[63]

These horrendous public humiliations were designed to deter other women from engaging in sexual liaisons with foreign workers, but they did not work. The cases of forbidden sexual relations went on increasing after 1943. Not all of them ended in the sort of extreme public humiliation that befell Dora von Cabitz. Far more typical is the case of 'Frau Kohl', a tram-car worker. She was accused of having an affair with an Italian worker by her brother-in-law on 17 December 1941. During her Gestapo interrogation, Kohl denied that the relationship with the Italian was of a sexual nature. He was merely teaching her Italian. She sometimes let him stay in her house overnight, but he always slept downstairs on the sofa. She wanted to divorce her husband, who often beat her up. The Gestapo warned her not to have any further contact with her Italian friend.[64]

Another extensive problem for the Gestapo to deal with during the war-time period was general misbehaviour by foreign workers in factories. The Nazi regime increasingly relied on foreign workers to sustain its armaments programme as Allied pressure increased during the latter stages of the Second World War. Of the 388,000 arrests carried out by the Gestapo between January and September 1943, 260,000 involved 'the breaking of work contract by foreigners'.[65] In armaments factories, foreign workers often made up 33 per cent of the workforce. The overwhelming majority were, in effect, under-nourished slave labourers. In the first six months of 1944, 32,236 Russian workers in coal mines were recorded as 'fatalities'. In reality, they had been deliberately starved to death.[66]

To ease the burgeoning case load of the Gestapo, plant managers were given special powers to deal with 'eastern workers', including being able to order three days' imprisonment in the labour camps attached to many factories. Many cases were dealt with by the Gestapo. Robert Ledux, a French worker, was reported to the Gestapo in February 1944 for loafing at a Krupp armaments factory. A foreman had asked him to move some heavy iron, but he refused, saying: 'No food, no work.' A fight then broke out between him and the foreman and he was subsequently placed in a re-education camp by the Gestapo.[67]

Cases involving suspected collaboration between communists and foreign workers were always thoroughly investigated by the Gestapo. The case of Hermann Haus (born 1892) in Duisburg provides a typical example. Hermann was married, with four children, and listed his occupation as 'shoemaker'. He was working at the infamous chemical company IG Farben in the west Rhineland city of Krefeld at the time he first came to the attention of the Gestapo.[68] On 1 March 1943, he was reported to the Gestapo by a factory manager for allegedly making communist statements and for urging foreign workers to work slowly to impede the German war effort.

The Gestapo interviewed a wide range of workers in the factory in order to find out whether the allegations were true. The manager told the Gestapo that during meal breaks Hermann disassociated himself from his German colleagues and preferred to spend time with foreign female workers, especially those from Belgium and in particular a certain woman named 'Mrs Pellus'. They'd struck up a close friendship after she reportedly comforted and supported Hermann's wife while she was pregnant. When a foreman told Mrs Pellus off for leaving the workplace thirty minutes early, Hermann intervened very strongly on her behalf.

There were also allegations that Hermann was inciting workers to engage in industrial sabotage. A foreman named Fritz Kruger suspected that he had been agitating the workers to work slowly, but he could offer no direct evidence for this. A second foreman called Aloys Engelhart described Hermann as 'short-tempered, tardy and undisciplined', but he offered no evidence concerning the allegation that he had agitated the workers to engage in sabotage.

A German female worker told the Gestapo that Hermann reprimanded her for working too hard. This woman had once given him one of her shoes to repair, but instead of asking for a payment, he asked her to go on a date with him. She turned him down. Afterwards, Hermann kept niggling her over minor issues. Two other female foreign workers also gave statements to the Gestapo.[69] One claimed Hermann had an affair with at least one foreign worker in the factory. This was a very serious allegation, which carried a maximum death sentence. Another female co-worker, who was married, said Hermann often made overt sexual advances towards her too.

Other German female workers claimed Hermann was always asking foreign workers 'not to work too much'. It was further alleged that Hermann was providing POWs, who worked in the factory, with stolen oil. The factory manager speculated to the Gestapo that Hermann was either a communist bent on industrial sabotage or a sexual predator, obsessed with foreign female workers. Every trouble with the foreign workers was due to Hermann, his line manager concluded.

The Gestapo interrogated Hermann about all these allegations. They could find no evidence he was either a communist or a union agitator, or that he was inciting industrial sabotage for political purposes. From 1911 to 1920, he'd been a loyal soldier of the German army. He worked diligently as an unskilled labourer at IG Farben for four years. Portraying all the accusations made against him as mere spiteful gossip, Hermann singled out the line manager who had made the original denunciation as having a long-standing personal dislike of him. None of the sexual allegations made were true, he said. He denied having an affair with Mrs Pellus. She and her husband were friends of him and his wife.

The final Gestapo report concluded that there was no evidence to support the view that Hermann incited slow work or sabotage in the factory. His version of the various sexual allegations was clearly accepted. Hermann was released from 'protective custody' on 6 March 1943. He'd been in detention for just five days. Herr Kurberg, the manager of the IG Farben plant, wrote to the Gestapo stating that he didn't want to lose Hermann because he was 'such a good worker'. It was decided that he would be transferred to another factory.[70]

It's clear that the Gestapo did not completely eradicate communism from working-class areas, but committed communists were clearly fighting an increasingly losing battle. All the Gestapo cases we've looked at involving alleged communists were investigated thoroughly and exhaustively. Numerous witnesses were brought in for questioning. Each case was treated with professional diligence and efficiency. A clear final assessment was made of the exact danger each individual posed to the 'National Community'. The Gestapo reserved its harshest treatment for known KPD activists, especially those who had previous 'political' convictions. These individuals were placed in 'protective custody' once any hint they were still committed to the communist cause came to light. It was a denunciation from a working-class or lower-middle-class member of the public that spurred the Gestapo into action in every case looked at here.[71]

The acute observation of former Gestapo officer Hans Gisevius that many individuals in working-class communities showed an increasing willingness to co-operate with the Gestapo seems correct based on the cases examined here.[72] It appears that the pressure to conform to the key National Socialist concept of a united 'National Community' (*Volksgemeinschaft*) had penetrated even the working class by the late 1930s. In these altered circumstances, the denouncement of the 'enemies of the people' now became a patriotic duty. Previously private domains such as the workplace, the beer hall and the petrol station were no longer free of political interference. An unguarded comment in any of these places could and often did lead to a Gestapo investigation.

As Robert Ley, the head of the Labour Front, put it: 'The only people who still have a private life in Germany are those who are asleep.' For communists this was true.

Chapter 5

Denounce Thy Neighbour

It's been estimated that 26 per cent of all Gestapo cases began with a denunciation from a member of the public.[1] In contrast, only 15 per cent started because of the surveillance activities of the Gestapo.[2] Denouncers came from a wide variety of social backgrounds. It was rare for upper-class or educated middle-class citizens to report dissident behaviour.[3] Members of the lower middle class and blue collar working class were overrepresented among the denouncers. Middle-class professionals made up less than 10 per cent of those who denounced.[4] About 80 per cent were male. Men contacted the Gestapo after witnessing incidents in places of work or leisure. Women made up about 20 per cent of all denunciations. They usually accused husbands, relatives and neighbours, typically in domestic situations.[5]

One study of 213 denunciations from the Gestapo case files in Düsseldorf showed that 37 per cent denounced someone else to resolve a personal conflict.[6] The best form of defence for those denounced was to cast doubt on the accuser. Gestapo officers became adept at discovering the underlying motive of denunciations. It was rare for a denouncer to suffer any consequences for making false allegations. One exception was a case that began one afternoon in a Bavarian beer hall in a small rural town. Two complete strangers struck up a conversation in the course of a lengthy drinking session. One of the men became so drunk he briefly blacked out. When he woke up, his drinking companion told him he'd been talking in his sleep about committing treason against Hitler's regime, and a prominent local Nazi Party member overheard his comments. This local Nazi contacted the man who had uttered the anti-Nazi comments a few days later, threatening to denounce him to the Gestapo unless he paid him silence money. The man paid a total of 350 Reichsmarks to the Nazi Party member, and was close to bankruptcy when he decided to report the matter to the Gestapo. The blackmailer was found, arrested, tried and sentenced to death.[7]

The law which provided the legal basis for denunciation was the catch-all 'Decree for the Protection of the Nationalist Movement against Malicious Attacks upon the Government', enacted on 21 March 1933. It contained the following provisions:

1. Whoever purposely makes or circulates a statement of a factual nature which is untrue or grossly exaggerated or which may seriously harm the welfare of the Reich or a [German federal] state or the reputation of the National Government or of a state government or organisations supporting these governments, is to be punished, provided that no more severe punishment is decreed in other regulations, with imprisonment up to two years and, if he makes or spreads the statement publicly, with imprisonment of not less than three months.
2. If serious damage to the Reich or a [federal German] state has resulted from this deed, penal servitude may be imposed.
3. Whoever commits an act through negligence will be punished with imprisonment of up to three months, or by a fine.[8]

This decree was supplemented on 20 December 1934 by the 'Law against Malicious Attacks on State and Party'. This added a fourth clause, punishing by imprisonment all 'rabble-rousing remarks' made against any personalities of the State or the Nazi Party. Paragraph 42 of the 1937 Civil Service Law made it a duty of all state employees to report anti-state activities to the Gestapo.[9] All these laws were an open invitation to denounce anyone who made derogatory remarks about the Nazi regime. Prison sentences for such offences varied between one and six months. Contrary to the popular assumption, there was not a flood of denunciations. The Munich 'Special Court' dealt with 4,453 of cases under these laws between 1933 and 1939, but only 1,522 of those denounced were convicted.[10] In 1937, there were 17,168 cases of 'Malicious Gossip' reported to the Gestapo throughout the whole of Germany.[11]

A typical denouncement case began on 15 September 1933 when Friedrich Weltbach, a worker in a copper factory in the Rhineland industrial city of Duisburg, contacted a Nazi Party factory organisation called the National Socialist Enterprise (NSJB) to report that his elderly factory foreman Heinrich Veet (born 1876), in Duisburg, was repeatedly refusing to give the Nazi salute when greeting his colleagues, would not allow workers to listen to important radio broadcasts by Nazi leaders, and often made derogatory remarks about the Nazi regime.[12] The case was passed on to the Gestapo for investigation. A number of workers were questioned.[13] Friedrich Weltbach said he often came across Heinrich Veet in the factory social room. One day Friedrich said to him: 'Good morning' and gave the Heil Hitler salute. 'Don't give me that shit,' Veet replied, angrily. A second worker recalled that when he spoke in positive terms about Adolf Hitler in front of Veet, he said: 'Don't talk rubbish', adding: 'I will kick your arse if you give the Nazi salute in front of me.' The leader of the NSJB in the factory claimed that he installed a radio in the factory social room so that employees could listen to important speeches by Nazi leaders. One morning he invited some young apprentices to join him in the social room to listen to an important speech by Hitler. When Veet heard about this, he warned workers they could not leave their normal work duties just to listen to a speech. Karl Koptur, a technician in the factory, noted:'I saluted everyone with the Hitler greeting. But I noticed Veet never saluted me back. He told me he was happy just to say good morning.' The NSJB rep told the Gestapo that the management at the factory had been informed of the legal requirement of all workers to greet each other with the Nazi salute. A Gestapo report, dated 22 September 1933, concluded: 'Everyone in the factory hates him [Veet].'

Armed with such a wide array of seemingly convincing evidence of anti-Nazi behaviour, the Gestapo arrested Heinrich Veet and placed him under 'protective custody'. He was sent to a local concentration camp. Veet's brother Andreas appointed a local lawyer to try to get him released. He sent a personal testimonial, too, supporting his brother to the president of police in Duisburg. It mentioned that Heinrich had served his country as a soldier in the 1900 Boxer Rebellion, and the First World War. He'd been awarded the Iron Cross second class, and several other military medals during the course of a distinguished military career. In the 1920s, Heinrich joined the liberal 'German People's Party' (*Deutsche Volkspartei* – DVP). He often praised Kaiser Wilhelm, and would display the colours of the pre-1914 German flag at his home. He was very deeply opposed to socialists and communists, his brother concluded.

The manager of the copper factory sent an equally supportive letter to the Gestapo. It emphasised that Veet had worked for the company since 15 November 1918 and was 'a real German [patriot] who has always done his duty'. He could be a 'bit rough' in the way he dealt with work colleagues at times, but this was just his natural manner. It was not proof that he was fundamentally opposed to Hitler's government.

On 16 October 1933, Wilhelm Wagener, the lawyer acting on behalf of Heinrich Veet, sent a letter to the Gestapo pleading for his release from the concentration camp. 'Veet is an old fashioned conservative', wrote Wagener. 'He is finding it difficult to make the adjustments to the new Nazi regime, but this does not mean he is in any way opposed to the state.' The accusations against him by his colleagues, he added, were all personally motivated. To further aid his case, the owners of the factory agreed to offer Veet an early retirement package if he was released.

The letter from the lawyer clearly made a big impression. The Gestapo decided to release Veet, without charge. He signed the following declaration: 'I promise that in future I will never do anything against the wishes of the state. The police have told me I will be put in prison if I do this again.'[14]

As many denouncers were work colleagues, the case of Heinrich Veet might seem typical. But it was extremely rare for subordinates to denounce superiors. It was usually the other way around. In this case, the denouncer, a committed Nazi, took his allegations to a National Socialist factory organisation, which passed it on to the Gestapo. The denouncer was initially able to persuade the Gestapo to believe his version of events, which was corroborated by several pro-Nazi young workers. The spirited intervention of Veet's brother enabled the original sentence to be overturned. The Gestapo was impressed by the testimonials provided by his brother, his employer and his lawyer. These were all upstanding members of the National Community. Their alternative portrayal of Veet as a patriotic and decent man, nearing retirement, encountering difficulties adjusting to the new demands of the Nazi regime proved compelling.

The Gestapo handled accusations against usually law-abiding citizens like Heinrich Veet with professional diligence and often surprising compassion. Gestapo officers held the view that the majority of German citizens posed no real political threat to the Nazi regime. Reinhard Heydrich often issued orders to Gestapo officers urging 'restraint' when questioning 'ordinary' German citizens.[15] In Gestapo interrogations of German citizens, phrases such as 'the suspect made a good impression' crop up frequently.[16]

It was not even unusual for an ordinary German to protest against high-handed actions by the Gestapo. A typical case began on 20 March 1934 when Karl Vort (born 1904) in Leoben, Austria, reported two Gestapo officers to the police for chasing him down a street in Düsseldorf, after an earlier argument in a restaurant, and assaulting him.[17] The two accused Gestapo officers (Bobel and Dittger) claimed they were carrying out an undercover surveillance operation on the night in question. They had received information that a weekly club night for mandolin players in a local club was being used as a cover to hold illicit anti-Nazi meetings organised by a group of local communists and former members of the SPD. When Bobel and Dittger arrived at the club they discovered it was closed down due to building renovation work. They went for dinner at a local restaurant, called the Trocadero. As they waited for their order to arrive, they overheard a heated argument at a nearby table during which a man made pro-communist statements in the company of a woman and another man. When the group got up to leave at the end of their meal, the two Gestapo officers approached the man who had made the pro-communist comments. They did not explain they were Gestapo officers. A heated row then broke out, which ended with the man, and his two companions, leaving the restaurant. A few moments later, it suddenly occurred to one of the Gestapo officers that the man who had just left the restaurant was a well-known former official of the KPD called Erwin. The Gestapo officers immediately left the restaurant and ran down the street after him, stopped him, and asked to see his identity documents. Karl Vort not only refused to show them his papers, but, according to the report of Bobel and Dittger, started to physically attack them. Blows were exchanged. A shop window was smashed during the fight, and all three sustained injuries. Bobel and Dittger denied being drunk on the night in question, and maintained that their version of events was true. They recommended that Vort should be charged with bodily harm and obstructing the police in the conduct of their duty.

The Gestapo made further enquiries into Karl Vort's background. He was seemingly living out of wedlock with a Miss Bohnstedt (who had been in the restaurant with him). The couple had a young child. A neighbour in their apartment-house told the Gestapo that Vort was 'opposed to National Socialism'.

This could not have been further from the truth. It turned out that Karl was an articulate medical student, an auxiliary policeman, and a committed Nazi who had recently applied for membership of the SA. A musician and a waitress, who witnessed the incident in the restaurant, recalled the heated argument between Karl and the two Gestapo men, but could not confirm whether Vort ever made any communist statements during the time he was in the restaurant. It seems highly unlikely he ever did.

During his interrogation, Karl Vort claimed the two Gestapo officers, who he claimed had been pretty drunk, started a pointless argument with him in the restaurant that evening. They never identified themselves as Gestapo officers. Feeling scared, Karl had left the restaurant with his companions. Bobel and Dittger then chased after him, caught up with him, and brutally attacked him. He had simply defended himself against this unprovoked assault. Because of his injuries, Karl spent ten days in hospital and incurred a large medical bill for his hospital treatment. He demanded compensation of 1,150 Reichsmarks from the Gestapo for his ill-treatment and injuries. A Brigade leader of the SA was brought in to try and conciliate between the two parties. No agreement was ever reached. The case was then passed by the Gestapo office to the public prosecutor. On 9 September 1934, he ruled that no measures should be taken against Bobel and Dittger, and the charges against Karl Vort for obstruction and assaulting police officers should be dropped too.

Vort refused to accept this decision. He began a civil action for damages against the Gestapo. He sent a letter to Rudolf Hess in Berlin complaining about his treatment. On 24 October 1934, the county court of Düsseldorf refused to deal with his civil law suit against the Gestapo officers because it was based on the assumption that they had acted arbitrarily when they stopped him in the street and asked to see his papers. In spite of this rebuff, Vort carried on trying to gain compensation from the Gestapo. He refused to give up. He sent a final letter of complaint to the Gestapo Headquarters in Berlin. On 11 January 1935, the Gestapo office in Berlin sent him a reply. It rejected his claim and emphasised that the version of events offered by the two Gestapo officers was correct.[18]

Complaints from people who claimed that a denouncement had ruined their lives were often sent to the Gestapo too. Karl Feedler (born 1903), in Oberhausen in the Ruhr region, asked the Gestapo to remove a clause in a previous conviction which prevented him from ever joining the German Army.[19] He had been denounced on 9 April 1935 by a customer in a beer hall who heard him say that it was not the communist Marinus van der Lubbe who had set fire to the Reichstag in February 1933, but a group of SS men, who were later killed in the 'Night of the Long Knives' to cover the matter up. For this trivial unguarded drunken comment, Feedler had been sentenced to two years in prison on 8 August 1935. He was not released until 1937.

In a letter to the Gestapo, dated 18 February 1942, Feedler wrote: 'It is a great and inconceivable honour to join the German Army. On account of a dingy affair in a pub, I was reduced to a second-class citizen. Nevertheless, I have always thought and felt like a true German [patriot], and therefore I wish to reclaim the right to join the army.' The Gestapo looked favourably on this request. A letter of support was sent by the Gestapo office to the local military commander, which stated:

For some time he [Feedler] has been a member of Stahlhelm [a nationalist pro-Army organisation] and of several Catholic youth organisations. He was educated as a Catholic. He made a speech in a beer hall in 1935, but was released from prison in 1937. He lives at the home of his parents, is a hard worker in a bakery factory, a member of the German Labour Front (DAF) and joins in annual collections for 'Winter Relief'. The Gestapo supports his claim.[20]

It is not known whether his claim was granted.

Denouncement was most often used for personal reasons. Married and unmarried couples and in-laws feature regularly in Gestapo case files. It was unusual for a husband to denounce his wife, but more common for wives to denounce husbands. It was not always easy for the Gestapo to pinpoint the exact reason why a wife had denounced her partner. A housewife in Mannheim told the Gestapo her husband was making derogatory comments about the Nazi regime. He was taken into 'protective custody' pending further enquiries. It was discovered that the woman had wanted the husband out of the way so she could continue a love affair with a young off-duty soldier in the family home.[21] In another case, two medical doctors were involved. The wife accused her husband of carrying out illegal abortions. This led to his arrest, interrogation, trial and conviction. He was sentenced to eight months in prison. His career was ruined. The allegation was true, but as the investigation unfolded, it became clear the true motive for his denouncement to the Gestapo was revenge. The wife had been infected with a sexually transmitted disease by her husband, who had been carrying on a love affair and refused to end it. After he was released, the man began divorce proceedings on the grounds that his wife had betrayed the vows of trust usually expected of a marriage partner. The judge granted the divorce and found the woman at fault, thus denying her right to maintenance payments.[22]

There was often a familiar narrative arc to Gestapo cases involving a wife denouncing a husband. The wife depicted herself as a loyal member of the National Community, a good mother and a loyal wife, who simply wanted the Gestapo to punish an obvious political dissident. The reality was frequently very different. Most husbands were denounced for underlying moral reasons. They were often carrying on love affairs or were chronic and violent alcoholics, whose marriages were teetering on the verge of divorce.[23]

A typical case began on 10 May 1939 when 'Frau Hof'

denounced her husband in Düsseldorf. She told the Gestapo her husband was 'left orientated. I cannot take it any longer. He always curses the government. He says he can never become a National Socialist. He has a loaded pistol and often threatens to shoot [me].' Her report made other allegations. Her husband had conducted an affair with a local prostitute. He repeatedly shouted verbal abuse at her, drank to excess and was unemployed. She could not have sex with him either, as he was 'sexually diseased'. The Gestapo investigated these various allegations in great depth. Herr Hof was asked to give his version of events. 'I must deny all charges against me,' he told the Gestapo. 'The report of my wife is just an act of revenge [by my wife], who apparently wants to get rid of me. It is not true that I beat up my wife.' The Gestapo report noted: 'From the whole episode it can be concluded that Frau Hof made these statements to get rid of her husband. Herr Hof has been warned. There are no grounds to pursue the matter further. He has been fined ten Reichsmarks for being in possession of an unauthorised weapon.'[24]

Gestapo officers did not generally regard working-class wives such as 'Frau Hof' as reliable witnesses. They felt anti-Nazi statements made within the home by German citizens were not a serious threat to the regime. It was often impossible to establish whether husbands ever made the anti-Nazi statements they were accused of. Similarly, Gestapo officers were often able to turn a blind eye to blood-curdling accounts by wives of the psychological, verbal and physical violence endured in these dysfunctional marriages.

Women often denounced other family members, particularly in-laws. These cases increased during war-time. They usually involved the wives of servicemen having love affairs with foreign workers. As an SD report noted: 'The consequences of adultery by a soldier's wife are seen to be grave. The husbands get disturbed at the [war] front when they are told about the change in the conduct of their wives by the neighbours.'[25] Letters home from German soldiers often express worries about the fidelity of the wives they left behind. They could not live up to the idyllic Nazi propaganda image of the faithful, self-sacrificing wife and mother. The Gestapo felt illicit love affairs carried on by the wives of soldiers fighting in the war undermined morale. In such cases the Gestapo could become a disciplining and moralising agency.[26] Of the 10,000 German women sent to concentration camps during the war, a substantial proportion were married women convicted of engaging in 'forbidden contact' with a 'non-Aryan', usually a foreign worker or a soldier.

One case began when a woman found a cache of letters in her brother's house strongly indicating that her sister-in-law was involved in a sexual love affair with a French worker called Michel Girault. She reported the matter simultaneously to her brother Erich and the Gestapo. Her sister-in-law Rosa Deeser (born 1916) was living in Duisburg when she was arrested by the Gestapo on 2 February 1943.[27] Rosa gave the Gestapo her own version of events. She worked as a shop assistant, and had been married since the age of eighteen to Erich, who was fighting with the *Wehrmacht* on the Eastern Front. She met Girault, in February 1942, in Detmold, at the home of a family friend she was staying with, while her husband was garrisoned in the city. She only spoke very briefly with him during her stay. In September 1943, she stayed with the same family again, this time for eight days, along with her children. One evening she went for a drink with Girault, and later that night the couple had sex together. In the following months she returned frequently to meet with Girault in Detmold. She was besotted with her French lover. 'I'd fallen in love with him,' she freely admitted. During a further visit, she told Girault she was pregnant, but this was a lie. She wanted him to give her some money to buy a dress, and thought this lie might induce him to do it. Rosa said the reason she embarked on the affair with Girault in the first place was because her husband had been violent towards her before he joined the army. She admitted telling Girault that RAF air raids were affecting the morale of the people of Duisburg, but she regretted saying this, and begged for mercy. Her house was searched extensively. She was physically examined by a doctor. No evidence of an abortion was detected. The Gestapo found no proof she might be passing on detailed information about the bombing raids, other than to her French lover. The Gestapo decided to let the family deal with the fallout from this affair. The case was dropped. As illegal sexual relationships between an 'Aryan' woman and a foreign worker often resulted in extremely harsh punishments, including execution, Rosa and Girault got off very lightly. There is no evidence Girault was ever questioned by the Gestapo about this love affair. What happened subsequently in Rosa's relationship with her husband, her sister-in-law or Girault is not known.[28]

Women often denounced boyfriends to the Gestapo too. This happened to Walter Remmer (born 1913) in Essen.[29] He was travelling on a train from Munich when he struck up a conversation with a woman from Offenbach. She was immediately smitten with him, and invited him back to her home. They began a sexual relationship that same evening. He then took up residence in her home. As Walter began to tell her more about his past, the woman became very suspicious about him. She denounced him to the Gestapo, believing he was most probably involved in opposition activity.

It soon emerged that Walter was an escaped prisoner on the run. On 18 June 1944, he underwent a detailed interrogation. He had been a soldier in the *Wehrmacht* and had been sentenced by court martial in Rome to a two-year prison sentence for stealing a pair of boots and a pair of gloves from an army service store and selling them. He served his sentence for these offences in an army prison camp in Hohenbrunn, in the district of Munich. On 1 December 1943, he escaped from the camp, wearing an SS uniform he'd stolen from the camp storeroom. He then went on the run using the alias 'Johann Weber'. He sent a letter to his sister telling her he had been discharged from the army. She sent him 400 Reichsmarks. With this, he bought civilian clothes and a train ticket from Munich to Offenbach, during which journey he met the woman stranger on the train.

While living with her, he became involved in an underground resistance group that distributed leaflets containing anti-Nazi slogans such as: 'Rise up people. Your Führer lies. Break the cross of the murdering.' Copies of these leaflets were discovered by the Gestapo in Frankfurt am Main and Kassel. Walter denied having any links to other opposition groups. He bravely refused to give the names of any of the people who had supported him. He was neither a Marxist nor a communist, and described himself to the Gestapo as a 'liberal nationalist'. He favoured a democratic government, did not want to overthrow the National Socialist government, and called Hitler, 'One of the greatest politicians of all time.' He admitted that he wanted Germany to end the war as he believed it was now certain to lose. The Gestapo looked further into his background, but failed to discover any links to other clandestine resistance groups. He was held in 'protective custody'. There is no hint in his file about his ultimate fate.[30]

The outbreak of the Second World War led to a heightened intolerance of any politically critical statements. A raft of new laws were introduced to deal with anyone who might try to 'stab the fighting front in the back'. This was something the Nazis repeatedly claimed had led to the German defeat in the First World War. Judges were advised to view themselves as 'soldiers on the home front' and to impose much harsher sentences.[31] All dissent was to be treated with zero tolerance. The number of 'Special Courts' increased from twenty-seven in 1938 to seventy-four by the end of 1942. Death sentences imposed within the existing judicial system rose sharply from 139 in 1939 to a peak of 5,336 in 1943.[32] Under a decree of 17 October 1939, concentration camps were removed from the scrutiny and jurisdiction of the civil courts. The practice of reporting 'unnatural deaths' in concentration camps to the Ministry of the Interior was no longer required.

The 'Decree on the Special Wartime Penal Code' came into force on 26 August 1939. It contained a new offence of 'Undermining the war effort' which carried a death penalty. On 7 September 1939 another law was brought in to stop Germans listening to foreign radio broadcasts. It contained the following provisions:

1. It is forbidden to listen to foreign radio broadcasts with intent. Contraventions will be punished by penal servitude. A prison sentence may be substituted in less serious cases. The equipment [the radio] will be confiscated.
2. Anyone who intentionally disseminates information gleaned from foreign radio stations which is liable to threaten the defensive capabilities of the German nation will be punished with penal servitude, in particularly serious cases with death.
3. The regulations of this decree do not apply to actions which are carried out in the performance of a duty.
4. The Special Courts are responsible for dealing with and passing judgments upon contravention of this decree.
5. Prosecutions under (1) and (2) are only to be initiated by the agencies of the State Police [Gestapo].
6. The Reich Minister for Popular Enlightenment and Propaganda [Dr Joseph Goebbels] will issue the requisite legal and administrative regulations for the implementation of this decree and, insofar as penal regulations are concerned, will do so in consultation with the Reich Minister of Justice.[33]

Most Germans were able to receive the German-language broadcasts of the BBC, and similar services from Russia, Switzerland, France and Luxembourg. As the post-war German leader Konrad Adenauer later recalled: 'It may seem surprising that I was so well informed about the course of the fighting.

The reason was that, apart from the time I spent in concentration camp or prison, I did not let a day pass without listening to several foreign broadcasts.'[34] The Justice Minister Franz Gürtner opposed the law. 'I fear', he wrote to Joseph Goebbels on 1 September 1939, 'that the decree of such an ordinance would open the floodgates of denunciations and all national comrades would stand more or less helpless *vis-à-vis* such denunciations'.[35] This was a genuine concern of the Gestapo too. German-language broadcasts of the BBC were able to reach the entire German population. In the period from 1 January to 30 June 1940, for instance, 2,197 people were arrested for listening to foreign radio broadcasts. A total of 708 of these cases ended up with a prison sentence of up to two years.[36] Only eleven people were given a death sentence for listening to foreign radio broadcasts.[37]

To induce fear, newspapers named and shamed those who were convicted. A typical report appeared in the Nazi Party newspaper the *Völkischer Beobachter* (People's Observer):

Johann D from Leverkusen-Rheindorf was sentenced to one year's penal servitude under the ban on listening to foreign broadcasts because he repeatedly listened to foreign radio stations. Also the Hanseatic Special Court in Bremen dealt with an accused person who listened to the Strasburg radio station on 7 September [1939] which was broadcasting the lie that the West Wall had been breached and that French troops were already at the Rhine and at the Moselle. The accused repeated these fairy tales the following day in his [factory] plant . . . Thus he was not sentenced for listening in but for spreading dangerous lies and he was given a term of penal servitude [hard labour] of one year and six months.[38]

People from all classes of German society were charged with listening to foreign radio broadcasts. It was an offence that relied heavily on public denunciations. Very few cases came from the spy network of the Gestapo. It became a question of whose version of events proved the most convincing. It was most commonly close relatives, neighbours, domestic servants and work colleagues who were the chief denouncers for this offence. On 17 November 1939 a house painter called Gregor, who lived in the town of Burgbrohl, in the Rhine Valley, denounced his brother-in-law Arnulf for listening to foreign radio broadcasts and making derogatory comments about Hitler. Under questioning, Arnulf admitted he had been listening to the broadcasts, but in mitigation he mentioned he was a veteran of the First World War and a loyal 'national comrade'. As the Gestapo dug deeper into the case, it soon became clear that the key motive for Gregor's denouncement was personal revenge. Only hours before he reported his brother-in-law to the Gestapo, a blazing row had occurred in the family home, during which Gregor, his wife and daughter were evicted from Arnulf's house. Arnulf spent three weeks in prison before he was released. Nevertheless, in February 1940, the Gestapo recommended to the state prosecutor that Arnulf be put on trial for listening to foreign radio broadcasts. On 27 September 1940, presiding judges decided to acquit him.[39]

In other cases, the Gestapo intervened when such leniency was offered by judges. One such case concerned a man who was denounced by a neighbour for listening to the broadcasts of Radio Moscow on 3 November 1939. Two months later, when the case was heard in a Special Court, the judge dismissed the charge due to lack of evidence. The Gestapo was unhappy with this outcome. The man was placed in 'protective custody' and then sent to Sachsenhausen concentration camp. He died there on 6 November 1940.[40]

Peter Holdenberg (born 1877) in Vluyn, a town in the Rhineland area, was accused of listening to foreign radio broadcasts by his neighbour. He was a Protestant, disabled and lived alone in a third-floor apartment in Essen at the time of his arrest by the Gestapo.[41] On 12 November 1941, Helen Stuffel, his next-door neighbour, and a tailor by profession, told her local Nazi Party branch that Peter was a regular listener to foreign radio broadcasts. The local Nazi Party branch passed on this information to the Nazi Party district office and they alerted the Gestapo.

Helen Stuffel gave a detailed statement to the Gestapo. She said that one of her neighbours, Irmgard Pierce, had told her that Peter was listening to foreign radio broadcasts. She boasted to the Gestapo that she listened through the adjoining wall of her flat for a fortnight to verify this claim. She heard him listening to programmes on the BBC and Radio Moscow every night from about 9.45 p.m. to 12 midnight. She'd then asked two of her neighbours to come to her flat to confirm her suspicions. All the women listened at the wall. The consensus was that Peter was definitely listening to foreign radio programmes. 'Holdenberg is a scaremonger,' she added. Another time Peter had supposedly told her: 'We [Germany] won't win the war and we should not win this war.' Digging the knife in deeper, Stuffel attempted to depict Peter as pro-Jewish too. He once allegedly told her that since Jewish shops closed down he could no longer pay for goods through instalment plans, which he always liked to do. She also heard him speak favourably about the Soviet Union. Finally, she speculated that as Peter was a book dealer and travelled around the country in the course of his business he was probably spreading all the false rumours he was hearing each night on the radio. 'He is very dangerous for the government,' she concluded.

The Gestapo brought in a range of other neighbours for questioning. These witnesses gave widely differing accounts. Irmgard Pierce said Stuffel's story was true. She called Peter a 'rabble-rouser and scaremonger'. When she once complained to him about having to go to the air-raid shelter every night, he answered: 'But if we are winning the war, then why do we need air shelters?' Another neighbour, Elisabeth Beck, corroborated all the accusations made by Stuffel and Pierce. The odds seemed stacked against Peter being treated leniently. Then three witnesses came forward to give evidence in his defence. The first was Katharina Hein, another resident of the apartment-house. All the allegations against Holdenberg were untrue, she said. She often had drinks with Peter and played board games with him on many evenings in his apartment. She never heard him listening to foreign radio broadcasts. The Gestapo felt Katharina's story was concocted to help Peter, and should be treated with caution. Klara Vogts, Peter's housemaid, denied he was anti-Nazi. She never heard him listening to foreign radio broadcasts while she was cleaning in the apartment. A third witness, Anton Ronnig, a bandmaster, said he was present when Peter talked about the war in front of Stuffel, but she had totally misrepresented that conversation. What Peter really said was not that he wanted Germany to lose the war, but that the forces of international capitalism did. He also pointed out that Stuffel herself had previously been very friendly with Jews, as many of them had been her clients in her role as a tailor.

Peter was arrested on 10 December 1941 and interrogated by the Gestapo. 'This is all a conspiracy,' he complained. 'I've had trouble with Stuffel in the past and Pierce always sides with her.' He denied all the accusations. They were merely the 'foolish gossip' of interfering busybodies, with an axe to grind. He had previously taken another neighbour to task for spreading a false rumour that he was listening to foreign radio broadcasts. He claimed that before 1933 he had not been a member of any political party, and he was most definitely not an opponent of the Nazi regime. He had been disabled since 1935, and since his divorce had lived quietly on his own.

On the following day, Peter attempted to commit suicide by hanging himself in his cell. He was found alive, rushed to a local hospital, but he died there on the following day.[42]

Countess Maria von Lingen, who lived in a castle near the south German town of Überlingen, was also denounced to the Gestapo for listening to BBC foreign radio broadcasts by three of her domestic staff: her housekeeper, nanny, and a kitchen maid. Her domestic staff switched on the radio one morning, while she was on holiday, and found it was tuned to the BBC foreign language service. Maria was brought in for questioning. 'I want to tell you something,' she told the Gestapo officer. 'I was not here. I was in Italy. Here's my [travel] pass, here's my travel permit and my re-entry permit . . . I can tell you I know nothing.' The Gestapo officer replied: 'You're responsible for what happens in your house.' The Gestapo decided to drop the case, because Maria's husband was killed in battle during the period of the investigation. Maria von Lingen later recalled what really happened: 'When the war broke, it was a prison offence to listen to foreign broadcasts. Of course one did it secretly. I always listened to the BBC, which one could receive very well.' Maria had an English friend and she was staying in the ancestral home during the time she was on holiday. It was her friend who listened to the BBC and forgot to turn the radio tuning dial back to a German station before she went to bed.

The Gestapo decided to investigate her 'English friend' more extensively. A Gestapo officer arrived at Maria's home a few weeks after the first interrogation. "He [the Gestapo officer] said: "You have a friend who is an English woman?" I said, "She's not English. She is, but she's also German. She married a German." The Gestapo officer told her that her friend had been accused of spying, and was being interrogated in Munich. "I have no idea what you're speaking about," Maria replied. "She never said anything to me [about spying]." Maria was questioned for ninety minutes before the Gestapo officer told her politely: "I must tell you that your testimony is in accord with what our colleagues in Munich have got, and the matter is closed."[43]

Another case concerning foreign radio broadcasts began on 10 November 1941 when Karl Kesler (born 1904) in Wuppertal was reported by the security guard of the metal factory in Düsseldorf where he worked as an accounts clerk for listening to BBC German-language broadcasts.[44] The accusation was the result of an everyday workplace conversation in which Robert Blingen, one of Kesler's office colleagues, told him that he suspected Karl was listening to enemy radio broadcasts, and was also forging factory luncheon vouchers. On 30 October 1941, when staff in the office were discussing new government measures to save iron for the armaments industry over lunch, Kesler suddenly commented: 'It's all fake [propaganda].' Blingen felt Kesler could only have gained this information by listening to foreign radio broadcasts. All the office staff complained to the management about this incident. They refused to work with such an 'unpatriotic colleague' any more. Kesler was sacked from his job on 1 November 1941.

In spite of this, the security guard still reported to the Gestapo that he suspected Kesler was listening to foreign radio broadcasts. He was arrested on 10 November 1941. He denied the allegations and felt he had been unfairly sacked. He claimed, in mitigation, that he was currently suffering from a severe mental illness. An innkeeper, also brought in for questioning, told the Gestapo that when Kesler had stayed there on a four-day vacation he never listened to foreign radio broadcasts or made any subversive comments. The case was passed on to the senior prosecutor in Düsseldorf for a final decision. He dropped the case, but ordered that Kesler be detained in a mental asylum. The director of the asylum sent a letter to the Gestapo on 5 January 1942 stating that Kesler's mental state had now greatly improved and he recommended his release, provided the Gestapo had no objections. The Gestapo approved his release, provided the doctors felt public safety was 'not endangered'. Kesler was released from the mental hospital. A month later, the Gestapo noted that he had begun a case for unfair dismissal against his former employer.[45]

It seems the denunciation of Kesler was motivated by a group of work colleagues who simply disliked him and wanted rid of him. The so-called allegations against him were extremely flimsy.

The offhand comment that Nazi propaganda might be telling lies about the need to hoard iron was hardly a major expression of anti-regime discontent. There was no convincing evidence produced that he ever listened to foreign radio broadcasts. Unusually, the Gestapo did not examine the circumstances of the alleged offence or the possible underlying motives of the denouncers. The decision as to why the public prosecutor sent him to a mental asylum is not fully explained either. It was most probably due to a previous medical history of severe mental illness, which might help to explain why he had trouble fitting in with his work colleagues.

It was in public places such as coffee houses, beer halls, hotels and restaurants that unguarded anti-regime or defeatist comments most frequently led to Gestapo denunciations. In the spring of 1938, an actor went for a meal in a restaurant near to Munich's central railway station. He struck up a seemingly friendly conversation with a married couple sitting at an adjoining table. He then made some comments that were highly critical of Hitler's foreign policy. The reaction of the couple suggested they disapproved of his unwelcome outburst. The actor hurriedly left the restaurant. The couple reported the incident to the Gestapo, and the actor was arrested two days later.[46] A similar case was reported by an SD contact man in Rhineland-Westphalia in July 1938. In a café a 64-year-old woman remarked to her companion at the table: 'Mussolini has more political sense in one of his boots than Hitler has in his brain.' The remark was overheard by other patrons and five minutes later the woman was arrested by the Gestapo who had been alerted by telephone.[47]

Rudolf Henning (born 1909) in Duisburg, a former member of the SS and a reserve policeman, was denounced by Marianne Kroll, a sales clerk, and Helmut Quest, a locksmith, for making 'defeatist comments' during a lengthy summer evening drinking session on 25 July 1944 in Remscheid in the Ruhr.[48] Helmut Quest told the Gestapo that on 8 August 1944 he'd unexpectedly bumped into unmarried Marianne Kroll, a former woman friend, in a beer hall called the 'Scenic Look Out'. He claimed she had a 'dingy [sexual] reputation'. Marianne told him she wanted him to meet a 'fabulous guy' she knew.

The following evening Marianne, accompanied by Rudolf Henning and a twenty-two-year-old female friend, went for a few drinks in Quest's apartment. Rudolf began making deeply critical remarks about Hitler and the Nazi regime as the alcohol loosened his tongue. The others warned him not to talk in such a critical manner about the Nazi regime in front of them. In spite of this awkward incident, all four of them left Quest's apartment and resumed their drinking session in a local beer hall. Rudolf continued making drunken anti-Nazi comments. At one point he said: 'Hitler is a brown head. The enemy is only seven kilometres away from the Austrian border. It's a pity that Adolf Hitler survived the attempted murder [of 20 July 1944] because otherwise the war would be over by now.' He then saluted another customer who walked by his table with a 'Heil Moscow' salute, and told his drinking companions: 'Some Gestapo men don't dare salute "Heil Hitler" any longer, because they know the war is lost.'

All these comments were reported to the Gestapo. Even though Rudolf was a former SS man and a reserve policeman, he was charged with 'high treason and the undermining of military strength' and placed under 'protective custody'.[49] This unusually harsh treatment against a German citizen was most probably due to the timing of the incident. It occurred just five days after Adolf Hitler had survived the famous 'Valkyrie' bomb plot led by Colonel Claus von Stauffenberg on 20 July 1944. Rudolf's ultimate fate is not known.

Speaking critically about Hitler's regime always risked the possibility of denunciation. Locksmith Johann Konte (born 1893) in Essen was denounced by Wilhelm Brunck, an off-duty SA man, on 2 November 1941 for making 'defeatist' comments during an argument in the street.[50] Brunck, along with a fellow

SA man, had been drinking in a beer hall for most of the day in question. At midnight, the two headed to another bar. As they walked along the street, they came across Johann, who they both knew. They asked him if he fancied joining them for a nightcap. Konte, clearly heavily under the influence of alcohol, snapped back at Brunck: 'You snotty-nosed brat. I ought to give you a bloody nose. How dare you speak to me? Two of my sons are at the [Eastern] front [in the war].' The two SA men ignored this. This only made Konte become more aggressive. He threatened to hit both of them and shouted: 'The SA consists of cowards and shirkers.'

This incident was reported to the Gestapo. Johann Konte was brought in for interrogation. He said he'd been on a pub crawl that day, and had consumed many glasses of beer. He couldn't even remember encountering the two SA men at all. He found it equally difficult to imagine he would ever have said such nasty things to them. The Gestapo officer noted in his report: 'Konte is a [German] nationalist, a funny guy, he's alright, but he was drunk that evening.' He suggested Brunck should be advised to drop his charge. He did. Here is yet another example of a Gestapo officer acting with understanding and compassion when dealing with a denunciation against a German citizen who was obviously loyal to the Nazi regime.[51]

Another key source of denunciations for the Gestapo came from local 'Block Leaders' (*Blockleiter*). These were assigned the task of keeping tabs on a block of homes, usually covering between forty and sixty residences. The essential requirement to become a 'Block Leader' was unswerving loyalty to the Nazi Party. They kept card indexes of every person living in the local neighbourhood, which included details of party membership, family status and occupational details.[52] They noted which families did or did not display Nazi flags, and whether or not they attended Nazi parades and rallies. They were also responsible for conveying party policy to the population, collected party membership subscriptions, organised funding drives and issued ration cards.[53] Most were of middle- or lower-middle-class origin. They could even recommend to local welfare authorities to withdraw state benefits from local 'work-shy' individuals. In working-class areas they were feared and hated. The Block Leader was often an important source of denunciations to the Gestapo. 'We never knew when our Block Leader would come nosing around,' recalls Ingeborg Tismer. 'We only knew that sooner or later he would.'[54]

Max Reich, aged thirty-seven, acted as a Block Leader in Berlin. During the summer of 1942, he noticed graffiti in a public toilet, which read: 'Hitler [the] mass murderer has to be murdered to end the war.' When visiting the same toilet on 28 October, he caught a seventy-three-year-old pensioner called Wilhelm Lehm chalking anti-Nazi graffiti in a toilet cubicle. He reported him to the Gestapo. On 8 March 1943, Lehm was sentenced to death by the 'People's Court', and executed on 10 May the same year.[55]

An underground SPD agent in Berlin offered the following assessment of the effectiveness of the supervision of Block Leaders:

The supervision is now so well organised that members of the illegal [resistance] movement can hardly meet in people's flats anymore. Every staircase now has an informer. This 'staircase ruler', as one might call him, collects Winter Relief contributions, runs around with all sorts of forms, inquiries about family matters, and tries to find out about everything under the sun. He is supposed to talk to housewives about prices and food shortages, he pushes into people's homes, he is supposed to find out about what newspapers people read, what their lifestyle is like . . . Effectively, every tenant is visited at least once a week by one of these block leaders and is pumped by him.[56]

Wilhelm Weffer, an industrial fitter, was Block Leader for a neighbourhood in the small Rhineland town of Tönisvorst.[57]

On 15 June 1942, he sent a letter to the local Nazi Party which claimed Johann Hack (born 1888) had insulted Hitler and was making defeatist comments. Johann was a married disabled railway worker, who lived with his wife Anna.[58] In his letter to the local Nazi Party, Weffer described Johann as a 'Marxist' and a 'big drunkard'. After a day of heavy drinking in a local beer hall Johann had reportedly made a number of anti-Nazi statements in front of four witnesses, including a member of the Hitler Youth. He said the army would fight the SS; Nazi Party leaders were all corrupt; the war against the Soviet Union was lost; and Hitler was an artist, not a brilliant military leader like Napoleon.

These allegations were eventually passed to the Gestapo. Hack was arrested on 24 August 1942. During his interrogation, he claimed that he was a patriotic German who had been awarded medals in the 'Great War'. He denied ever being a Marxist, but admitted to being a member of the socialist SPD between 1920 and 1921. He said he had insulted Hitler in the beer hall, but his words were uttered while he was drunk and should not be taken seriously.

The Gestapo office report from Krefeld, dated 25 August 1942, noted that the evidence of the Block Leader had shown Hack was guilty, and recommended a harsh sentence to act as an example to others of the consequences of agitating in public places against the Nazi government. The case was passed on to the public prosecutor. He recommended Hack be sent for trial. On 15 December 1942, the chief judge of the 'Special Court' in Krefeld concluded that Johann Hack, who had previously spent a month in prison in 1934 for anti-Nazi 'political stirring', and who was still 'backbiting and insulting Hitler and members of his government', should serve seven months in prison.[59]

One of the most bizarre denunciations the Gestapo ever dealt with came from an unskilled working-class labourer who denounced himself. His name was Adam Lipper (born 1892) in Völklingen, in the Saarland region. Between 1919 and 1935 the city was under French rule, due to the terms of the Versailles Treaty. After a referendum in 1935 it returned to German jurisdiction.[60] During the First World War, Adam served in the German Army, but was captured by the French Army. He was a POW from October 1916 until the end of the war. In 1924, Adam joined the French Foreign Legion and remained a member until 1935. During his time as a French legionnaire Adam became an alcoholic. He found the readjustment to civilian life very difficult. He worked in a coal mine, but left his job in 1938, giving no reason. He was now unemployed, in receipt of state benefits. He turned down several job offers brokered by his local employment office, and was drinking heavily.

On 1 March 1940, Adam Lipper walked into his local Gestapo office and asked to be placed in a concentration camp for six months to cure his chronic alcoholism. He claimed a spell in a concentration camp would cure him, and help him to become a loyal and hard-working member of the National Community. The Gestapo treated this bizarre request with suspicion. His background was examined in detail. His time as a soldier in the French Foreign Legion quickly came to light. He underwent a lengthy interrogation during which he promised to 'get up to something' if he was not placed in a concentration camp, though he never said what that 'something' was. When he continually stonewalled questions about what he had been doing in the Foreign Legion, the Gestapo decided to place him in prison, pending further enquiries. Those who had previously served in the French Foreign Legion were often viewed as potential spies. This possibility was soon ruled out. Adam seemed to have great difficulty even getting up in the morning. His alcoholism was common knowledge in the local community.

On 18 April 1940, after seven weeks of self-induced 'therapy' in a prison cell, without alcohol, Adam Lipper declared himself 'cured' and asked to be freed. The Gestapo sanctioned his release. His subsequent fate is not known.[61]

The defeat at Stalingrad in February 1943 led to a sharp deterioration of German public morale. Germans started telling jokes to each other that were increasingly critical of the regime, most notably, 'What's the difference between the sun and Hitler? The sun rises in the East, but Hitler goes down in the East.' On 8 July 1943 an SD report noted:

> The telling of vulgar jokes detrimental to the state, even about the Führer himself, has increased considerably since Stalingrad. In conversations in cafés, factories and other meeting places people tell each other the latest political jokes and in many cases make no distinction between those with a harmless content and those which are clearly in opposition to the state. Even people who hardly know each other exchange jokes. They clearly assume that any joke can now be told without fear of a sharp rebuff, let alone of being reported to the police [Gestapo].[62]

In reality, the consequences for those denounced for uttering anti-Nazi comments in the latter stages of the war were often fatal. A seventy-three-year-old retired army major was denounced in September 1944 by his son-in-law, who was a soldier on leave. He claimed his father-in-law was not only listening to foreign radio, but was also making frequent 'defeatist' remarks. The former major was arrested, tried and sent to prison. He died there on 11 March 1945.[63] Germans who tried to profit from the impact of Allied bombing raids were treated with equal harshness. Paula, a young woman from Cologne, with no criminal record, was reported to the Gestapo by a local neighbour after being seen leaving a bombed-out house carrying three tins of coffee, some old curtains and a dress. She was arrested by the Gestapo, interrogated and then publicly hanged.[64] Hugo Bauer denounced his landlord on 20 May 1943 for listening to foreign radio broadcasts, which he claimed he'd heard while passing the door of his apartment. The Gestapo felt the allegations were personally motivated, declared Bauer a 'parasite on the body politic' and sent him to Sachsenhausen concentration camp.[65]

The Nazi authorities became increasingly concerned about whether the public could cope with the psychological impact of Allied bombing. A secret SD report on civilian morale, in May 1944, noted: 'Many national comrades . . . have had the wail of the air-raid sirens, the rumble of the engines of attacking aircraft, the shooting of the flak and the explosions of the bombs continually in their ears and with the best will in the world can no longer free themselves from [negative] impressions.'[66]

It was after an RAF bombing raid on Essen on 1 May 1943 that firefighter Hans Elsäss informed the Gestapo that a local businessman had been shouting out anti-Nazi comments in the street in a crazed manner. The fireman was driving through the bombed streets of Essen at 7.15 a.m. when he heard a man repeatedly shouting 'Long live Moscow' out of his bedroom window at passers-by. This man was Walter Needen (born 1903). He was married and owned a prosperous local factory.[67]

Walter was brought in for questioning on 27 May 1943. He told the Gestapo that he had always been an opponent of communism, and a Nazi Party member since 1 May 1937. He was declared fit for military service in July 1940, but exempted because he was needed to run his factory on the home front. Walter said the reason he was so angry that night was because his factory and his house were both damaged during an Allied bombing raid. This prompted him to drink heavily throughout the night. In the morning, he opened his bedroom window, saw some young men on motorbikes, and shouted at them: 'Here we are in a Soviet paradise. Long Live Moscow!' He was so drunk he could not fully remember what he was doing or saying. His wife confirmed that he was extremely drunk at the time of the incident. Walter's explanation seemed credible. The Gestapo released him without charge.[68]

If the success of a police force is measured by the number of cases that end in a court conviction then the Gestapo can be classed as deeply inefficient in the way it dealt with cases of denouncement. A study of a sample of denouncement cases in the Würzburg area revealed that only 20 per cent of such cases ever went to court and 75 per cent of those failed to end up in a conviction.[69] Gestapo brutality is almost entirely absent in cases of denouncement involving 'ordinary' Germans, which reinforces the idea that while the Nazi terror system showed a brutal face towards a clearly defined set of opponents, it displayed a more professional and humane face to ordinary German citizens. By constantly acting as a seemingly 'honest broker' in matters of harmless gossip between members of the 'National Community' the Gestapo became an organisation that the law-abiding public felt it could trust.

The cases of denouncement examined here support the view that the Gestapo was predominantly a reactive organisation that relied heavily on public co-operation. The surprising leniency displayed in most of these cases was due to the fact that the accused were 'ordinary' German citizens and were not classed as a danger to the Nazi regime. The motives of denouncers in cases involving ordinary German citizens are not easy to categorise. Most were trying to display loyalty to the system, but others were attempting to use the Gestapo to settle personal scores.[70] Few of the allegations, though often mean-spirited, were rarely without any foundation. The outcomes for those accused varied widely for identical offences. The Gestapo often spent a great deal of time exhaustively examining what turned out to be very trivial matters. In many of the most blatant expressions of public dissent, heavy drinking plays a central role. The public progressively realised that uttering such comments in beer halls was dangerous. A study of denunciations in court files from the Bavarian city of Augsburg shows that 75 per cent of cases began with a denouncement in a beer hall in 1933, but by 1939 this had fallen to 10 per cent.[71]

During the final stages of the war, Nazi judicial authorities came to recognise that false denunciations were wasting a great deal of the time of the Gestapo. As a letter of 1 August 1943 from the Ministry of Justice in Berlin put it: 'The denouncer is – according to an old saying – the biggest scoundrel in the whole country. That is true in the first instance of those who, in spite of knowing better, falsely report a fellow citizen to the authorities in order to cause him some unpleasantness.'[72]

Chapter 6

The Racial War against the 'Social Outsiders'

The destruction of political and religious opposition had been the central objective of the Gestapo in the early years of Hitler's rule. From the mid-1930s onwards the Nazi regime began to use pseudo-eugenic terms to describe its more broadly defined 'racial enemies'. A racial hierarchy was established ranging from the 'most valuable' to the 'least valuable' members of the National Community. The work of the Gestapo now became more of a co-operative enterprise involving the criminal police (Kripo) and a wide range of welfare and health officials who were all determined to deal with a broadly defined group called 'Social Outsiders'.

In 1937, Reinhard Heydrich defined the role of the Gestapo and Kripo in overtly racial terms:

> The overall responsibility of the Security Police [SIPO] is to safeguard the German *Volk* as a total being, its life force and institutions from any kind of destruction or disintegration. Defensively it must repel the attacks of all forces that could in any way weaken or destroy the health of the life force . . . Offensively it must investigate and thus combat in an anticipatory manner everything oppositional so that this opposition cannot even develop into something destructive and disintegrative.[1]

Those classed as outside the idealised racially pure National Community (*Volksgemeinschaft*) would now be ruthlessly targeted. Those broadly defined as 'asocials' included: habitual criminals, homosexuals, sex offenders, prostitutes, the long-term unemployed, alcoholics, beggars, prostitutes, juvenile delinquents, street

Rudolph Diels, the first head
of the Gestapo.

The courageous Protestant Pastor
Paul Schneider, pictured as a
student in 1921.

The Gestapo Headquarters at 8 Prinz-Albrecht-Strasse, Berlin.
The building was destroyed by Allied bombing in 1945.

Two policemen survey the fire damage following the Reichstag Fire in February 1933.

Heinrich Himmler, leader of the S.S. (left), shakes hands with the creator of the Gestapo, Hermann Göring.

Ernst Thälmann, leader of the German Communist Party (K.P.D.). He was killed on Hitler's order in 1944.

Heinrich Himmler (left) with Ernst Röhm, the leader of the Storm Troopers, S.A.

Former German Chancellor Franz von Papen giving a speech in Austria.

Political prisoners undergoing forced labour at Dachau Concentration Camp, 1933.

Reinhard Heydrich, leading figure in the leadership of the Gestapo, the S.S., and the S.D.

The leader of the 'Confessing Church'
Pastor Martin Niemöller.

Wilhelm Frick, The Nazi Minister
of the Interior from 1933 to 1943.
He was executed in 1946.

Dr. Werner Best, leading figure in the administration of the Gestapo.

Dr. Robert Ritter, assisted by Eva Justin, takes a blood sample from a Gypsy.

Buchenwald Concentration Camp.

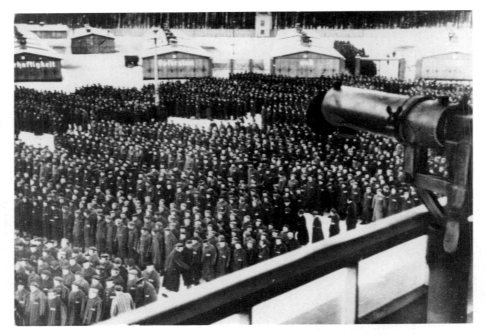

Morning roll call for inmates at Sachsenhausen Concentration Camp, 1936.

Clemens Graf von Galen, Bishop of Münster. He led the Catholic protests against Nazi euthanasia.

Otto Ohlendorf, head of the inland S.D. and commander of Einsatzgruppen D, the mass killing squad that committed mass murder in the Soviet Union. He was executed in 1951.

Local Germans walk past a smashed Jewish shop in Magdeburg,
the morning after Kristallnacht in November 1938.

A meeting of leading figures in the Reich Security Main Office R.S.H.A. in Berlin in
1939 (Left to right, Franz Huber, leader of Gestapo in Vienna, Arthur Nebe, head of
Kripo, Himmler, Heydrich and Heinrich Müller, head of the Gestapo.)

Gestapo mug shot of Peter Penk, accused of being a communist sympathiser.

Gestapo mug shot of Luise Vögler, denounced for her alleged Pro-Soviet sympathies.

Gestapo mug shot of Helmut Hesse, a brave Protestant religious dissident.

gangs and Gypsies. A 1944 draft law for the 'Treatment of Community Aliens' defined 'asocial outsiders' as individuals who:

1. Show themselves in their personality or in the conduct of their life, and especially in the light of any unusual deficiency of mind or character, unable to comply by their own efforts with the minimum requirements of the national community;
2. (a) owing to work shyness or slovenliness, lead a worthless, unthrifty or disorderly life and are thereby a burden or danger to the community;
   Or
   display a habit of, or inclination towards beggary or vagrancy, idling at work, larceny, swindling or other less serious offence, or engage in excessive drunkenness, or for any such reasons are in breach of the obligation to support themselves;
   Or
   (b) through persistent ill-temper or quarrelsomeness disturb the peace of the community;
3. show themselves, in their personality or in the conduct of their life, mentally disposed towards the commission of serious offences.[2]

For decades before the Nazis came to power, the pseudo-scientific discipline of eugenics claimed that only selective breeding could reduce the number of criminal and anti-social individuals in society. The term 'eugenics' was first coined by the British scientist Francis Galton. The phrase 'racial hygiene' was first used in a book by the German doctor Alfred Ploetz in 1895, which argued the case for the superiority of the German 'Aryan' race. Eugenic ideas were popular in a variety of other countries. Many biological scientists concluded that human differences were hereditary and unalterable. The implication was that the human race could only be improved by better breeding, as happened with racehorses and elite breeds of dogs. The science of eugenics became not only popular, but respectable, viewed as modern and grounded in science. In Britain, a Eugenics Society was established in 1902. In 1909, University College, London appointed a Professor in Eugenics. Sterilisation laws were introduced in Switzerland (1928), Denmark (1929) and Norway (1934). Sweden retained sterilisation laws until 1975. The most wide-ranging programme of sterilisation occurred in the USA, where no less than thirty-nine American states, beginning with Indiana in 1899, sterilised the mentally and physically handicapped. The number of people sterilised in the USA between 1907 and 1932 has been estimated at 12,145.[3] Social policies designed to improve the 'racial stock' were accepted in many other countries such as China, Brazil and India.[4]

In 1920 two German doctors – Karl Binding and Alfred Hoche – published a book called *Permission for the Destruction of Life Unworthy to be Lived*. It identified a number of individuals of 'no social or economic use', most notably, 'incurable idiots' and the mentally handicapped. The authors also suggested the terminally ill should be given the right to an assisted suicide. Leading Nazis supported these ideas with vigour and wanted to push them further if they gained power. They became passionate followers of the theories of the eugenic scientists. Hitler's utopian promise to create a conflict-free and racially pure 'People's Community' struck a chord, especially with middle-class voters who found the tough law-and-order stance of the Nazi Party very attractive. 'The explanation they gave at party meetings,' a woman from Düsseldorf recalls, 'went something like this. The riff-raff has to be cleared off the streets! Repeat offenders, sex criminals and parasites on the Folk Community . . . will be re-educated in the camps to do honest work. They will be taught discipline and cleanliness.'[5]

Within days of the Nazis coming to power in 1933, Frick, the Interior Minister, set out the welfare spending priorities of the new government. All 'racially sound and healthy people' would have money spent on them, but there would be a severe programme of public spending cuts for those classed as 'inferior

and anti-social' and new radical policies to 'prevent the repro-
duction of severally handicapped people'.[6] On 14 July 1933, the
draft Law for the Prevention of Hereditary Diseased Progeny
was published. It took legal effect from 1 January 1934.

Compulsory sterilisation was allowed for anyone suffering from
congenital feeble-mindedness, schizophrenia, manic-depressive
psychosis, epilepsy, Huntingdon's Chorea, hereditary blindness,
deafness and severe physical disability. It also made it possible for
chronic alcoholics to be nominated for sterilisation too. Subsequent
amendments turned a narrowly defined medical measure into
one which allowed doctors and social welfare authorities to cite
'social reasons' for sterilisation. Around 60 per cent of those
sterilised were defined as 'feeble-minded'. Estimates of the total
number of people sterilised in Nazi Germany between 1933 and
1945 range from 350,000 to 400,000.

The first step in every sterilisation case was a recommendation from a public health service doctor, a social worker or the
director of a state mental asylum, a care home or a prison.
Welfare officials trawled through medical records, school reports,
and employment and police records. The person nominated for
sterilisation was then sent a letter which contained the date of
an appointment with a local doctor. At this meeting, the physi-
cian would decide whether the patient would be sterilised or
not. A total of 220 Hereditary Health Courts were established
to administer the system. These were presided over by two
health service doctors and a lawyer. A further eighteen courts
dealt with appeals. Appeals had to be dealt with in a month.

Official statistics compiled by the Reich Ministry of the
Interior show that in 1934, the first year the law became oper-
ative, 32,268 people were forcibly sterilised. Of these, 17,070
(52.9 per cent) were classed as 'feeble-minded', 8,194 (25.4 per
cent) deemed 'schizophrenics', and 4,520 (14 per cent) were
epileptics. Among the others, 201 were blind and 333 deaf.[7]
There were 4,000 appeals against compulsory sterilisation orders,
but only 441 of these were successful. Proceedings in the appeal

courts often lasted less than fifteen minutes, due to the high number of cases being dealt with each day. Men were sterilised by vasectomy and women by fallopian tube ligation.[8] Around 5,000 women died of post-operative complications arising from this complex surgical procedure.

Some eager local doctors, trying to curry favour with their Nazi paymasters, started unilaterally nominating their own patients. By 1942, 38,000 German doctors were members of the Nazi Party, which represented over 50 per cent of the total.[9] One doctor successfully proposed sterilisation for a young woman who had two 'illegitimate' children. He then looked up her family history, and nominated ten of her relatives. Maria von Linger recalled that her uncle suffered from severe depression and tried to commit suicide: 'The attempt failed. It was reported to the local health office by his doctor. And he had a forced sterilisation. The man got the shock of his life. He was a very handsome man.'[10]

In 1937, family doctors were being asked by state officials to pose questions when interviewing candidates for sterilisation regarding the occupational life of the individual, their surroundings and whether they had stood the test of life. Intelligence tests were added to the process of determining sterilisation, which included general knowledge questions such as 'Who discovered the USA?' or 'When was Columbus born?' Doctors primarily nominated individuals from poor working-class backgrounds for sterilisation. The better-off were able to employ lawyers to fight against compulsory sterilisation. In Hamburg, a group of academics even produced a map of anti-socials in the city. It noted the largest concentration of 'asocials' was in a rough dockland slum area that had previously been a communist stronghold.[11] The criteria used to sterilise most able-bodied people became so elastic it could have applied to virtually anyone. It became widely accepted within police, welfare, academic and medical circles that anti-social behaviour was a hereditary trait. The reasons given by doctors for sterilisation became ever more dictated by quite obvious social and especially class prejudices. The notes of a doctor considering a nomination on a local vagrant on the grounds of 'moral feeble-mindedness' are fairly typical:

In his social work file he is described as a beggar or vagrant who has come down in the world. He is in receipt of fifty per cent war injury pension because of TB on the lungs and intestines. He spends his money very irresponsibly. Smokes a lot and sometimes gets drunk. He has repeatedly been an inmate at Farmsen [a homeless shelter]. He usually leaves the institution to go tramping. He has previous convictions for resisting arrest, breach of the peace, public slander and grievous bodily harm. In his welfare files it is reported that he has often disturbed the operation of the service and physically attacked officials.[12]

Vagrants and beggars were seen as classic 'asocials'. In 1933, 500,000 Germans had no fixed abode. The Nazis issued every homeless person with a 'Vagrants Registration Book'. It recorded their movements between towns and cities and noted stays in homeless shelters. Those who did not produce it to the police on demand were classed as 'disorderly wanderers' and often detained indefinitely in concentration camps. In September 1933, 100,000 vagrants were rounded up in a huge swoop by the criminal police. They were soon released as there were no concentration camps large enough to house them at that time. In 1934, a local Nazi Party official in Kassel proposed a radical 'solution' to the problem of vagrants in a letter to a leading state functionary:

The goal of legislative and administrative measures should not be to follow the line of least resistance and channel the travelling people along orderly lines. The aim must be to remove entirely the destitute vagrant's right to exist. It cannot be denied that this aim will only be achieved with great difficulty, but if ever there was a fitting time for achieving it, it is now, when the state is in a position to act if there is resolute cooperation between the judiciary and the police.[13]

One increasingly cited reason for sterilising 'anti-social' people such as vagrants was a very loosely defined 'disorder' called 'moral mental retardation'. It had no medical basis at all. A report on 450 sterilisation cases undertaken by the racial hygiene division of the Public Health Department in 1936 noted that none of those sterilised with this 'condition' had a 'deficit in intelligence' at all, but they did exhibit what one official termed 'a complete indifference to moral values'. Another equally vague 'illness' used to justify sterilisation was called 'hereditary mental retardation'. In the university hospital at Göttingen 58 per cent of all women sterilised were recorded as suffering from this very loosely defined disorder.[14]

The Nazi regime set up 'Advice Centres for the Improvement of Genetic and Racial Health'. Women engaged to be married were given a leaflet called the 'Ten Commandments for the Choice of a Spouse':

1. Remember that you are a German.
2. If you are genetically healthy you should not remain unmarried.
3. Keep your body pure.
4. You should keep your mind and spirit pure.
5. As a German you should choose a spouse of the same or Nordic blood.
6. In choosing a spouse ask about his ancestors.
7. Health is also a precondition of physical beauty.
8. Marry only for love.
9. Don't look for a playmate but for a companion for marriage.
10. You should want to have as many children as possible.[15]

Nazi racial policy increasingly viewed poor problem families as useful guinea pigs for social experiments. In Bremen in 1939, the local authorities decided to investigate whether troublesome anti-social families could be turned into well-adjusted members of the National Community. Nazi social-engineering projects started to develop. In 1936 a sealed-off, controlled 'asocial' council estate was set up in Hashude on the outskirts of the city. It cost 600,000 Marks. It consisted of eighty-four houses constructed in vandal-proof concrete and iron, in an L-shape, with no back entrances. Every front door was visible to an observation tower, manned by armed guards. A double hedge hid a barbed-wire fence which surrounded the perimeter.

The families sent to the Hashude estate were selected by social workers. The parents all had a long history of severe social problems, including heavy drinking, vandalism and petty crime convictions. They were nearly all in conflict with their existing neighbours. Their children were disruptive in the local areas in which they lived and were not attending school. At Hashude, these problem families were heavily supervised and monitored on a daily basis for the first six months. The men were forced to suffer heavy labouring work, the women were given long bouts of house cleaning, and children forced to attend school lessons in an in-house kindergarten. Bad behaviour and rule breaking were treated with zero tolerance. If the behaviour of the family improved they were allowed to live in the terraced houses on the estate. In July 1940, the facility was closed down. Many local well-behaved families felt these problem families should not be rewarded with good houses for bad behaviour. A list of what happened to the final eighty-four families at Hashude survived. It showed that fifty-nine of the families had improved to such an extent they could be allowed to be housed within the local community once again, a further seven were deemed to have 'improved', but eighteen were classed as 'completely unreformed'. This novel experiment in Nazi social engineering was hugely expensive and was never repeated else-where.[16]

One group Himmler and Heydrich decided could not be

reformed were repeat criminal offenders. One of the less well-known aspects of Nazi Germany is the way the regime brutally persecuted long-term criminals. On 24 November 1933, the Law against Dangerous Career Criminals allowed 'unlimited preventive custody' for any person convicted twice of any criminal offence. If a criminal had already been sentenced twice for a prison term of six months then a judge was allowed retrospectively to pass a sentence of fifteen years for the current offence. A sub-clause in this law allowed courts to order castration for sex offenders over the age of twenty who had already committed more than one offence. Between 1934 and 1939, 1,808 prisoners were forcibly castrated. Around 70 per cent were convicted paedophiles. Convicted rapists were the next largest category group subject to castration. Most castrated sex offenders were aged between thirty and fifty and came from the poorest backgrounds. Criminologists in Hitler's Germany regarded the policy of using castration against sex offenders as a success, pointing to a re-offending rate in sex crimes of under 5 per cent.[17] Crime statistics do record some surprisingly large falls in sexual convictions in the Nazi era. These decreases were very dramatic during war-time, when most men aged between eighteen and forty were serving in the armed forces. Between 1939 and 1943, the number of rape convictions fell from 7,614 to 2,212, representing a 72 per cent drop, and sexual offences against children under fourteen decreased from 6,285 to 2,480, representing a fall of 60.5 per cent.[18]

After 1 January 1934, anyone defined as a 'dangerous habitual criminal' did not even have the right to release after serving a prison sentence. The police also regarded this policy as a huge success. In March 1932, for example, there were sixty-seven serious armed robberies in Berlin, but in March 1934 this had reduced to twelve.[19] By early 1935, this law was being applied to all repeat offenders. By 30 April 1938, only 701 repeat offenders had been released from prison at all. The use of these open-ended punishments proved extremely traumatic for prisoners.

Franziska, who had a number of convictions for minor thefts, gave vent to her frustrations in a letter to her family: 'I'm totally embittered sitting here and not knowing why and for how long . . . I will lose my mind if this goes on like this . . . This is a slow suicide.'[20] Another prisoner called Gustav, branded by prison officials as 'work-shy' and a 'persistent thief', made the following appeal to the court: 'I deny that I am an "incorrigible thief". When I committed my offences I was pretty young and barely aware of my crimes . . . which repulse me today and which I will definitely not commit again. During almost all my thefts I was suffering hardship [and] during my last thefts which I committed in 1930 I rarely took more than I needed to live.'[21]

In March 1937, Kripo mounted large-scale raids on repeat offenders. These resulted in the arrest of 2,752 people, including burglars (938), thieves (741), sex offenders (495) and swindlers (436). Only 372 were ever released and 68 died in custody.[22] Underpinning this policy of 'two offences and you're inside for good' were statistical crime surveys which showed that repeat offenders committed most of the crimes. A survey of crime statistics, undertaken by the Reich Ministry of Justice in 1937, noted that 72 per cent of repeat offenders received their first court sentence before the age of twenty-one. It was felt that after this age it was unlikely offenders could be reformed, and confining them in prison indefinitely was therefore the best solution for the National Community.[23] The harsh sentencing policy against petty criminals appears to have had little impact on reducing these offences. The number of petty thefts actually went up from 44,352 in 1939 to 82,828 in 1943, an increase of 71 per cent.[24]

On 14 December 1937, the Interior Ministry issued a new decree called 'Preventative Crime Fighting'. This extended 'preventative police custody' to all persistent offenders who 'endangered' the public. This was a catch–all measure primarily used against anyone whose conduct did not please the Gestapo or the police. Arthur Nebe, head of Kripo, was a keen supporter of the increased use of 'preventative custody'. The overall crime rate in Nazi Germany as a whole did fall from 444,036 offences in 1937 to 266,223 in 1940. The fall in offences perpetrated by 'repeat offenders' was just as dramatic, decreasing from 171,430 in 1937 to 86,668 in 1940.[25] Criminals had been excluded from the Sterilisation Law, but the officially sanctioned disease of 'hereditary feeble-mindedness' allowed prison governors, working with prison doctors, to order the sterilisation of prisoners. Between 1933 and 1939, a total of 5,397 prisoners were forcibly sterilised (4,909 men and 488 women). Many were defined as suffering from mental illness or viewed as 'seriously asocial', and included a high proportion of vagrants, serious alcoholics and prostitutes. Reports of prison doctors frequently used phrases such as 'mentally inferior' or 'too stupid for words' to justify a sterilisation order. For women, being 'morally unstable' or 'sexually wayward' was seen as a valid enough reason to end their right to have children.[26]

During war-time, the harsh treatment of habitual criminals intensified. On 5 September 1939, the decree against National Pests was introduced. This targeted three criminal elements: the blackout exploiter, the thief and the anti-social saboteur. The Decree against Violent Criminals of 5 December 1939 offered courts much greater powers to deal with gangsters and violent offenders too. The prison population grew from 120,000 in 1939 to 200,000 by 1945.[27] On 20 August 1942 Adolf Hitler told a justice official that it was wrong to keep 'criminal vermin in prisons' while the 'most superb' examples of the German race were being sacrificed on the battlefield. The implication was that criminals in prisons were still being afforded favourable conditions. Otto Georg Thierack, the new Justice Minister, immediately took up this challenge. In a clandestine agreement with Himmler's SS he began a secret extermination programme aimed specifically at killing 'asocial' prisoners. Those selected were transferred to concentration camps to undergo 'annihilation through labour', which was a euphemism for starving and working prisoners to death. The 'general transfer' of 'asocial' prisoners began in October 1942, but individual transfers of selected prisoners continued until the end of the war. The prisoners nearly all went to the German-based concentration camps. Kripo, often assisted by the Gestapo, organised the operation. Prisoners were transported to the concentration camps in large lorries and special trains. By the end of April 1943, about 14,700 prisoners had been sent to the concentration camps (13,100 men and 1,600 women).[28] A typical transferee was a petty criminal called Richard. He had a long list of convictions for minor theft, including stealing a garden hose from a farm. He was sent to Mauthausen concentration camp on 29 November 1942. He died two months later. Overall, it's been estimated that 20,000 prisoners were sent to the concentration camps and very few of them survived. By 1944, 7,736 of the 10,231 prisoners taken to Mauthausen had been starved to death or executed.[29] The murder of German long-term prisoners is yet another example of the broad genocide policy carried out by the Nazi regime.

Another group the Nazis classed as social outsiders were the long-term unemployed. The punishment for being unemployed in Nazi Germany became forced slave labour, even though such an offence never officially existed. On 26 January 1938, Heinrich Himmler informed the Gestapo and Kripo of his plan to mount nationwide surprise raids during what he called the 'National Campaign against the Work Shy'. The decree defined the 'work-shy' as anyone fit to work who had given up a job twice for no clear reason. The Gestapo had never targeted the long-term unemployed in such a way before. Local employment offices were asked to supply information to Gestapo officers on the names and addresses of individuals. The ulterior motive of this sweep against the unemployed was not simply racial. Himmler wanted to dragoon surplus labour for use in the factories that were now being attached to the concentration camps.

The order issued to the Gestapo insisted that only those 'willing to work' should be seized, and defined the following as not suitable for arrest: heavy drinkers, Gypsies, old people, vagrants and habitual criminals. 'Operation Work Shy' began on 21 April 1938, and lasted for nine days. According to one report, 1,500 'asocials' were seized and transported to concentration camps.[30] Heydrich felt the Gestapo had defined the 'asocial' unemployed much too narrowly. Kripo was asked to mount a more vigorous set of raids on the long-term unemployed. On 1 June 1938, all Kripo police districts were set a target to arrest 200 unemployed 'asocials' in their own area. Between 13 and 18 June 1938, Kripo officers arrested 8,000 broadly defined 'asocials', including not just the long-term unemployed, but vagrants, beggars, criminals and even some Gypsies. Lists of those arrested included violent drunks and pimps. These arrests were designed to send out a clear warning to all 'asocials' in the underclass that if they remained unwilling to work they would end up in a concentration camp. All the people arrested during 'Operation Work Shy' were taken straight to the new concentration camps of Flossenbürg, Mauthausen and Neuengamme, which were no longer designated purely for 'political' and 'religious' opponents. Many of the other concentration camps were no longer designated purely for political and religious opponents either. In October 1938, of the 10,188 prisoners held in Buchenwald, for instance, 1,007 were 'career criminals', and 4,341 defined as 'asocials'.[31] By 1939, the concentration camps held more than 10,000 'asocials'. In Sachsenhausen, 1,600 political prisoners were suddenly confronted with 6,000 'work-shy' inmates.

The uniforms of 'asocials' in the concentration camps were marked with a black triangle. Their stay was supposed to 'educate them' to make them reliable members of the National Community. Unlike the political, religious or criminal groups, the 'asocials' lacked any group solidarity. The SS guards regarded them as lazy, stupid and cowardly. Only homosexuals and Jews ranked below the 'asocials' in the concentration camp hierarchy.

Most were simply vulnerable, isolated and often disorganised individuals, who had been unable to conform or cope with life. The mortality rate of 'asocials' was much higher than for political and religious prisoners. Many died when they had to endure hard labour outdoors in stone quarries in the winter months. Political prisoners, viewed by SS guards as principled and hardworking individuals, were out-sourced the task of assigning the new 'asocials' to hard-labour tasks. On 18 June 1940, the Reich Main Security Office (RSHA) ordered that no 'asocials' or habitual criminals should ever be released from concentration camps or prisons. As the camps filled up with 'asocials', a much more brutal regime emerged, involving forced slave labour, increased punishments and even medical experiments.

German teenagers also found themselves caught up in the battle to secure social conformity. The Nazi regime set a very high standard on child behaviour. Social workers employed by the Youth Welfare Office had the right to apply for a care order against children living in 'asocial' families. The number of young people committed to care homes and youth detention centres rose dramatically. By 1941, 100,000 youngsters were locked up in such institutions. Most were sent for 'preventative purposes' by social workers. The crime rate for juveniles bucked the general trend of a falling crime rate. Offences committed by young people actually increased from 17,458 in 1939 to 52,469 by 1942.[32] In March 1940, the Decree for The Protection of Young People prohibited youngsters from attending dances and amusement parks after 9 p.m. or to drink alcohol, smoke or loiter on the streets. Schools were asked to report the non-attendance of pupils to welfare authorities. The Youth Court at Hanau sent Emmi Krause to a youth detention centre in March 1939 for repeatedly missing school, after she was spotted by police in the company of young men and off-duty soldiers late at night, near the local central railway station.

The records have survived for one of the toughest youth detention centres at Breitenau in northern Hesse. It was originally an adult workhouse, but served as a detention centre for children and teenagers during the Nazi era. The staff were poorly paid, overworked and lacked training. George Saurbier, the director, believed wholeheartedly in the 'racial' mission of the Nazi state. He had a low opinion of what he called the 'low life' inmates and their families. In reports of meetings with visiting parents he often described them as 'biologically inferior scum' or as 'mentally retarded'.[33] He gave the girls in care sedative drugs to curb their 'sexual urges', but a colleague from a nearby insane asylum advised him to adopt a different and less expensive method to deal with the 'promiscuous girls' in his care when he wrote in a letter: 'One only gets through to these girls by disciplining them. If those sort of things happen here then we lay them on a bed and put them on water soup and the most restricted diet until they are thin and ugly. Then things tend to go all right . . . In my experience you get nowhere by drugging them.'[34]

It proved cheaper to starve inmates. The daily cost of feeding an inmate at the Breitenau centre fell from forty-eight to thirty pfennig per day between 1934 and 1939. That equated to two slices of bread in the morning and clear soup for lunch and dinner. Children ran away from the homes due to these starvation rations. Many sad and lonely children wrote heart-rending letters to their parents, usually asking for some food, such as the following from a young boy called Rolf: 'Please don't think badly of me for writing so often, but it's so cold here and I already have cold fingers. I'm still in the house of misfortune . . . Now I won't be home for Christmas, please don't forget me and send me something. See for once if you can get together half a Stollen [German Christmas Cake] and some ginger and if possible a couple of Advent biscuits and a couple of sweets.'[35]

During war-time, the Gestapo became increasingly concerned about why young people were forming dissident groups. The activities of two youth groups came under particular scrutiny. The first was the Edelweiss Pirates, primarily composed of boys aged between fourteen and nineteen, who lived in the working areas of Cologne, Düsseldorf, Essen, Wuppertal and Duisburg. The 'Pirates' were linked to a number of other subversive youth gangs, notably the 'Raving Dudes', the 'Navajos' and the 'Kittlebach Pirates'. The Gestapo was determined to hunt these young 'rebels without a cause'. It was initially difficult for the Gestapo to distinguish their behaviour from juvenile delinquency.

A Cologne 'Special Court' judge described the members of the group:

> The regulation uniform of the Edelweiss Pirates is short trousers, white socks, a check shirt, a white pullover and scarf and wind-cheater In addition, they have very long hair. A comb is worn in the left sock and a knife in the right one. In so far as girls belong to the gangs, a white pullover or waistcoat is worn. In the warmer months they leave town in their hundreds on foot, by bicycle or train. They alternate between gatherings and trips. Normally, they meet at night on street corners, in doorways or in parks. They sing their own songs . . . There is little homo-sexuality. Instead they practice sexual intercourse with the female members.[36]

The more the 'Pirates' were harassed, the more they became determined to resist. One of their favourite tactics was to ambush and attack members of the Hitler Youth in the newly built urban subways. They daubed anti-Nazi graffiti on public build-ings too. A report by the Reich Ministry of Justice noted: 'In addition to harmless ringing of doorbells, they have beaten up pedestrians. In some cases they have smeared human excrement on the faces of national comrades.'[37]

On 17 July 1942, a branch of the Nazi Party in Düsseldorf sent the following report on their activities to the local Gestapo:

> The said youths are throwing their weight around again. I have been informed that assemblages of young people have been

more conspicuous than ever, especially since the last bombing raid on Düsseldorf. These youngsters . . . hang around in the late evening with musical instruments and young females. Since this riff-raff is to a large extent outside the Hitler Youth and adopts a hostile attitude towards the organisation they represent a danger to other young people.[38]

The Düsseldorf Gestapo compiled detailed files on the members of nineteen groups of Edelweiss Pirates who were operating between 1938 and 1944. They provide interesting information about the social characteristics of the group. They were mostly working-class teenagers, aged between sixteen and nineteen, who had previously been members of Catholic youth organisations and attended elementary schools. A majority had lost their fathers in the war. They were not part of the 'asocial' long-term unemployed or juvenile delinquents. Most had full-time jobs, with average earnings per month of a hundred Reichsmarks. These were the self-assured members of the working class, unwilling to conform to the rigid discipline demanded by the Nazi regime, but with no strong political opinions.[39] The Gestapo was advised by the Ministry of Justice to make a distinction between leaders, active members and passive followers of the Edelweiss Pirates. In minor cases, a warning was advised. Youth custody was used as a last resort. The leaders were to be 'prevented from continuing their gang activity by the toughest punishments', which involved detention in a youth 're-education' camp.[40] In December 1942, the Gestapo mounted a series of raids in the Rhineland region to put a halt to their teenage rampage. In Düsseldorf, ten groups composed of 283 youths were arrested; in Duisburg, ten groups were broken and 260 were arrested, and eight groups in Essen and Wuppertal, totalling 196 people, were captured. Most were charged with painting anti-Nazi graffiti and distributing anti-Nazi leaflets.[41] Two years later, the Gestapo acted much more ruthlessly. On 10 November 1944, the Cologne Gestapo arrested and then publicly hanged thirteen members of the Edelweiss Pirates in the working-class Ehrenfeld area of the city. The aim was to deter others from continuing to belong to such groups.[42]

A quite different type of popular youth protest emerged during the war-time period: 'Swing and Jazz Youth'. Its followers were predominantly educated members of the affluent middle class, located in big cities, most notably Hamburg, Berlin, Stuttgart, Frankfurt and Dresden. They admired American jazz and swing music, set up illegal clubs, usually in the cellars of the spacious homes of their parents, and organised dance nights. Gestapo reports on the swing movement constantly stress the free and open attitude towards the sexuality of their followers. A report by a Hitler Youth spy at an illegal swing festival in Hamburg in February 1940 gives a particularly vivid description of their activities:

> The dance music was all English and American. Only swing dancing and jitterbugging took place. At the entrance stood a notice on which the words 'Swing prohibited' had been altered to 'Swing requested' . . . The dancers were an appalling sight. None of the couples danced normally; there was only swing of the worst sort. Sometimes two boys danced with a girl; sometimes several couples formed a circle, linking arms and jumping, slapping hands, even rubbing the back of their heads together.[43]

Swing youth members had money and wore fashionable clothes. They were not anti-fascist, but were apolitical hedonists who wanted to establish a counter-identity from the one being peddled by the Nazi regime. They were strongly influenced by the culture of Germany's capitalist and democratic Western allies, particularly the USA and Britain. These non-conformist youth and counter-cultural groups were a small minority, but they show that some young people in the big cities were becoming disillusioned with the rigid conformity of Hitler's Germany long before the war ended.

Street-walking prostitutes were also viewed as a major problem in the big cities by the Gestapo. They were defined as 'genetically diseased carriers of venereal disease' and as 'a danger to the family life of the Third Reich'.[44] Under the 1927 Law for Combating Venereal Disease, enacted by the democratic Weimar government, prostitution had been decriminalised, and state-run brothels were banned. This allowed prostitutes to solicit on the streets.

In May 1933, the Nazi government made publicly soliciting for trade by prostitutes illegal. A series of anti-prostitute raids followed. In Hamburg, for example, 3,201 were arrested and 274 forced to undertake medical treatment for venereal disease.[45] In August 1934, a prostitute called Rosa was arrested by Kripo for stealing forty Reichsmarks from a client she'd slept with, who reported her to the police. The prosecutor called Rosa a 'debased and dangerous street-whore' and asked the judge to take account, when sentencing her, of a similar offence she had committed in 1927. She was sentenced to sixteen months' imprisonment, but this turned into indefinite confinement, and she was never released.

After 1936, however, the Nazi regime began to display a contradictory attitude towards prostitution. Prostitutes were treated as a necessary menace. Himmler felt organised brothels helped prevent youth drifting towards homosexuality and could even act as a reward for soldiers during war-time.[46] In a secret directive issued by the Ministry of the Interior, dated 9 September 1939, brothels were legalised once again, but soliciting on the streets remained illegal. Prostitutes were now registered, examined by health officials and required to work in regulated brothels. Prostitutes who operated outside brothels were dealt with harshly. On the evening of 21 September 1942, a ship stoker walked into a Gestapo office and reported that a local prostitute, who had passed on a venereal disease to him, was soliciting men in a beer hall in Hamburg's notorious Reeperbahn area, and he gave a description of what she looked like. A Gestapo officer was swiftly dispatched to the bar and promptly arrested her. She signed the following statement: 'I haven't been working for the past nine weeks and I earned too little in this time. I practised prostitution. I did not know I had a sexual illness [this had not yet been diagnosed]. I had not seen any sign of it. I had the intention of settling in a brothel and continuing with prostitution.' She was placed under 'preventive custody' and sent to prison.[47]

Women who had several sexual partners were often reported to the Gestapo and Kripo for anti-social behaviour. On 14 August 1941, the Kripo in Essen ordered the 'preventive arrest' of a woman after being informed by a local welfare worker that a local divorcee was leading a 'promiscuous life'. She had been seen frequenting local bars, in the company of several men, while leaving her children home alone. The children were taken into care. She was eventually picked up by Kripo while wandering the streets of Duisburg alone in a drunken state. She was sent to Ravensbrück concentration camp and ended up being transported to Auschwitz. She died there on 23 July 1942.[48]

By 1942, there were twenty-eight regulated brothels in Berlin alone. Kripo supervised and regulated all of the brothels. They were also established for foreign workers, using foreign female workers as prostitutes. German citizens were forbidden from using these. Believe it or not, brothels were even opened in many concentration camps to provide what Himmler called an 'incentive' and 'reward' for the hard-working privileged male prisoners known as 'Kapos'. Many of the women forced into prostitution came from the Ravensbrück concentration camp. Prostitutes were replaced frequently due to exhaustion. By 1944, there were brothels at the eight major German-located concentration camps. Female prostitutes were forced to work in these brothels. It's been estimated that a total of 31,140 women acted as prostitutes in the Nazi concentration camps.[49]

The Gestapo took a completely different attitude towards

homosexuality. Public persecution of homosexuals was not new or unique to Nazi Germany. It was defined as a criminal activity in most countries during this period.[50] Himmler saw the open and free-spirited 'Cabaret' gay club culture of Weimar Berlin as 'the symptom of a dying race'. He often gave morally infused lectures to the SS on the subject, with titles such as 'The Dangers of Homosexuality to the German Race'.[51] In one speech he said, 'All homosexuals are cowards; they lie like Jesuits. Homosexuality leads to a state of mind that doesn't know what it does.'[52]

A policy statement issued by the Nazi Party in the Weimar era outlined its stance on homosexuality quite clearly:

> Anyone who thinks of homosexual love is our enemy. We reject anything which emasculates our people and makes it a play thing for our enemies, for we know life is a fight and it is madness to think that men will ever embrace fraternally. Natural history teaches us the opposite . . . We therefore reject any form of lewdness, especially homosexuality, because it robs us of our last chance to free our people from the bondage which now enslaves it.[53]

The notorious paragraph 175 of the Criminal Code deemed sexual intercourse between men aged twenty-one and over as punishable by a prison sentence. As sexual penetration had to be proved to secure a conviction, the number of convictions under this law was extremely low during the Weimar era. In 1935, the law was widened to include any 'unnatural act'. This made it much easier to prosecute homosexuals. Between 1933 and 1935, using the old 175 Act, 4,000 men were convicted. Between 1936 and 1939, using the new catch-all law, close to 30,000 men were found guilty.[54] Paragraph 175 did not apply to lesbians. They were viewed by the Nazi regime as 'sexually deviant', but same-sex activity between women, contrary to popular myth, was never criminalised in Nazi Germany. Gestapo case files show most gays arrested under the 175 law were between eighteen and twenty-five. They came from a wide variety of social backgrounds. During Gestapo interrogations, homosexuals were forced to divulge intimate details of their sexual experiences dating back to their early childhood. Their confessions contain statements such as: 'I will never engage in this perverted activity again.'[55]

Unfortunately, due to the difficulties of being gay in the Third Reich, we tend to view such people through the documents left behind by their persecutors. Rarely do we hear the personal voice of a gay person who lived at this time. Yet Gad Beck has left a startling account of his experiences as a gay Jewish man living in Berlin. He suggests that in the German capital it was not difficult to lead a gay lifestyle and avoid detection:

I came out, as you say nowadays, in a totally nonchalant fashion. It just happened . . . I never talked about it openly with my parents, but it wasn't necessary. They knew. My first relationship was with a picture-perfect boy named Otto . . . We would have sex after sports or going swimming and soon I started visiting him at home. Sometimes we could even have fun there since his father worked during the day . . . Otto was not the only one . . . Another playmate was Martin who liked fooling around in broad daylight on the S-Bahn [the suburban railway system]. The train was crowded and we would stand really close together and touch each other, rubbing a bit, fumbling around and grabbing. No one around us would notice or care to notice . . . I was virtually unaware of how the political climate was becoming increasingly distressing and oppressive.[56]

The Gestapo established a special section to deal with homosexuality at its Berlin HQ in October 1934. Most local offices in the big cities had similar dedicated officers dealing with homosexual cases. Index cards were created on all active homosexuals. Research Institutes were set up, notably the Institute for Psychological Research and Psychotherapy in Berlin in which gays were 're-educated' and, 'if cured', were released to lead what the Nazis called 'normal lives'. The psychiatrists who worked at this institute believed heterosexual males were often seduced into becoming homosexuals by other homosexuals. The therapy therefore concentrated on trying to stop homosexuals from seducing others and encouraging them to adopt a heterosexual lifestyle upon release. In cases where it was felt a person could not be converted away from their homosexuality, then castration was recommended prior to release. On 1 October 1936, a Reich Central Security Office for combating Homosexuality and Abortion was established. In prosecutions against Catholic priests and monks, evidence was often fabricated alleging homosexuality. In one case against a monk, the Gestapo star witness was a mental patient who claimed he'd been sexually assaulted by the monk. When the prosecuting lawyer asked him to identify in court the man who had carried out these assaults, the man pointed to the judge. The case collapsed. The Gestapo drive to suggest there was a 'gay plague' spreading through the Catholic Church was a total failure. Most cases were thrown out by the judiciary. Only fifty-seven priests and seven monks were ever sentenced under Paragraph 175.[57]

Homosexuality remained a criminal offence during the Nazi era. Kripo, the courts and the prisons handled the great majority of such cases. Kripo and the Gestapo often discussed cases. Many of the homosexual cases handled by the Gestapo ended up with the accused person being sent to a concentration camp. In prisons, homosexuals wore ordinary prison uniforms, with no identification marks. It's been estimated that, between 1933 and 1945, around 100,000 homosexuals were given prison sentences for 175 offences, and 50,000 served some time in a concentration camp.

In the concentration camps, homosexuals wore a pink triangle on their striped uniforms. They were often kicked, beaten and humiliated. One homosexual victim later described his first day at Sachsenhausen concentration camp: 'When my number was called, I stepped forward, gave my name and mentioned Paragraph 175. With the words "You filthy queer, get over there, you butt fucker," I received several kicks, then was transferred to an SS sergeant in charge of my [camp] block. The first thing I got from him was a violent blow to my face that threw me to the ground.'[58] Such incidents of violence feature heavily in most of the survivor testimony of gays who ended up in Nazi concentration camps. Eugen Kogon, a political prisoner, recalled: 'The fate of homosexuals in the concentration camps can only be described as ghastly. They were often segregated in special barracks and work details. Such segregation offered ample opportunity to unscrupulous elements in positions of power to engage in extortion and maltreatment.'[59] The SS guards believed gays were fixated on sex and needed strict supervision to prohibit any sexual activity. 'One block was occupied by homosexuals,' recalls one gay survivor. 'We could sleep only in our nightshirts and had to keep our hands outside our blankets.' SS guards inspected the homosexual barracks to ensure that this rule, which was designed to prevent gays from masturbating, was adhered to.[60] Homosexuals were not just isolated within the camps, but also from the outside world. Very few families were willing to stand by their sons. On the contrary, most relatives were ashamed they had a family member who was a homosexual.

More alarmingly, they were singled out for horrific medical experiments. At Buchenwald, for instance, hormone experiments were conducted by the notorious Danish doctor Carl Vaernet and the German surgeon Gerhard Schiedlausky. Vaernet believed homosexuals could be 'cured' via a combination of castration, followed by injections of high doses of male hormones. The procedures led to huge complications for those selected, excruciating pain and death. Surviving documentation reveals the Danish doctor was completely clueless about what he was trying to achieve. The evaluation of blood tests and urine samples was utterly shambolic. The tests only halted when a yellow fever epidemic spread through the camp.[61]

A final group the Nazis considered a danger to the 'purity of the German race' were Gypsies. They endured discrimination, stigmatisation and ostracism before 1933, but they became trapped in a triangulated crossfire of Nazi eugenic, anti-social and racial policies. There were around 28,000 Sinta and Roma people living in the Third Reich in 1933. They were a numerically small minority who we now know came to central Europe from northern India in the fifteenth century via Egypt. 'Gypsies as they really are', noted the popular Nazi magazine *New Race*, 'are Nomads of another race, who because of their vermin and filth and stench remain foreign to us to this day.'[62] In 1936 a Reich Office for the 'Fight against the Gypsy Nuisance' was established.

The persecution of the Gypsies was directed by the research of a highly respected academic: Dr Robert Ritter. He was born in Aachen in 1901. He qualified as a doctor and was then awarded a doctorate in psychology and a specialist post-graduate certificate in child psychiatry. He came to the subject of Gypsies after publishing several academic books and articles on anti-social youth and the 'biology of criminality'. He considered crime and anti-social behaviour to be rooted in the hereditary and social background of individuals. Ritter created a large research institute of doctors, social workers, psychiatrists and anthropologists. This was funded by the German government and special SS funds. His rigorous methods enabled his findings to be viewed as cutting-edge research. Ritter undertook a comprehensive study of all Gypsies living in Germany between 1936 and 1940. His team interviewed thousands of Gypsies and compiled a detailed card index, which later proved invaluable when Gypsies were selected for transportation to Auschwitz. In the final report of his exhaustive research project, published in 1940, he concluded that because Gypsies 'inter bred with Asiatics' and 'anti-social elements within the German Lumpenproletariat' in deprived areas of the big cities they had 'polluted their Aryan blood'. Ritter felt 'pure Gypsies', which he defined as the classic travelling Gypsies, posed no threat to society and should be left alone. It was the gypsy 'half-breed' who lived in the poorest sections of the big cities that were defined as 'racially suspect'.

One of Ritter's key research assistants was the ambitious young academic Eva Justin. She completed an influential PhD on 148 Gypsy children at a care home. She treated the children like animals in a zoo, measuring their heads, noting the colour of their eyes, their height, the shape of their noses and ears. She photographed each of them, and encouraged them to play sport and go on long carefree walks. She concluded that the morals and behaviour of Gypsy children in care homes and in their leisure time was much worse than when they lived with their parents. She concluded these children could never assimilate within the National Community and advised that compulsory sterilisation was the best method to deal with them.[63]

A number of cities set up special camps for Gypsies to park their caravans and wagons, but to isolate them from the local community. These were not exactly concentration camps, as Gypsies could come and go as they wished, but the conditions in them were awful. Few had adequate supplies of water, gas, street lighting or sewerage. In March 1939, it was reported that 40 per cent of Gypsies in such camps had scabies.[64] Alongside the policy of controlling and harassing Gypsies, a more sinister approach began to emerge. Gypsies were increasingly defined as a 'racial problem'. There were calls from leading officials in the Gestapo and Kripo to deal with the 'Gypsy menace' more harshly. The chief of the rural police in the district of Esslingen in the south German state of Württemberg wrote a letter to a senior Nazi official on 11 March 1937 offering a radical way to deal with the Gypsy population in Stuttgart:

The Gypsy is and remains a parasite on the people who supports himself almost exclusively by begging and stealing . . . The Gypsy can never be educated to become a useful person. For this reason it is necessary that the Gypsy tribe be exterminated by way of sterilisation or castration. With the help of such a law the Gypsy plague would soon be eliminated . . . Such a measure would not cost the state very much money.[65]

On 8 December 1938, Himmler issued an equally menacing decree called 'Combating the Gypsy Plague', which spoke of the need to tackle the Gypsy problem in terms of 'the inner characteristics of that race'. Himmler ordered the special Reich office on Gypsy affairs to 'compile information on all Gypsies in Germany and to decide on all measures necessary for combating the Gypsies'.[66] All Gypsies were now required to be registered, undergo a 'racial biological examination' and carry an identity card classing them as: (i) a pure Gypsy (ii) mixed race Gypsy (iii) 'non-Gypsy itinerant' – essentially a travelling vagrant. This decree gave the police extra powers to ban Gypsies from travelling in groups of several families, and allowed police to take into custody anyone defined as an 'asocial Gypsy'.

The onset of the war brought a further tightening of the net. Gypsies were no longer allowed to leave their place of residence, without special permission. They were subjected to compulsory labour and classed as 'Community Aliens'. In 1939, the SD reported that Gypsy fortune tellers, who were very popular at fun fairs, were offering negative predictions on the outcome of the war. Shortly after, Heydrich issued a decree banning Gypsy fortune telling altogether. Any Gypsy fortune teller found breaching this order was taken into 'preventive custody'. A forty-seven-year-old Gypsy fortune teller called Anna, arrested by Kripo, was sent to the all-woman Ravensbrück concentration camp in February 1940 for defying this order. She died there on 14 May 1942. Emma, another Gypsy fortune teller, aged thirty-six and a mother of six children, was arrested in June 1940. She agreed not to engage in fortune telling ever again. She was sentenced to three months in prison. In March

1943, she and her six children were all sent to Auschwitz. It's unlikely they survived.[67]

The policy of deporting Gypsies developed slowly. In May 1940, 2,500 Gypsies were transported to camps in Nazi-occupied Poland and used as forced labour. On 16 December 1942, there was a sudden and dramatic change of policy. Himmler ordered the mass deportation of Gypsies to the deadly Auschwitz-Birkenau concentration camp. Himmler decreed, however, that 'pure Gypsies' who had previously led a travelling lifestyle should be exempted from these deportations. Himmler had a strange fascination with 'pure gypsies'. He believed they were descended from the original ancient 'Aryan' tribes. Arthur Nebe, head of Kripo, informed officers that 'Himmler intends that in future "racially pure gypsies" be allowed a certain freedom of movement so that they can move around in a fixed area, live according to their customs and mores and follow an appropriate traditional [Gypsy] occupation'.[68]

In a letter on 3 December 1942, Martin Bormann, political secretary to Hitler, complained about Himmler's exemption of 'racially pure' Gypsies from the deportation order: 'Such a special treatment of racially pure Gypsies would represent a fundamental departure from presently applied measures for fighting the Gypsy plague and would not be understood by the population and the lower ranks of the party leadership. The Führer too would not approve it if a segment of the Gypsies are given back their old freedom.'[69] Three days later, Himmler met with Hitler, and was able to overcome his reservations. The racially pure Gypsies were exempted. A memo from the Ministry of Justice, dated 17 February, noted that: 'New research has shown that among the Gypsies are racially valuable elements.'[70]

Kripo, not the Gestapo, took charge of the deportations of Gypsies. They selected people based on the card index and racial assessments supplied by the Ritter Institute. Kripo was given *carte blanche* to decide who was deported or exempted. Once again, so-called 'racial' criteria became a matter of social judgement. Kripo officers often called for 'expert' opinion from the 'Racial Hygiene Research Centre' within the Public Health Office when deciding difficult cases. The following vague report, dated 10 July 1944, heavily flavoured with social prejudice, attempts to categorise the 'racial character' of a family who were accused of being Gypsies, but denied they were:

> Although the membership of the Gypsies in terms of blood is denied by family X, the racial diagnosis as regards the members of family X is undoubtedly 'Gypsy'.
>
> This verdict is based on
>
> 1. Racial and psychological features
> 2. Anthropological features
> 3. Genealogical date
> 4. The fact the family is regarded as Magyar by Hungarians.
>
> These few facts alone are sufficient on their own for family X to be regarded as presumptively Gypsy . . . The gestures, affectivity and overall behaviour are not only alien type but in fact positively indicate Gypsy descent.[71]

The deportation of Gypsies to Auschwitz began on 1 March 1943 and was concluded by the end of the month. Those sent to Auschwitz were only allowed to take personal clothing and food for the train journey. In the deportations of Gypsies, Kripo was given even more powers over selection than the Gestapo was given during the deportation of Jews. The number of Gypsies exempted from transportation to Auschwitz-Birkenau varied from region to region. In Magdeburg, nearly all Gypsies in the area ended up being deported. The city of Giessen, in the state of Hesse, deported 14 of 25 Gypsies. In Munich, around 141 out of 200 were deported. In Oldenburg, a Catholic area, only four Gypsies out of 84 were deported.[72] A total of 13,000 'half-breed' Gypsies were deported from Germany and Austria in March 1943. It's thought that around 15,000 out of the original 28,627 Gypsies in Germany and Austria survived the deportations.

Every 'half-breed' Gypsy over the age of twelve who was exempted from deportation was expected to give consent to be sterilised. The key role Kripo played in these sterilisation orders shows how this supposedly civilian criminal detective force had become indistinguishable from the Gestapo. Kripo had become the 'racial policing' wing of the Gestapo. The sterilisation of Gypsies in Germany did not follow the normal procedure of a recommendation by a doctor followed by an assessment by the hereditary health courts. Kripo simply asked local authorities to give consent to sterilisation orders. Gypsies who agreed to sterilisation were classified as 'socially adjusted'. If anyone refused, Kripo officers threatened them with dispatch to a concentration camp and deportation. A Gypsy called Johann, who had served in the army, was exempted from deportation due to his war record. On 13 May 1943, the Kripo office in Nuremberg ordered his sterilisation. Johann refused to give his consent. A Kripo officer threatened him with being sent to a concentration camp. Johann refused again. He was then arrested as an 'asocial', and placed under 'preventive police custody'. He was told he would be transported to Auschwitz. The next day, Johann finally agreed to be sterilised and was released.[73] It's been estimated that between 2,000 and 2,500 Gypsies who were exempted from deportation were sterilised between 1943 and 1945.

Hilda, a young German girl, recalls a particularly poignant tale of the day she met some Gypsies during the war-time period when the deportations to Auschwitz-Birkenau were taking place:

I was visiting this local church fair, a carnival. They had a merry-go-round with different stands and booths. And then I saw this girl come in a kind of Gypsy caravan. She had some sweets. I had his beautiful pink paper. I gave it to her as a present. I can still see us there sitting together. She had a rag doll. I think she was nine or ten. She said nobody should touch that doll as it was special. Then she told me, and I had to swear I wouldn't tell a soul, that there were other Gypsies who went from town to town with a fair, but they had been put in a camp and then gassed. So I whispered, 'But that can't be. I mean just because they are Gypsies . . . what crime did the commit?' 'No,' the girl replied: 'You don't understand, they are being killed just for *being* Gypsies.' The doll she showed me had been given to her by someone who was later gassed. I never spoke about this meeting to my parents as I promised this girl I would keep her secret.[74]

Chapter 7

Persecuting the Jews

At 11.03 a.m. on the morning of 11 March 1933, Ludwig Förder, a Jewish lawyer, was sitting in his office in the main court building in Breslau.[1] The door was suddenly and violently kicked open. Bursting into the room came two burly Nazi storm troopers shouting: 'Jews – get out.' In a police statement later in the day Förder described what happened next:

> I saw Siegmund Cohn, over 70 years old, a member of the bar, was sitting in his chair, as if it had been nailed down. He was unable to move. Several of the brown shirts attacked him . . . An SA man jumped on me, beat me twice on the head causing profuse bleeding. The blows landed close to the scar of my wounds from the First World War . . . The SA man looked around, pointed at me and asked the judge: 'Is this a Jew?' . . . The old man believed he had no right to lie to the thug and answered: 'Yes – this is a Jewish lawyer.' Then the thug turned to his friends: 'Take the Jew out.' An SA man was standing at the door and when I passed, he kicked me violently in the back and made me fall over judge Goldfarb, who was also the head of the Jewish community . . . He then turned to me in shock and asked: 'To what authority should I apply to complain about this scandal?' I replied: 'I believe there is no such authority left.'[2]

Anti-Semitic incidents such as this came as a huge shock to Jews in Nazi Germany. Jews formed a miniscule minority. Between 1871 and 1931 they never exceeded 1.09 per cent of the population. In 1933, 525,000 Jews were living in Germany, with 144,000 of them living in Berlin. By 1939, just 300,000 Jews remained. From 1940 to 1944, 134,000 German Jews were deported to the slave labour and extermination camps in Poland. The total number of German Jews killed in the Holocaust has been estimated at 160,000. German Jews who survived were mostly in mixed marriages or were the children of such unions.[3]

Jews had resided in the Germanic areas of Europe for centuries. They periodically suffered persecution. The 1871 German constitution offered Jews full citizenship rights. Religious conversion to Christianity was allowed too. Many Jews integrated and assimilated with the German majority. From 1881 to 1933, 19,469 Jews converted to Protestantism, for example. During the First World War, 100,000 Jews signed up to fight and 70,000 served at the front, with 30,000 of them receiving bravery awards. A total of 12,000 Jews were killed.

The rate of intermarriage between Jews and German Christians increased rapidly before Hitler came to power. In 1901 to 1905, 15 per cent of Jews were married to non-Jews. By 1933, this figure had increased to 44 per cent. Jewish assimilation in Germany was progressing at a faster rate than in any other European nation. Assimilated Jews became indistinguishable from Gentiles. 'I suspect if someone had asked my father or mother in 1930 or 1931: "What are you?," they would have said "German",' recalls Claus Moser, the son of a Jewish banker, born in 1922. 'My father was in the First World War. He got the Iron Cross. My parents would never have denied their Jewishness, but first came being German. I'm sure before Hitler came to power, although I went once a year to the synagogue with my father, it wasn't a big deal.'[4]

Klaus Scheuenberg, born in 1925, recalled:

My father was, like many middle class German Jews, a naïve, apolitical individual. When Hitler came to power he created a new [military] decoration, the Front Fighter's Cross. The cross was sent to everyone who had fought on the front in the last [First] world war, along with a huge certificate [from Hitler] that began, 'My dear comrade'. The Nazis didn't have a list of who was Christian and who was Jewish yet, so my father was sent one. After he got it, my father said, 'Hitler can't be all that bad. Look, he's awarded me this medal.' How naïve![5]

Jews in Germany were prominent in business, commerce, culture and the professions. In 1933, 61 per cent were employed in business and commerce, compared to 18 per cent of Germans. About 40 per cent of Germans were employed in industry, compared to 22 per cent of Jews. Only 2 per cent of Jews worked in agriculture, compared to 29 per cent of Germans. Between 1929 and 1932, 25 per cent of all employees in the retail trade were Jewish. Jews owned 41 per cent of all iron and scrap firms and 57 per cent of metal businesses. They were very prominent in banking and the financial services sector of the economy. In 1930, 43 per cent of leading positions in German banks were held by Jews. In 1928, 80 per cent of the leading members of Berlin's stock exchange were Jewish.

Jews also prospered in the professions. In 1933, 381 Jewish judges and state prosecutors, and 16 per cent of lawyers, were Jewish. Jews held 12 per cent of all university lecturing posts, and an additional 7 per cent of academics were Jews who had converted to Christianity. About 10 per cent of doctors and dentists were Jewish. From 1905 to 1931, ten of the thirty-two Germans awarded Nobel prizes for science were Jewish. They were highly visible in the arts, film, the theatre and journalism. In 1930, 80 per cent of all theatre directors in Berlin were Jewish, and 75 per cent of the plays produced there were written by Jews.[6]

The amazing success of Jews in so many areas of German society was deeply resented by a large number of Germans. As Ursa Meyer-Semlies, a German Gentile, born in 1914, remembers:

It was said 'The Jews are our misfortune'. It was always said through propaganda, they are a small minority and have the most important positions, especially in every city, in every large place, and they have all the stores in their hands. I didn't think anything about it, but at once one became aware of it. And one looked around . . . the big textile stores, cigar shops . . . music supply stores, jewellery shops were all in the hands of Jews. On the Memel River were big coffin works, located there to be close to the supplies of logs floated down the river. The Jews had that too.[7]

Ellen Frey, also born in 1914, claims many Germans held similar negative attitudes. 'The Jews,' our parents told us, 'are everywhere. They're in the theatre, at the highest positions. They're sitting everywhere and have us in the palm of their hands. That's what our parents told us. They sort of push us Germans aside and take all the best jobs . . . Yes one thought perhaps it's very good if they leave, so we get a turn . . . That was the opinion back then.'[8] Erna Tietz, a German Christian, born in 1921, claims it was commonplace for Germans to say in conversation: 'When dealing with Jews pay close attention because "The Jew" always works happily for his own pocket.'[9]

In 1934, Reinhard Heydrich spelled out the fate that awaited Jews inside Nazi Germany:

The Jews' possibilities for living are to be curtailed, and not simply in the economic sense. Germany must be for them a country without a future, in which the residual older generations can certainly die, but in which the young cannot live, so that the stimulus to emigrate remains acute. The methods of rowdy anti-Semitism are to be rejected. One does not fight rats with a revolver, but rather with poison and gas.[10]

The persecution of the Jews was a stage-by-stage process. The Nazis wanted to force Jews out of the economy, to alienate them from their neighbours and then drive them out of Germany. Those Germans who had mixed with Jews socially before Hitler came to power subsequently marginalised them and then ostracised them. There were 400 different anti-Jewish laws enacted by the Nazi regime. Jewish community leaders described this as 'Judicial Terror'. Jews were excluded from jobs in the civil service, the legal profession, secondary schools and universities.

The first concrete measure taken against the Jews came on 1 April 1933 with a one-day national boycott of Jewish shops. Nazi storm troopers stood menacingly outside Jewish stores holding up placards with slogans such as: 'Whoever eats Jewish products will die from them!' Arnold Biegelson, a Jewish clerk, recalled:

SA men stood in front of the smeared display windows carrying large signs which read 'Don't buy from Jews'. My mother, who didn't look Jewish at all, was stopped by an SA guard after leaving one of the shops. He said: 'You can see the sign, but you go in anyway. We'll remember your face.' We didn't take those threats seriously. At that time, we were still allowed to move around freely.[11]

A week after the boycott, the Jewish newspaper *Jüdische Rundschau* (Jewish Panorama) published an article entitled: 'Wear it with pride, the Yellow Star' by Robert Weltch, a leading figure in the Zionist community:

The National Socialist press calls us the 'enemy of the nation' and leaves us defenceless. It is not true the Jews betrayed Germany. If they betrayed anyone, it was themselves . . . Because the Jew did not display his Judaism with pride, because he tried to avoid the Jewish issue . . . The Jew is now marked by the Yellow Star . . . A powerful symbol is to be found in the fact the [Nazi] boycott leadership gave orders that a sign 'with a yellow star on a black background' was to be pasted on boycotted shops.

The regulation is intended as a brand, a sign of contempt. We will take it and make it a badge of honour . . . Jews, take it up, the Star of David and wear it with pride![12]

Weltch seriously underestimated how difficult life was becoming for Jews. Effigies of Jews were burned during SA parades. Copies of the violently anti-Semitic newspaper *Der Stürmer* appeared on street-advertising display pillars. The front cover featured physically repellent and grotesque images of Jews.[13] On 20 August 1933, local people in Würzburg complained to the Nazi district leader about a German woman having a sexual relationship with a local Jewish man. The SS humiliatingly paraded the man through the streets, wearing a sign that read: 'I have lived out of wedlock with a German woman.' The Jewish man was placed in 'protective custody' by the SS for two weeks. This action was completely illegal, as there was no law at this stage prohibiting sexual relations between Jews and non-Jews.[14]

The assumption by many German Jews that extreme Nazi anti-Semitism of this kind would fizzle out proved illusory. As Claus Moser remembers:

You have to remember I would be passing shops that said "Jews, don't buy here". It was all around. I think I was frightened with all these endless brown shirts and black shirts everywhere. All round the town were these little advertising towers on the streets on which they would show horrible pictures of Jews. I thought what a disgusting, horrible time, but we'll get through this and in a year or two these horrible people will be gone. It then began to be one's main consciousness that one was Jewish and the sense of danger gradually increased.[15]

Gad Beck, born in 1923 into a well-to-do Berlin family, had been one of the most well-liked pupils in his class before Hitler came to power. 'Then all of a sudden strange things started happening,' he recalled:

'Herr Teacher can I sit somewhere else?' said one pupil. 'Gerhard has sweaty and stinking Jewish feet.' Children are often more direct and brutal than adults. That sort of rejection really hurt. At lunch, I told my family what happened. My parents' reaction disappointed me and confused me totally. They evidently didn't take the event seriously. Soothingly, they babbled on about how things would soon calm down.[16]

Contrary to popular myth, the Gestapo did not place a high priority on persecuting law-abiding Jews in the first two years of Hitler's rule. In the city of Krefeld, only eight Jews were arrested by the Gestapo during the whole of 1933, and seven of those were active communists.[17] Most Jews who ended up being questioned by the Gestapo were those who responded vociferously to anti-Semitic insults in public places. On 17 August 1935, a fifty-five-year-old Jewish woman became agitated with two youths in Cologne city centre. She saw them selling a newspaper, with the headline: 'Whoever is involved with Jews pollutes the nation'. 'It's disgusting for you to sell that newspaper,' she told the youths. They reported her comments to a local SS officer and she ended up being interrogated by the Gestapo. She claimed her comment was fired off in anger, without thinking of the possible consequences. This case was subsequently dismissed by the public prosecutor.[18]

This incident occurred during the summer of 1935 when Nazi anti-Semitic agitation was escalating in many German cities and towns. Jewish shops endured a fresh wave of boycotts. Impromptu signs were erected on the road boundaries of many towns and villages with the slogan: 'Jews are not wanted here'. In some places, Jews were banned from libraries, cinemas, swimming pools, beer halls, bowling alleys and parks. Jewish cemeteries were routinely vandalised by marauding SA teenage gangs. There were strong calls by Nazi activists for the introduction of new laws banning marriage and sexual relations between Jews and non-Jews.

Responding to this 'pressure from below', Hitler decided to clarify the legal status of Jews. The Reichstag was summoned to a special session in Nuremberg on 15 September 1935, and a new set of far-reaching Reich citizenship laws was agreed. The 'Nuremberg Laws' became an integral part of the Nazi drive to enhance the 'biological purity' of the German race. No 'full blooded Jew', meaning a person with two sets of Jewish parents and grandparents, was now deemed to be a German citizen or allowed to marry or have sexual relations with anyone who was Aryan. Jews were not even allowed to employ 'pure blooded German women' under the age of forty-five as domestic help. Nor were they allowed to raise the German flag any more. For old Jewish 'Great War' veterans this was a bitter pill. Jews of 'mixed parentage' consisting of a German 'Aryan' and a Jew (known as *Mischlinge* –'cross-breed') were classed as 'subjects of the state', which denied them full citizenship rights. Hitler presented the Nuremberg Laws as providing the foundation for 'peaceful co-existence between Germans and Jews'.[19]

'The Nuremberg Laws, in the absence of interpretive regulations', Norman Ebbut, *The Times* Berlin correspondent, commented,

> are being used to justify every type of indignity and persecution, not by individuals, but by the established authorities . . . The opportunities offered by the new laws are unlimited . . . Any individual can report his Jewish enemy or competitor as having been seen in company of 'Aryan' women, or trump up alleged business obligations from the past . . . Unless some attempt is made in high quarters to check the ferocity of the anti-Semitic fanatics, the Jews will be condemned, as it were, to run round blindly in circles until they die. This is the process to which the term 'cold pogrom' has been applied.[20]

A legal definition laid down the differences between 'pure' or 'full Jews' (*Volljuden*) and 'half-Jews' (*Mischlinge*), who were the children of mixed marriages between German 'Aryans' and Jews. A 'full' Jew was any person with three or more Jewish grandparents. The '*Mischlinge*' were divided into two categories: (i) first degree: a person with two Jewish grandparents – the nearest to a German citizen, and (ii) second degree: those with one Jewish grandparent. Both categories were not considered 'Aryans', but those defined as a '*Mischlinge*', particularly those of the first degree, mostly survived deportation and extermination during the Holocaust.[21] In mixed marriages, the Jewish partners were safe from deportation, provided they did not get divorced and especially if they had children.

Cecile Hensel, a good-natured young girl, born in 1923, lived in the small university town of Erlangen. Her father was the noted philosopher Paul Hensel, who died in 1931. She counted among her ancestors Moses Mendelssohn, known as 'The German Socrates', and the celebrated composer Felix Mendelssohn. Free spirited and open hearted, Cecile grew up knowing very little about political events in Nazi Germany. Her liberal-minded father told her: 'Big cities have a university, but small towns are a university.' Cecile was just eleven when her mother explained the Nuremberg Laws to her:

I was brought up as a Christian in the Lutheran faith. My mother was an Aryan. I said to my mother, 'What is a *Mischling*?' She replied: 'It's a person who no longer fits in.' Everyone wants to belong, and I didn't belong now. I was turned by these laws into an outsider. I can remember when somebody at school said to me, 'You're Jewish.' I replied, 'I have a very famous Jew as one of my ancestors, Moses Mendelssohn, that's true, but I'm not Jewish.' Then this girl said to me in a loud voice: 'Ah his name was Moses, you see, he was a Jew!' Then I got thrown out of school. It was such a terrible time. I stayed at home all the time, like a prisoner. When I awoke in the morning, I was terrified. When I went to bed in the evening, I was terrified.[22]

Dorothea Schlosser, another 'half Jewish' girl, born in 1921, who lived in Berlin, had a very similar experience: 'My aversion to Hitler began with a remark made by the principal of my school. He said: "There are Jews and there are Christians, but worst of all are the half-breeds." That really hit home . . . I cried a lot in that period. I used to look at myself in the mirror and think, "Are you really that horrible?"'[23]

After the Nuremberg Laws many Jews realised they were fighting a losing battle and fled abroad. 'One thing I remember more clearly than anything else is the day we left Germany in April 1936,' recalls Claus Moser, whose family left for Britain:

What I find most extraordinary to rethink is that there I was, a thirteen-year-old boy, carrying a cello, going to England. This journey was momentous, except that I and my brother did not know we were going for ever. It was a journey into the unknown. I don't think I had the feeling I was escaping death. I think I felt Germany had turned into a horrible country. A disgusting country. We Jews are the focus of all the horrors. So although we were not escaping immediate violence, it was a feeling of enormous relief when we left.[24]

With the benefit of hindsight, it may seem surprising that more German Jews did not see the approaching calamity. Women, perhaps, seemed to grasp the dangers for Jews more quickly. 'The women protested strongly in the home,' a Jewish woman recalls:

They would say to their husbands: 'Why should we stay here and wait for eventual ruin? Isn't it better to build up a concrete existence somewhere else, before our strength is exhausted by the constant physical and psychic pressure? Isn't the future of our children more important than a completely senseless holding out?' All the women, without exception, shared this opinion; while the men passionately spoke against it. I discussed this with my husband. Like all the other men, he simply couldn't imagine how one could leave one's homeland.[25]

The Nuremberg Laws allowed Jews to be arrested for a new crime: 'race defilement' (*Rassenschande*).[26] It criminalised sexual relations between Jews and non-Jews. This made it easier for Jews to be denounced to the Gestapo for breaking the law. It was, therefore, only after the introduction of the Nuremberg Laws that the Gestapo became more heavily involved in Jewish persecution. The Nuremberg Laws applied to all Jews and German 'Aryans' who either had an extra-marital sexual relationship with each other or were suspected of having one. Jewish and 'Aryan' men were supposed to be punished equally. In reality, Jews charged with this offence were treated more harshly during interrogations. German 'Aryan' women rarely faced any custodial punishment, but Jewish women were often held in 'protective custody'. Convicted 'Aryan' men received shorter sentences than Jews, but after their release they were treated as social pariahs too. German 'Aryan' women often lost the custody of their children after being accused of having sexual relationships with Jews.[27]

Many Gestapo offices set up dedicated 'race defilement' sections. In Berlin, the Gestapo often used entrapment techniques. A number of teenage girls and prostitutes were recruited by the Gestapo for the express purpose of luring Jewish men into compromising sexual situations. Elsewhere, the Gestapo mounted prying surveillance operations on couples suspected of being involved in illegal sexual relationships. There were often raids on the homes of couples to catch them in the act of sexual intercourse.

Between 1935 and 1940, 1,900 people were convicted of 'race defilement'. The number of prosecutions differed widely in each region. In Hamburg, between 1936 and 1943, 429 'race defilers' were put on trial. In Frankfurt during the same period only 92 were convicted. The average sentence was eighteen months for this offence. Those convicted served sentences in normal prisons or in prisons using hard labour. In March 1936, the Gestapo complained to the Ministry of Justice that sentences passed by judges for this offence were too lenient. Heydrich demanded that sentences of penal servitude be applied more regularly.[28]

The detection of cases of 'race defilement' by the Gestapo came primarily from denouncements from the public. The historian Robert Gellately's study of 'race defilement' cases in the area of Lower Franconia showed that 57 per cent of such cases began with a denouncement from an ordinary German citizen. As Gellately states, 'without the active collaboration of the general population it would have been next to impossible for the Gestapo to enforce these kinds of [anti-Jewish] racial policies'.[29] In the files for the city of Düsseldorf, there are 255 such cases concerning Jewish men and 137 German men on 'race defilement' charges. The Gestapo required a much higher level of corroboration in cases of 'race defilement' than for minor political offences. Three people were required to corroborate any charge or it was dismissed, with a stern warning and a promise of future surveillance. This stipulation kept the number of cases ending up in court at a low level.[30]

Those charged with 'race defilement' tended to be under forty and came from diverse backgrounds. A judgment administered to a Jewish man in the Hamburg Court in November 1937 noted: 'The fact that the accused and the witness [his German partner] had known one another since 1920, and they have had a lasting relationship since 1927, could not be regarded as a mitigating circumstance, since the relationship continued for one and a half years after the passage of the Nuremberg Laws and was only terminated through the arrest of the accused.' He was sentenced to thirty months of penal servitude.[31] A well-to-do Jewish businessman called Karl, who was married to a German 'Aryan' woman, was denounced anonymously for 'race defilement'. The letter to the Gestapo claimed he sexually abused his workers and housemaids. The Gestapo found the charge was groundless.[32]

In another case, a twenty-year-old Jewish housemaid described having sex with two 'Aryan' German men in full pornographic detail during a confession to the Gestapo that runs to several single-spaced typed pages. Rather than simply asking the woman to admit to sexual intercourse, which was all that was required for a conviction on a 'race defilement' charge, the Gestapo officer clearly wanted to hear the full intimate sexual details. Some Gestapo officers evidently gained some prurient pleasure from listening to women, usually under the age of forty, discussing these intimate sexual encounters.[33]

Jews appear in Gestapo files for a range of other reasons. Prominent Jews were often put under close surveillance and harassment. Many of these files are quite extensive and were frequently updated. The extremely bulky case files of Siegfried Kleff, Michael Steinbeck and Josef Kahn are typical. Dr Siegfried Kleff (born 1882) was a Jewish Rabbi. He lived in Düsseldorf with his wife Lilli.[34] In February 1937, he became the chairman of the Düsseldorf section of the National Association of Jewish Congregations in Germany. This organisation helped Jews to emigrate. In March 1937, the Gestapo in Berlin sent information to its Düsseldorf branch informing it that Siegfried was suspected of wanting to fraternise with Germans, and asking whether he was really the committed Zionist he claimed to be. In May 1937, Siegfried was fined twenty Reichsmarks for mentioning a banned newspaper to his Jewish congregation. On 19 August 1937, Kleff made a request to emigrate to the Netherlands. On 30 August 1938, the Gestapo not only refused to let him go, but promptly confiscated his passport. During the *Kristallnacht* pogrom of 9–10 November 1938, Kleff was placed in 'protective custody' in a local concentration camp, but released twelve days later. A new entry in his Gestapo file appears on 21 November 1941 which records that 315 books had been confiscated from him. The final entry in his file is dated 21 January 1942. It blandly records that Kleff had been transported to Poland. Certain death awaited him. In all this time, the Gestapo had never subjected him to a single interrogation.[35]

The Gestapo placed Michael Steinbeck (born 1880), a medical specialist, under similar surveillance, on suspicion he might be involved with the Freemasons. The Nazi regime was extremely hostile to Freemasonry. In *Mein Kampf*, Hitler had claimed Jews used the organisation as a secret network to gain control and influence over business and financial organisations. Nazi antagonism towards Freemasonry was therefore closely linked to anti-Semitism.

Steinbeck was originally born in Bucharest and lived in Duisburg with his wife Margarete.[36] The file contains a lot of material about his activities over a lengthy period. The Gestapo discovered an invitation for Steinbeck to attend a meeting of a Masonic Lodge on 22 March 1937. Whether he actually attended is not mentioned in his file, but it is noted that this particular Masonic Lodge was being dissolved at that time. There are a large number of leaflets in his file from a seafaring association called the 'Fraternity of Free Mariners' in the Rhineland. It seems Steiner had been active in this organisation during the Weimar period, and had acted as the editor of one of its periodicals called 'Devilfish'. A copy of an article by Michael Steinbeck is also in his file. He introduced himself in the article as a doctor who had been in charge of a hospital in Tangier in Morocco, financed by a Muslim charity, during the First World War. Steinbeck goes on to make critical comments about the German authorities, who had seemingly driven a local farmer to suicide. He also claimed that anyone who had worked abroad was treated with suspicion when they returned. All this concerned matters that had occurred years before the Nazis came to power. The Gestapo arrested him in 1937 for being involved in a Masonic discussion group. There was also some suspicion that he might be involved in 'race defilement'. No charges were ever brought against Michael Steinbeck by the Gestapo and his ultimate fate is unknown.[37]

Josef Kahn (born 1886), was living in Düsseldorf with his Jewish wife Emilie when he was arrested by the Gestapo for being part of a group that studied and discussed the politically neutral international language of Esperanto.[38] There are letters in his file from a German 'Aryan' woman of a personal nature that brought him under suspicion of 'race defilement' too. The Gestapo arrested Kahn on 26 April 1937 in the Hotel Fürstenhof in Düsseldorf at the end of a meeting of local Esperantists. He was interrogated on 1 May. Kahn told the Gestapo he had served as a soldier and wireless operator in the 'Great War'. During the Weimar era, he voted for liberal parties. He claimed to be a German nationalist, and supported 'all measures of the Nazi-government, except those concerning Jews'. He admitted to being a member of the German branch of the Esperanto Association since 1911. He lectured frequently on the subject, and regarded his work for the organisation as purely recreational and totally apolitical. Josef Kahn was released on 5 May 1937. No charges were brought against him. His ultimate fate is not recorded.[39]

It was during 1938 that the persecution of Jews escalated most dramatically inside Nazi Germany. A special decree of 26 April 1938 obliged all Jews to record all their wealth in terms of money and goods. In June 1938, police were ordered to rearrest any Jew who had completed a sentence for breaching the Nuremberg Laws, and transfer them to a concentration camp. By the autumn of 1938, up to 75 per cent of all Jewish businesses had been closed down.

On 7 November 1938, Herschel Grynszpan, a seventeen-year-old German-Jewish refugee living in Paris, found out that his Polish parents had been deported from Hanover to Poland. He was surprised, shocked and angry. He walked into the German Embassy in Paris carrying a loaded revolver, with the aim of killing the German ambassador. The first person he encountered was a minor German official called Ernst vom Rath. Without any warning, the teenager fired five shots at him. Three bullets missed, a fourth grazed vom Rath's chin, but the fifth lodged in his stomach. Two days later, Ernst vom Rath died of his wounds in a Paris hospital. There was a bitter irony in vom Rath's portrayal as a slain 'German patriot' in German newspapers. He had recently been under surveillance by the Gestapo because of alleged 'anti-Nazi attitudes' and allegations of homosexuality. In his trial, Herschel Grynszpan claimed he had been involved in a homosexual relationship with the diplomat. Whether this allegation was true has never been fully resolved. A news blackout, ordered by Joseph Goebbels, prevented these details from being known outside the court at the time.

The murder of this minor diplomat was to have enormous ramifications. On the night of 9–10 November 1938 violence and destruction was unleashed on Jews throughout Germany in a manner never seen before in Hitler's Germany. *Der Stürmer* called it 'just revenge' for vom Rath's murder by a 'Jew Pig'. 'Action against Jews will shortly be underway,' wrote an excited Joseph Goebbels in his diary. 'They are not to be interrupted. However, measures are to be taken in co-operation with the Order Police for looting and other measures to be prevented. The arrests of about 20–30,000 Jews are to be prepared.'[40]

Many Jews had been attacked, robbed and murdered before, but those crimes were mainly committed by brown-shirted SA thugs taking the law into their own hands. Now, the Hitler government organised a nationwide anti-Jewish pogrom. Heinrich Müller, the head of the Gestapo, sent a memorandum to local Gestapo offices at 11.55 p.m. on 9 November reporting the violent actions against Jews that were already being undertaken. Müller told Gestapo officers to stop the looting, but not to impede the setting fire to synagogues or the vandalising of Jewish shops that was going on.[41] In a telegram at 1.20 a.m., Reinhard Heydrich gave more detailed orders as to how the demonstrations should be organised:

For instance, synagogues are to be burned down when there is no danger of fire to the surrounding buildings. Business and private apartments of Jews may be destroyed, but not looted. The demonstrations that take place should not be hindered by the police. As many Jews, especially the rich ones, are to be arrested as can be accommodated in existing prisons. Upon arrest appropriate concentration camps should be contacted immediately in order to confine them in these camps as soon as possible.[42]

This well-orchestrated night of horror became known as *Kristallnacht* ('Night of the Broken Glass'). These anti-Jewish riots were reported throughout Germany. Nazi thugs and SS men set alight synagogues and prayer houses. Irreplaceable objects of huge religious value were tossed on to a funeral pyre of pure anti-Semitic hate. Individual Jews were beaten up, homes and businesses ransacked. Around ninety-one Jews were murdered and thirty thousand Jews were arrested, allegedly 'for their own safety'. Approximately ten thousand Jews were sent to the three main concentration camps: Dachau, Sachsenhausen and Buchenwald. Nearly all the Jews arrested were released within six weeks. In a press release, Joseph Goebbels claimed German actions were 'understandable'.

It seems some ordinary Germans were shocked by the wanton violence and destruction of *Kristallnacht*. A secret report compiled by socialist informants for the exiled SPD noted:

The brutal measures against the Jews have caused great indignation among the population. People spoke their minds openly, and many Aryans were arrested as a result. When it became known that a Jewish woman had been taken from nursing her child, even a police official said this was too much. 'Where is Germany heading, if these methods are being used?' As a result, he was arrested too. After the Jews, who are going to be the next victims, this is what people are asking. Will it be the Catholics?[43]

One day after *Kristallnacht*, two women – Helene Kohn and Margarethe Fischer – denounced a German 'Aryan' called Leopold Funk, because he had talked openly in the street about the anti-Jewish violence in what was described as a 'startling and annoying manner'.[44] The two women reported his angry outburst to a policeman and Funk was arrested. He was held in 'protective custody' in Stuttgart pending further Gestapo investigation. The two women claimed that, as they had passed him in the street at around 11 a.m. on 10 November, he had been standing outside a 'smashed Jewish shop', and he had called those responsible for the vandalism a 'bunch of dogs' and 'Huns' who had attacked Jews, whom he described as 'harmless people'. The Gestapo interrogated Leopold on 14 November 1938. He said he never knew the smashed shop was owned by Jews. His outburst was merely a general and harmless rant about the destruction of property occurring in his local community on that night. He claimed he did not see Jewish people as 'harmless' and expressed loyalty to the anti-Semitic policies of the Nazi government, 'without any reservations'. The Gestapo officer, in his report on the case, felt Leopold's statement about not knowing it was a Jewish shop was 'implausible'. After serving six days in prison, Leopold Funk was released, without any charge. When the Gestapo officer who originally dealt with the case found out about this lenient sentence he complained to a Gestapo official in Stuttgart that the case should have been dealt with by a 'Special Court' and a much harsher sentence imposed.[45]

Those who were willing to show any sympathy with the plight of the Jews were a diminishing minority, as a Social Democrat report from December 1938 makes clear:

The broad mass of the people has not condoned the destruction, but we should nevertheless not overlook the fact that there are people among the working class who do not defend the Jews. There are certain circles where you are not very popular if you speak disparagingly about the recent events ... Berlin: the population's attitude was not fully unanimous. When the Jewish synagogue was burning, a large number of women could be heard saying, 'That's the right way to do it – it's a pity there aren't more Jews inside it, that would be the best way to smoke out the whole lousy lot of them.' . . . If there has been any speaking out in the Reich against the Jewish pogroms, the excess of arson and looting, it has been in Hamburg and the neighbouring Elbe district. People from Hamburg are generally not anti-Semitic.[46]

The exodus of Jews leaving Germany increased after *Kristallnacht.* 'Countless new regulations went into effect in the next few months that made it virtually impossible for Jews in Germany to maintain any semblance of their normal middle class lives,' Gerhard Beck, recalled:

Radios, telephones and valuables were confiscated. We were no longer permitted to run businesses, buy books or newspapers, own motor vehicles, or use public transportation, and times for buying groceries were limited. The Nazis introduced the *Judenbann*, off-limit zones for Jews. That meant Jews were prohibited from using certain streets, public places and facilities in the city, such as theatres, cinemas, or public bathhouses or swimming pools. Jews who didn't have a Jewish-sounding first name were forced to add either 'Sara' or 'Israel' to their name and a 'J' was stamped on our passports. It was absolutely prohibited for Jews to attend 'Aryan' educational institutions, and many Jewish organisations were disbanded. If that weren't enough, the Jews were forced to pay repair costs for all that had been destroyed on *Kristallnacht;* one billion Reich marks had to be paid to the German government as an 'atonement penalty'.[47]

Conditions for Jews continued to deteriorate. On 19 September 1941, all Jews over the age of six were required to wear a yellow Star of David, with the word 'Jew' (*Jude*) in black letters in the centre. Jews tried to remain law-abiding in order not to attract the attention of the Gestapo. One Jewish woman, denounced to the Gestapo for uttering critical comments about the regime, told a Gestapo officer during her interrogation, on 4 July 1941: 'As a Jew, I am very careful about making statements of any kind, and I weigh every word in advance.'[48]

SD reports on the public reaction to the introduction of the yellow star show it was well received by the German public. In August 1941 an SD report in Biefeld reported that local 'Aryan' Germans felt the measure would deter the population from having any further associations with Jews. An SD report from September 1941 on the introduction of the yellow star noted:

> The above named police order has evoked genuine satisfaction in all classes of the population. It constituted the major topic of conversation on Saturday and Sunday. Time after time one hears the opinion that now the Jews in Germany have lost every possibility of concealing themselves. Generally it is pointed out that only through this order will the complete effectiveness of the restrictive measures against Jews' use of cinemas, restaurants and markets be achieved.[49]

The Gestapo pursued Jews who tried to evade regulations concerning the yellow star or for not using the official Jewish names of Sarah and Israel. A twenty-three-year-old German man, who had a Jewish father and German mother, signed a police statement in March 1944 for a minor traffic offence using his own surname rather than 'Israel'. The police passed on this information to the Gestapo. The man was promptly sent to a concentration camp. It was then decided he would be transported to Poland, which would have meant almost certain death in the Holocaust. His employer wrote a long letter to the Gestapo pleading for mercy. It worked. He was released, with a stern warning over his future behaviour.[50]

Many Jewish women in mixed marriages with 'Aryan' men often refused to wear the yellow star. A Gestapo officer wrote of a Jewish woman who he had arrested for this offence:

It has always been a cheap excuse to claim that one did not know anything. The Jewess Helena claims to know nothing about laws relating to the Jews. It is typical of Jews to give such lame excuses. In reality they just assume that if they are not known as Jews [and married to Aryans] they need not bring it to notice on their own. So far so good and if their racial identity becomes public they can get away with a mild fine. Lately, Jews in mixed marriages are committing this offence. Therefore, it seems necessary to impose a jail sentence instead of a fine.[51]

On 1 October 1941, when the first deportations to Poland began, the Reich Association of German Jews recorded that 163,696 Jews still remained in Germany.[52] By this time, as well as facing a wide range of other restrictions, Jews were not allowed to use buses or trains, go to museums or art galleries, own cars, buy flowers, eat in restaurants, or sit on deck chairs. Each Jewish residence was required from 13 March 1942 to display a white paper star at the entrance. Jews were not even allowed to keep pets. It was extremely difficult for Jews to grasp the enormous tragedy that engulfed them. It is hard to understand the consequences of a tidal wave in the hours of darkness.

Most deportations of German Jews took place from October 1941 to the summer of 1942. During this period, more than a hundred thousand Jews were transported by trains to ghettos in Lodz, Riga and Minsk and to the extermination camps at Belzec and Auschwitz-Birkenau. The only Jews who remained in Germany after this wave of expulsions were those in mixed marriages and their children. The Nazis created what they called a 'model concentration camp' at Theresienstadt to give the misleading impression to the outside world that there was nothing sinister about these deportations. The decision to deport Jews from the Old Reich (*Altreich*) was influenced by Adolf Eichmann's successful forced emigration of 50,000 Austrian Jews. Heydrich decided that the creation of large-scale ghettos in Germany would breed disease and crime, which might affect the social cohesion of the general population.[53]

Eyewitness accounts and post-war war trials show how the Jewish deportations in Nazi Germany were carried out. Jews were transported in most cities during the hours of darkness or very early in the morning. It's difficult to know whether Jews knew their fate would be extermination. Rumours circulated widely in Germany about the mass shootings in the Soviet Union, during the latter months of 1941, but Jews in Poland, when the deportations began, were not being gassed. It is questionable to argue that Jews must have known, but went anyhow without protesting, or that Germans must have known too, but did not protest. The vast majority of Germans appear to have been indifferent to the ultimate fate of the German-Jewish population. Years of vicious propaganda demonising Jews as physically repellent, parrot-nosed demons seeped into even the most previously open minds. Posters, films and newspapers were full of these anti-Semitic images on a daily basis. As Max Reiner recalled: 'I couldn't pick up a German newspaper any more. Jews . . . Jews. It seemed as if there were no other subjects. They exceeded themselves in insults, threats, ridicule.'[54]

In Cologne, a 1954 Gestapo trial revealed that 11,500 Jews were transported in eighteen different transports that began on 21 October 1941. By the end of 1942, 80 per cent of all Cologne's Jews were deported. The pattern of each transport followed a similar procedure. Himmler's RSHA in Berlin sent a letter or telegram to the head of the local Gestapo office ordering them to assemble a transport of Jews to a specific ghetto in Poland or a designated concentration camp.

The Gestapo was responsible for organising the Jewish deportations. There was a set of official guidelines on the process, which listed all the regulations surrounding them. Every stage of the process was meticulously recorded. Gestapo officials contacted leaders of the local Jewish community requesting them to prepare a list of deportees. Valerie Wolfenstein, the daughter of a Jewish architect, described how the process operated in Berlin: 'The persons received a letter notifying them what day they were to be ready. They had to make a list of all their property and take it to the office of the Jewish community. The Gestapo delegated all the preliminary work to this office.'[55] Each deportee was then informed of the date and time of their deportation and assigned a number, but this letter often arrived just two days before departure. At the Jewish community office, deportees were required to sign a declaration which stated that as a Jew they were an enemy of the state and all their property now belonged to it. The Gestapo issued guidelines on how the private possessions Jews had left in their homes were to be auctioned off. These macabre auctions of confiscated Jewish property occurred alongside the deportation process.

The Gestapo out-sourced the decision on the individuals who should be deported to local Jewish community leaders, but retained a final say on each deportee. The Gestapo co-operated closely with Jewish orderlies, appointed by the Jewish community, and Kripo to transport Jews from their homes to the deportation centres. Once they reached there, the Gestapo carried out a number of final checks on them. Every person was checked against the typed transportation list and obliged to display their call-up number prominently on their clothing. Luggage was then searched. Property, cash and valuables were liberally confiscated by Gestapo officers. Jews were only allowed to take a single suitcase of belongings with them and were forced to buy their own one-way ticket to oblivion. Witnesses report that people were 'herded like animals' on to the waiting trains.[56] There was little sign of compassion by the Gestapo during the whole process.

It is known that some Germans helped Jews in hiding and

provided them with food, clothing and shelter. It has been estimated that there were around five thousand Jews in hiding, and 1,402 hidden Jews emerged in 1945 in Berlin.[57] One of them was Rolf Joseph, who worked at the IG Farben factory in the Lichtenburg district. He decided to go underground and live illegally in order to escape transportation during the summer of 1942. 'For the first four months we had no shelter,' he later recalled. 'Hundreds of "illegals" as we called ourselves were living like us: we would ride in the S-Bahn [overground] or U-Bahn [underground] till late at night, always in fear of being stopped to show our identification cards with the large "J" on them. We spent nights in parks and woods and when the weather was very bad in railway station washrooms.'[58]

Rolf was arrested at Berlin's *Wedding* station by the military police, who examined his identification card and checked it against a list of those defined as 'deserters'. The Gestapo interrogated him for several days, as he later explained:

> The Gestapo insisted on knowing where I had been living. I assured them that I had no shelter. Everyone [at the Gestapo office] refused to believe it. Time and again they demanded the names of the people who were sheltering me, but I refused to give them any. Then they took me into a cellar, tied my hands and feet, strapped me on a wooden box and gave me twenty-five lashes with a horsewhip on my naked buttocks. I had to count out each stroke.[59]

The Gestapo often became entangled in messy disputes over the possessions Jews had left behind in their homes prior to deportation. A typical case involved the disposal of the furniture of a Jewish woman who was sent to the Theresienstadt concentration camp. [Sara] Martha Peet (born 1892) in Bingen on the Rhine, lived in Düsseldorf at the time of her deportation.[60] Her landlord had informed the Gestapo that as a divorced Jewish woman she had no right to remain in Germany. The

Gestapo soon established that Martha Peet had been married to a German 'Aryan', but they were now divorced. This left her in an extremely vulnerable position. The couple had two children, who were considered as having 'German blood' and therefore exempt from transportation. A son, aged seventeen, lived with his mother. A daughter, aged nineteen, lived with her father. The Gestapo decided that transportation should be applied to Martha Peet. The lawyer representing her former husband, Paul, claimed the furniture of his ex-wife on behalf of his children, after she had been transported to Theresienstadt. The Gestapo agreed to this request. Her son was placed under the custody of her husband. There is no record of what subsequently happened to Martha Peet after her transportation. Her chances of survival were extremely slim.[61]

Public reactions to the deportations are not extensively recorded, but most German citizens knew about them, and hundreds of thousands witnessed them first-hand. In Bavaria, only one official government report on the deportation of Jews, dated 10 December 1941, has survived. It claimed the population 'took note of the fact approvingly'. An SD report for the district of Minden recorded:

> Although this action by the state police [Gestapo] was being kept secret, the deportation of the Jews was discussed in all sections of the population. Accordingly, a great number of comments were collected to measure public attitudes. Individual statements that one should thank the Führer for freeing us of Jewish blood were overheard. A worker said, for example, 'that had the Jews been taken care of fifty years earlier, then we would not have had to endure either a world war or the current war'.[62]

In some places misgivings over the deportations were observed. An SD officer, observing a transport of Jews from Detmold on 28 July 1942, noted the following public misgivings:

The Jews assembled before the transport in the market place in Lemgo. The fact occasioned the population to appear in truly great numbers . . . It was observed that a large part of the old citizens, supposedly also [Nazi] party members, negatively criticised the transport of Jews from Germany. A position against the transport was taken more or less openly for all possible reasons. It was said that, as it was, the Jews in Germany were certainly condemned to die out, and that these measures, which represented a particular hardship for the Jews, were therefore unnecessary . . . A significant case of standing up for the Jews occurred during a transport of Jews in Sabbenhausen. Here the wife of a teacher attempted to give Jews sausage and other foodstuffs . . . The woman was arrested.[63]

As we have seen, it was only Jews in marriages with German 'Aryans' or the children of such unions who stood any chance of being excluded from deportation. The Nuremberg Laws had outlawed German–Jewish unions. Mixed marriages were divided into two categories. Jewish women married to German 'Aryan' non-Jewish men and their children were defined as being in a 'privileged marriage' and were not subject to most of the anti-Semitic laws, including the wearing of the yellow star. They were also exempted from deportation. The children of these marriages enjoyed similar privileges, provided they had not practised the Jewish religion or attended Jewish schools. Divorce meant some of these privileges were lost for the Jewish partner, but not for the children. Jewish men married to a German 'Aryan' woman in a childless marriage were in a 'non-privileged marriage'. Childless Jewish women married to German 'Aryan' men were in a similar position. Some Jews in non-privileged marriages were still required to wear the Jewish yellow star, and to use their official Jewish names.[64] The Jewish partner in these marriages remained in a precarious position. In early 1943, there were still 12,117 'privileged' and 4,551 'non-privileged' marriages.[65]

The loyalty of German women who were married to Jewish partners was very powerful. The most high-profile protest against the deportations came from the 'Aryan' wives of Jewish husbands. One unprecedented demonstration began on 27 February 1943 when German authorities in Berlin announced that all remaining Jews would be deported. Around two hundred German women converged outside the administrative office of the Jewish community in Berlin on *Rosenstrasse* to oppose this decision. The women shouted repeatedly: 'Give us back our husbands.' Over the next week, the protest grew. It eventually involved a thousand women. On 6 March 1943, Joseph Goebbels, the Nazi Gauleiter of Berlin, decided to release the 1,700 intermarried Jews being held in the *Rosenstrasse* building. It was an amazing U-turn. Goebbels was concerned about the damage the demonstration was having on public opinion. This spirited action by a group of German 'Aryan' women saved the lives of their Jewish husbands.[66]

There were some spouses who used the general climate of anti-Semitism to rid themselves of inconvenient Jewish partners. In March 1944, a sixty-three-year-old German 'Aryan' man and his sister denounced his estranged Jewish wife to the Gestapo on the grounds she had said Hitler had murdered children and the Jews would seek revenge. The couple had been married since 1908. The Gestapo fast-tracked the divorce of the couple. The woman was no longer in a privileged marriage. The Gestapo sent her by train to Auschwitz. She died there.[67]

There were widespread regional variations in the Gestapo's treatment of German–Jewish marriages and the children of such unions. It was absolutely vital for anyone involved in such unions to avoid coming to the attention of the Gestapo. The tragic story of Helene Krabs (born 1906) illustrates this point quite graphically.[68] Helene, who was Jewish, was married to a German 'Aryan' called Paul Krabs, but the couple had no children, and were therefore in a 'non-privileged marriage'.

The case began when Paula Berngen, a neighbour, who had

been friendly with Helene and her husband for many years, reported to the Gestapo 'in confidence' on 1 May 1942 her 'strong suspicion' that the Krabs couple were hiding a Jewish woman called Edith [Sara] Mayer in their home. Edith had been transported to the Riga ghetto, but had amazingly managed to escape and return to Germany with her German 'Aryan' fiancée, twenty-two-year-old Heinz Henzen from Cologne, who had rescued her. This couple were deeply in love, and wanted to leave Nazi Germany so they could marry.

A quite amazing series of events now developed. The Gestapo soon established that Edith and Heinz, who had begun their illegal relationship in 1940, were certainly not being hidden at the Krabs' apartment in Solingen. Their whereabouts were unknown. On 20 May 1942, Helene Krabs was brought in for questioning by the Gestapo. She said she made her living as a tailor. Ever since 1932, she had completely ceased to participate in Jewish religious life. In 1933, she married her German 'Aryan' husband Paul, who had no affiliation to any religion at all. Helene described Edith Mayer as a 'remote relative'. She knew about her deportation to Riga, but she denied seeing her in recent weeks or that she had ever allowed her to hide at her home.

The next day Paula Berngen was asked to provide further details of her allegations. She said Edith and Heinz had knocked on the door of her apartment at around 2 p.m. on 1 May 1942, while she was having lunch with her husband Willi. She invited the couple in. Edith told her she had been released from the Riga ghetto. Heinz said he was of 'Aryan descent' and the couple wanted to get married, but needed to emigrate from Nazi Germany to do so. At 4 p.m. Paula Berngen accompanied the couple to the Krabs' apartment. A week later, Heinz returned to her apartment to thank Paula for her hospitality and to say goodbye. He told her he was now returning to Berlin for the time being, but that Edith was going to stay with the Krabs. Paula never believed Edith had been legally released from the

Riga ghetto, but was convinced she had escaped and was quite obviously on the run. This was why she reported the matter to the Gestapo. She said Helene Krabs must be lying if she had told the Gestapo she'd not seen the couple or given them shelter.

Further detailed enquiries were now undertaken by the Gestapo. Letters went back and forth between several Gestapo offices throughout Germany. New and startling details began to emerge. The Gestapo office in Wuppertal reported on 18 June 1942 that Edith Mayer had been living in Lengenfeld, in Saxony, when she was 'evacuated' to the Riga ghetto on a Jewish transport train that had left on 8 December 1941. The Gestapo office in Düsseldorf tried to establish whether Mayer had been released from the ghetto, which was deemed highly unlikely, or had somehow miraculously escaped. On 22 July 1942, the senior prosecutor of the county court of Feldkirch, a town in Austria, close to the Swiss border, reported that Edith and Heinz had been arrested while trying to cross the Swiss border. Heinz was charged with 'race defilement' due to his illegal relationship with Edith, and with avoiding service in the German army. It turned out that Heinz had travelled to Riga and then rescued Edith from the Riga ghetto.

Heinz Henzen underwent a lengthy Gestapo interrogation on 21 August 1942. He made a startling new allegation. He claimed that Paula Berngen already knew of his relationship with Edith, and she had promised to help the couple. Edith had asked Paula to keep some new clothes and other possessions in safe keeping for her until she returned to collect them. Heinz further claimed that the couple had stayed for eight days with the Berngens, and then for three days with the Krabs family. The testimony of Heinz revealed an ulterior motive behind the original denouncement made by Paula Berngen: she had been asked by Edith to hold a number of valuable possessions in safe keeping before she was transported to the Riga ghetto. Paula had never expected she would have to give them back. Heinz also supplied the Gestapo with the names of three other people who had helped the couple while they were on the run. He was placed in a concentration camp pending trial. His ultimate fate is not recorded.

Edith Mayer, the Jewish escapee, was now interrogated. She told the Gestapo Heinz had indeed rescued her from the Riga ghetto in April 1942. He undertook this dramatic escape mission in a lorry he borrowed from an employee of Organisation *Todt*, which was responsible for the building of the German motorways (*Autobahnen*). After rescuing Edith, Heinz drove from Riga to Königsberg and then abandoned the lorry. The couple then travelled by train to Berlin, and finally ended up in Solingen. Edith told a completely different story from Heinz about what happened when they arrived there. She said she alone had stayed for eight days with her relatives Paul and Helene Krabs. She had never stayed with the Berngens at all. Heinz then departed for Cologne to stay with his parents, and the couple arranged to meet up later. She said the Krabs were very scared about putting her up, but they didn't want to turn her adrift. Helene and Heinz were later reunited in Berlin. They then went to Königswinter in Hesse, where they stayed with a family for three days, after which they moved on to Bludenz in Vorarlberg, an Austrian district close to the Swiss border, before they were arrested. Edith was placed in a concentration camp. Her ultimate fate is not recorded in the Gestapo file. It is unlikely she survived.

The Gestapo now had the full story, but there were still contradictory statements about exactly where Edith and Heinz had stayed. The Gestapo believed the Krabs had definitely hidden Edith Mayer and had helped her to remain at large after her escape from the Riga ghetto. Paul Krabs, a skilled lathe operator in a local factory, and Helene Krabs continued to deny that Edith Mayer or Heinz Henzen had ever stayed with them. On 22 August 1942, they were informed about the statements Heinz and Edith had made, which showed this was untrue.

On 1 September 1942, a Gestapo report on recent developments in the case recorded that Helene had been placed in a
concentration camp. Paul was sentenced to three months in
prison. It was further noted that the Berngens would have to
be interrogated once again. If they had any property belonging
to Edith then it must be confiscated. On 7 September 1942,
Helene Krabs finally gave a full confession. She said that in the
autumn of 1941, Edith had asked her to take care of some
possessions, which included towels, duvet covers, dinnerware,
some pieces of silver, wine decanters and a china coffee set.
The Berngens, who were present at this meeting, promised
Helene they would keep Edith's belongings in safe keeping
until she returned to collect them.

On 11 September 1942 a letter was sent from the manager
of the metalwork factory where Paul Krabs worked. It requested
that Paul should be released from prison urgently as the factory
had to deliver important war munitions. On 15 September,
Paul admitted that both Henzen and Mayer had stayed at his
home, but claimed they slept in separate rooms. 'I am the
victim of my own kindness,' he concluded. On 18 September
1942, the Gestapo released Paul Krabs until the important work
in the munitions factory was completed. On 20 October 1942,
his three-month prison sentence was suspended for a further
six months. There is no record to indicate Paul ever returned
to prison.

The Gestapo now interrogated Paula and Willi Berngen to
try and discover what happened to Edith's possessions. On 9
September 1942, Paula Berngen admitted she had indeed sold
the belongings of Edith Mayer, after she was deported to the
Riga ghetto. Her original shameless denouncement had been
designed to hide this fact. The next day, forty-seven-year-old
Willi Berngen gave his side of the story. He said he had known
Edith Mayer and Paul and Helene Krabs for many years. He
had originally met Paul at a choral society, but in 1933 Paul
had been expelled on account of him having a Jewish wife.

Willi first met Heinz in 1940 while he was socialising at the Krabs' home. Heinz told him his parents were deeply opposed to his relationship with Edith. Willi had warned the young man time and time again of the danger of such an illegal relationship between a Jew and an 'Aryan'. Willi knew Edith had been deported to the Riga ghetto. He was, therefore, really surprised when the couple appeared at his home. As soon as the couple left, Willi told his wife to inform the Gestapo. His wife had already sold Edith's possessions for 120 Reichsmarks, which was quite a tidy sum in those days. Apart from returning these proceeds to the Gestapo, Paula and Willi Berngen suffered no other consequences whatsoever for their actions.

The ultimate punishment for Helene Krabs had not yet been determined by the Gestapo. On 29 September 1942, a Gestapo report noted that as Helene was four months' pregnant she had been moved from a concentration camp to a prison. The charges were deemed serious enough for her to be held under 'protective custody' as a 'threat to the state' in Wuppertal prison. A Jewish person helping another Jewish person to evade justice constituted a very serious offence in the eyes of the Gestapo. A further Gestapo report, dated 14 October 1942, pointed out that Paul and Helene Krabs had been married for ten years, without producing any children. It was suggested in the Gestapo report that Helene's pregnancy was a desperate attempt to turn her marriage into a privileged one to try and escape deportation.

On 6 November 1942, the Gestapo suddenly decided that Helene Krabs should be transported to the notorious Auschwitz-Birkenau concentration camp in Poland. Paul Krabs begged the Gestapo for mercy on behalf of his wife in two letters in early December 1942. In one letter he writes, 'My wife was only acting in a compassionate manner. She simply felt a loyalty to her relative. It was an impossible situation for her. I beg for mercy on her behalf.' The Gestapo refused to change its decision. On 10 December 1942, the Gestapo reported that Helene

Krabs had been sent to Auschwitz–Birkenau. Rudolf Höss, the camp commandant, was informed about her pregnant state.

On 3 January 1943, Helene Krabs was murdered, along with her unborn child, in Auschwitz. As was usual with German Holocaust victims, the authorities at the camp recorded a different story. In a letter from the administration office at Auschwitz to the Gestapo, dated 8 January 1943, it stated that Helene had died of angina in the camp hospital. The corpse had been cremated, and her ashes placed in a garden for the urns of the dead.[69]

This was another lie.

Chapter 8

The Gestapo on Trial

O n the evening of 23 April 1945, Heinrich Müller, head of the Gestapo, entered Adolf Hitler's Berlin bunker, beneath the bomb-ravaged Reich Chancellery. He had been summoned there by the Nazi dictator, who was convinced a spy was leaking information to the Allies. Müller began an investigation to find the culprit. He soon established that the person must be someone who could leave and return to the bunker without arousing any suspicion. He concluded the chief suspect was SS General Hermann Fegelein, the husband of Eva Braun's sister Gretl, and a close ally of Heinrich Himmler. Fegelein had missed six of the last military briefings in the bunker. He was finally located and arrested in Berlin, underwent a brief interrogation and then confessed. He was summarily executed on 28 April in the garden of the Reich Chancellery. This was the last investigation of Heinrich Müller's career in the Gestapo. Müller was last seen alive on 2 May 1945. Then he stepped out of the bomb wreckage surrounding the bunker and disappeared. What happened to him remains an unsolved mystery to this day. The most likely scenario suggests he was killed in a Soviet bombing raid. His identity papers were found on a corpse and buried in a Berlin cemetery by SS man Walter Leuders. A death certificate for Müller has survived in Berlin's registry office. It is dated 15 December 1945. It lists the cause of death as 'killed in action'. Not everyone believes Müller was killed. Leading Jewish Nazi hunter Simon Wiesenthal was convinced Müller cheated justice and lived under a false identity, possibly in the Soviet Union or South America. In 1963, West German authorities tried to resolve the mystery by exhuming Müller's remains in Berlin and subjecting them to forensic examination. The results proved remarkable. The remains in the coffin were those of three individuals, none of whom was Müller.[1]

Heinrich Himmler, driving force behind the Nazi terror system, also escaped from the Berlin bunker on 23 April 1945 like a rat deserting a sinking ship. He was secretly trying to broker a peace settlement with the Allies. Hitler was incandescent with rage when he discovered this betrayal by someone he thought was one of his strongest allies. Himmler conveyed some vague peace proposals to the Allies, via the Swedish diplomat Count Folke Bernadotte. The Allies rejected his proposals. Himmler went on the run in the Flensburg area, using forged identity papers, under the assumed name Heinrich Hitzinger. He shaved off his moustache, changed into civilian clothes, stopped wearing his glasses, and wore a patch over his left eye. His disguise fooled no one. He was captured by British troops at a checkpoint on the road to Bremervörde and taken to a local internment camp at Lüneburg. As a doctor examined him, Himmler bit on a deadly poison cyanide capsule and died a few minutes later. The man who had created the vast terror system that included the Gestapo had cheated justice.[2]

Most of the other leading members of the Gestapo were arrested too. One exception was Adolf Eichmann, who was briefly detained in a US internment camp, but escaped. He ended up in Argentina in 1952, living under an assumed name: Ricardo Klement. He even gained employment in the German-owned Mercedes-Benz factory in Buenos Aires. His wife and two sons left West Germany to join him, without arousing suspicion.

The other major Nazi war criminals faced a single trial, organised by the victorious Allies, at the International Military Tribunal at Nuremberg. The legal principles of the trial were decided at a conference in London in the summer of 1945. The accused were charged on three counts: (i) Crimes against Peace (ii) War Crimes (iii) Crimes Against Humanity. Article 10 of the protocol underpinning the trial stated that key groups and organisations within Nazi Germany could also be declared criminal by the tribunal. The trial took place between 14 November 1945 and 1 October 1946. There were 403 public court sessions. It was presided over by Briton Sir Geoffrey Lawrence.

A key part of the proceedings at Nuremberg was a sub-trial of the Gestapo, which was branded a 'criminal organisation', along with the SS and the SD, the intelligence wing of the SS. US lawyer Colonel Robert Storey was the leading prosecution counsel in the Gestapo trial. He argued that the Gestapo, which he defined as a 'state organisation', was in a close relationship with the SD in carrying out its activities. One of the key defendants at the Nuremberg trial was Hermann Göring, who had established the Gestapo in Prussia in February 1933. The categorisation by Storey of a single repressive system of Nazi terror, staffed by people collectively responsible for Nazi war crimes, proved a compelling argument during the trial.[3] The evidence gathered by the prosecution to support this argument was very detailed. Amazingly, the criminal police (Kripo) and ordinary police (Orpo) were excluded from the indictment, on the grounds they remained civilian organisations in the service of a totalitarian state during the Nazi era.

Defence counsel for the Gestapo was the German lawyer Dr Rudolf Merkel. He called several members of the Gestapo as defence witnesses. Central among them was Dr Werner Best, head of the administration and personnel department of the Gestapo HQ in Berlin between 1936 and 1940. He took the stand on 31 August 1946. Best depicted the Gestapo as an innocent and harmless state organisation which took its orders from state leaders. According to Best, the Gestapo was little different from the criminal police. This line of defence acted as a template for other Gestapo officers in other post-war trials.

It was Werner Best who originally shattered the myths surrounding the Gestapo, many years before historians ever dealt with the subject in detail. The main essentials of the later revisionist interpretation of the Gestapo are laid out quite clearly in Best's testimony and ran as follows. The vast majority of Gestapo officers were transferred from the political or criminal police force. They were poorly paid, with salaries below those of detectives in the criminal police. If any officer refused a transfer from the police division to the Gestapo, Best claimed, 'Disciplinary action, with the result they would have been dismissed from office, with the loss of the acquired rights, for instance, their right to a pension' would have followed. The average Gestapo officer was no different in background and professional outlook from a criminal detective. 'It is not the case, as it is often argued and still being asserted,' argued Best, 'that the Gestapo was a network of spies, which kept track of the entire people. With the few officials, who were always busy, anything like that could not be carried out.' The Gestapo was, according to Best, a reactive organisation which relied primarily on 'reports coming from the general public', and he suggested most of these were personally motivated. All major cases of treason were always handed over by the Gestapo to the criminal courts for sentencing once an investigation was complete. Almost half of all staff who worked for the Gestapo were administrative officials, with ordinary civil service backgrounds. A police background was central to the appointment of all Gestapo officers. The Gestapo did not run the concentration camps, and Best never thought the 'life and health of inmates were being endangered in them'. Gestapo officers were constantly in touch with the families of inmates who were frequently kept informed about release dates. Gestapo officers even advised families on welfare payments they might be entitled to while their relatives were in custody. Best claimed that 'enhanced interrogations' were only carried out using strict guidelines, and used in serious cases of treason, but 'confessions were in no way extorted' from prisoners during questioning. Orders to Gestapo officers always came from the top downwards, and they had to be followed without question.

'I was in no position to prevent my superior from carrying out measures he had ordered,' Best concluded.[4] In 1948, Best, who was Reich Governor of Denmark between 1942 and 1945, was sentenced to death by a Danish court for war crimes. This sentence was reduced to twelve years on appeal. Best was released in 1951 due to a Danish amnesty concerning Nazi war criminals.

Another Gestapo officer, Karl-Heinz Hoffmann, took the stand on 1 August 1946. He served in senior line-management positions in Gestapo offices in Koblenz and Düsseldorf, then moved to a key supervisory position in Office IV-D of the RSHA in Berlin before being appointed as head of the Gestapo in Nazi-occupied Denmark in 1942 under Werner Best. Hoffmann had gained a university degree in law. In 1937, he joined the Gestapo, at the age of twenty-five, as a graduate entrant, without any previous police experience. He was soon promoted to the post of Deputy Political Adviser. In testimony, he claimed all the Gestapo officers he worked with in the localities were criminal policemen who began their careers in the Weimar period and were then transferred into the Gestapo. The case load of the Gestapo in Koblenz and Düsseldorf consisted primarily of combating treason, mostly by communists, dealing with church dissidents, and implementing policies surrounding the treatment of Jews. Hoffmann explained to the court how most Gestapo cases were dealt with:

> The great majority of cases were dealt with by means of a warning by the [Secret] State Police when the results of the inquiry were negative. In those cases where custody was necessary, we saw to it that the perpetrators were brought before the court. Protective custody was only given for a short time in all those cases where the matter was not ready to be brought to the court. Protective custody by being transferred to a concentration camp was only proposed by the Gestapo if the personality of the perpetrator, judged by his previous behaviour,

gave one to expect that he would continue to be an habitual offender against the regulations.[5]

Hoffmann claimed it was a cardinal principle of Gestapo regulations that officers should maintain strict secrecy surrounding their work. On the question of whether physical cruelty and torture were used during interrogations, Hoffmann replied, bluntly: 'Brutal treatment and torture were strictly prohibited and were condemned by the courts ... I remember two [Gestapo] officers in Düsseldorf, who were sentenced [to prison] for maltreatment of prisoners by a regular court.' In Denmark, however, Hoffmann admitted 'enhanced interrogations' were used far more frequently, especially against resistance organisations, but he maintained these were not extensive and were enacted under war-time conditions.

Hoffmann claimed the treatment of the Jewish question was handled exclusively by Eichmann's office in the RSHA in Berlin, where he operated in a separate office. Eichmann's work was regarded by the Gestapo as strictly confidential. He signed all the orders for the deportation of the Jews. If anyone asked Eichmann what orders he was carrying out in regard to the 'Jewish Question', he always replied that he was implementing 'special missions ordered by the highest authorities and that, therefore, it was unnecessary for the other departments to countersign, and thus be able to state their own opinion'.[6]

The defence case for the Gestapo was very ably handled by Dr Rudolf Merkel. He mounted a strident defence against the prosecution charge which alleged that the Gestapo was a 'criminal organisation' and its officials should take collective responsibility for its 'crimes against humanity'. Merkel argued that under German law, dating back before Hitler came to power, individuals could be found guilty of specific crimes, but not organisations. To establish collective guilt, Merkel argued, the tribunal needed to prove Gestapo officers were not acting

229

legally, in accordance with the German law that existed at the time their actions took place.

Merkel portrayed the Gestapo as a state, non-Nazi institution. Its officers had a long-standing addiction to carrying out orders, obediently, and without question. He claimed this was a distinctly German character trait which the prosecution needed to understand. The omnipotent power of the Gestapo was a myth, claimed Merkel, spread by Nazi propaganda: 'The approximately 15,000 to 16,000 Gestapo officers in question, even if they had watched and spied on people, would have been far from adequate for the purpose.' A second myth Merkel rejected was the Allied claim that the Gestapo was full of committed Nazis. In reality, said Merkel, it was staffed by members of the existing political and criminal police force. Any assimilation by these 'ordinary' men of Nazi ideas was a very slow and incomplete process. At the outbreak of the war, only 3,000 Gestapo officers were even members of the SS. This represented less than 20 per cent of the total number of Gestapo officers. Merkel also cast serious doubt on the commonly held belief that the Gestapo arrested people using 'protective custody' orders and then sent them straight to concentration camps without trial. Merkel produced evidence which showed protective custody orders were 'governed by exact regulations' that were decided by higher authorities, including the public prosecutor and the courts. As for the charge that the Gestapo used 'enhanced interrogations' extensively, Merkel argued this was not the case at all inside Germany, especially before the war-time period. Such methods were only used in very 'exceptional cases', and only on the order of the highest authorities. Gestapo officers were instructed repeatedly that 'any ill-treatment during interrogations' was strictly prohibited.

According to Merkel, those Gestapo officers who were transferred into the Einsatzgruppen and took part in mass killings in Poland and the Soviet Union were not acting as Gestapo personnel or under Gestapo orders when they carried out these murders. During the deportation of the Jews from Germany, Merkel conceded the Gestapo did prepare the evacuations, in liaison with local Jewish community leaders, but he maintained they were carrying out 'decrees and orders originating from much higher authorities', particularly from the office of Eichmann in Berlin, who gave no details to local Gestapo officers of the ultimate purpose of the Jewish transports.

Merkel concluded his defence by stating that it was not his duty to excuse the crimes of the Nazi regime or to whitewash individuals within the Gestapo who had disregarded humanity and committed war crimes, but he concluded that on the basis of the detailed evidence he had presented, the Gestapo could not be classed as a criminal organisation.[7]

On 30 September 1946, the Nuremberg judgment was delivered. It decided the Gestapo was a criminal organisation, which performed its functions with the close co-operation of the SD. The judgment laid out the extent of the criminality of the Gestapo. Its officers had arrested and interrogated all the people who ended up in concentration camps. It played a central role in the persecution of communists, religious groups, Jews and a wide variety of opponents. It played a key role in the persecution and deportation of Jews. The Gestapo arrested individuals and transported them to concentration camps to undertake 'death through slave labour', not only within Germany, but throughout Nazi-occupied Europe. It was implicated in the mistreatment and murder of prisoners of war and foreign workers inside Nazi Germany. Many Gestapo officials took part in the mass killings in the Soviet Union. Given all these crimes against humanity the Nuremberg judgment concluded that all Gestapo officers and executive administrative officials were collectively responsible for the criminal acts of the Gestapo. Only minor clerical and ancillary workers were excluded from the judgment, and those individuals who had ceased employment with the Gestapo before 1 December 1939. Hence, the Nuremberg judgment suggested that the Gestapo only became a fully functioning criminal organisation after the Second World War began. In effect, this ruled out the possibility of Gestapo officers facing punishment for crimes they committed before then.[8]

Twelve of the twenty-two key Nazi defendants received death sentences, including Hermann Göring, who killed himself with a cyanide capsule on 16 October 1946, the day on which he was supposed to be executed. Wilhelm Frick, the Minister of the Interior, who had attempted to prevent Himmler's SS taking over the Gestapo and the criminal police between 1933 and 1936, was hanged. Ernst Kaltenbrunner, the Chief of the Reich Security Main Office (RSHA), which included Office IV of the Gestapo, was also executed. Kaltenbrunner tried to suggest in his testimony that Heinrich Müller ran the Gestapo without any interference or supervision from him. The remaining defendants received prison sentences varying from ten years to life. Franz von Papen, the man who helped bring Hitler to power, was acquitted.[9]

The classification of the Gestapo as a criminal organisation theoretically opened the way for all its key officials to be prosecuted. Yet there was no major follow-up collective Gestapo trial ever held. The majority of former Gestapo men were initially interned in Allied detention camps. Most served sentences of up to three years. It's been estimated that in the first year of the Allied occupation of Germany, 250,000 people, associated in one way or another with the Nazi regime, were placed in a variety of Allied internment camps.

Between 1945 and 1949, Germany was divided into four occupation zones administered by the four victorious allies: Britain, the USA, the Soviet Union and France. On 23 May 1949, the democratic Federal Republic of Germany (FRG) was created from the eleven states within the three Allied occupation zones administered by the USA, Britain and France. The communist German Democratic Republic (DDR) began to function as a state in the Soviet zone of occupation from 7 October 1949. Due to the onset of the Cold War, Berlin remained divided between the Allies.

The Allied authorities empowered German courts to pursue individual war crimes cases through the courts either under existing German law, which was quite restrictive, or under Allied Control Council Law no. 10 of 20 December 1945, which allowed retroactive prosecutions for war crimes, crimes against humanity and crimes against peace. There were twelve subsequent war trials of high-ranking Nazi figures held between December 1946 and April 1949, most notably, of the judiciary, the military, doctors, government officials and the murderous *Einsatzkommando* leaders. The most high profile of these was undoubtedly the *Einsatzgruppen* trial, which took place from 15 September 1947 to 10 April 1948. It had twenty-three defendants, ten of whom had held high-ranking positions in the RSHA in Berlin. Only Gustav Nosske, head of IVD5 at the Berlin HQ, was directly attached to the Gestapo. He was involved with Nazi-occupied Eastern Territories. Otto Ohlendorf and his co-defendants pleaded 'Not Guilty' to all charges. All claimed they were following Hitler's orders for the 'Final Solution', and thought they were free from any personal legal responsibility for the mass murders they carried out. They were not murderers, they claimed, but accomplices. The final judgment rejected this line of defence. A total of fourteen defendants received the death penalty in the Einsatzgruppen trial, including Otto Ohlendorf.[10]

To deal with less serious war crimes offenders, denazification trial courts (*Spruchkammer*) were established in the western zones of occupation. They were staffed by lay people. There were real problems in pursuing Gestapo officers in the post-war period. The vast majority of Gestapo files had been destroyed either deliberately or in Allied bombing raids, which had deliberately targeted police and government buildings in all the major cities during the latter stages of the war. Even the infamous Gestapo HQ at 8 Prinz Albrecht Strasse in Berlin was completely destroyed early in 1945 and a vast treasure trove of important documents lost for ever. It was only in the Rhineland that a large number of files survived, most notably, the Düsseldorf files, used in this study. It seems this office was simply remiss in not destroying the files before the Western Allies took control of the city. Without these files the entire way in which the Gestapo operated would have been hidden from history. Finding witnesses for war trials was no easy task for prosecutors either. Many lived in occupied territories now controlled by the Soviet Union. The vast majority of Jewish victims had perished in the Holocaust and could no longer speak. Many Germans who had suffered at the hands of the Gestapo were reluctant to testify. The Law for the Liberation from National Socialism and Militarism of 5 March 1946 allowed individuals incriminated in Nazism, including Gestapo officers, the chance of exoneration by producing evidence from relevant witnesses.

The decisions and sentences of the denazification courts varied widely, but extreme leniency became the norm. There were five categories of offender defined: (i) Major Offenders: these were subject to arrest, trial and imprisonment; (ii) Offenders: these included leading Nazi Party activists; (iii) Lesser Offenders: these were given probation; (iv) Followers and Fellow Travellers: these faced possible minor employment restrictions; and (v) Exonerated: no sanctions. Based on the Nuremberg judgment, all Gestapo officers should have been defined as 'Major Offenders', put on trial and imprisoned. This never happened.

The aim of those who entered the denazification process was to achieve the highly prized certificate of blamelessness, which meant being classed as 'Exonerated'. This became jokingly known as a 'Persil Certificate' (*Persilschein*), the reference being to the popular detergent Persil, which promised in TV adverts to wash clothes 'whiter than white'. It was suggested that Nazi war criminals were trying to turn their old brown shirts clean and white too. The majority of Gestapo officers ended up being classed as 'Exonerated', as did the overwhelming majority of all West Germans who entered the denazification process. In the state of North-Rhine Westphalia, which covered 4 million people, only ninety former Nazis were ever placed in the top two categories. It was as if no one was ever really a Nazi in the first place.[11]

The task of denazification tribunals was huge. Millions had been tangled up in the criminal web of Hitler's criminal and genocidal regime. More than 3 million Germans went through the denazification process. In the end, it became a matter of filling out a bland tick-box questionnaire that an overstretched official read and signed, without much close scrutiny. Between 1945 and 1948, the US Opinion Survey (OMGUS) section conducted twenty-two surveys into the extent of possible continuing support for the Nazi regime. It discovered 77 per cent thought the extermination of Jews was 'unjustified', but when asked if Nazism was a bad idea just 53 per cent replied 'Yes'. Respondents cited 'race policy' and 'atrocities' as reasons for this response. Only 21 per cent thought Nazism was 'bad' before the Second World War began. When asked if Germans believed the extent of the numbers killed in the Holocaust, 59 per cent said 'Yes'. The question, 'Did you know what went on in the concentration camps?' prompted 51 per cent to record that they did, but 40 per cent claimed complete ignorance. When asked why people were sent to concentration camps, 57 per cent said 'for political reasons'. On the question of whether Germans were in favour of bringing to trial all those Nazi perpetrators who murdered civilians, a whopping 94 per cent said 'Yes'. This shows that the German public was not originally opposed to a vigorous policy of bringing war criminals to justice.[12] This did not last long, however. According to a 1950 opinion poll, the number of West Germans who felt the Nuremberg trials were fair had fallen to 38 per cent.[13]

The period of Allied occupation rule from 1945 to 1949 stands out as the only really sustained attempt to deal with Nazi war criminals, even though the actual level of prosecutions in the period was very small. In the 'Judges' Trial' of 1947 only 16 defendants were even brought to trial. Evidence was heard from 128 witnesses, many of whom testified about the complicity of judges and lawyers in persecuting key target groups. Only four of the accused received a life sentence in the Judges' Trial. The rest were given prison sentences varying between five and ten years. Believe it or not, seventy-two of the judges of the infamous 'People's Court' were re-employed by the West German Federal Republic. In total, around 80 per cent of all former legal employees were allowed to keep their jobs. The West German legal system was underpinned by Hitler's judiciary and lawyers. The full transcript of the Judges' Trial was not even published in West Germany until 1996.[14]

Gestapo officers sought character references during the denazification process, which went on until 1953. Most had little difficulty finding people willing to describe them as humane, professional, understanding and non-violent. One Gestapo officer Otto Dihr, born on 15 January 1902, was determined to clear his name. He was, on the surface, a classic Gestapo 'ordinary man'. He left school without any qualifications. In 1922, he became a policeman. He was a traffic cop in the Weimar period. There was seemingly nothing sinister at all about this supposedly 'good cop'. After 1934, Dihr became a member of the Krefeld Gestapo. He only joined the Nazi Party in 1937. During his period as a Gestapo officer he dealt with cases involving communists, Jehovah's Witnesses and homosexuals.[15] He was never disciplined by his superiors for exceeding the regulations of 'enhanced interrogations'. Dihr wanted to be classed as 'Exonerated'. He could then receive his generous occupational pension. He produced impressive character testimonials to support his case. Erich Heinzelmann, a Gestapo colleague from Cologne, offered a glowing reference. Ironically, a *Heinzelmann* is a mythological figure in north German folklore, a kind of little ghost, who comes in the night, does all kinds of work, and cleans the house, but only as long as he is undetected. A woman, from the Krefeld typing pool, who worked with Dihr, described him as charming and highly professional at all times.

Some of those Dihr had interrogated described him as 'professional and humane'.

Then suddenly some of Otto Dihr's victims came forward to tell a completely different story. Imgard Mendling, a Jehovah's Witness, gave a statement on 30 January 1948 in which she outlined a brutal beating she had endured by Dihr in Düsseldorf. This had left her bleeding profusely and in unendurable pain. Karl Lummers, a typesetter from Krefeld with communist sympathies, claimed he was repeatedly 'hit and kicked' by Dihr during an interrogation. Josef Ritting, arrested in September 1935 for distributing communist leaflets, was also interrogated by Dihr. He was hit in the face several times, then attacked with the leg of a chair and kicked brutally while his feet were tied together. Two other Gestapo officers joined in this brutal beating. Josef passed out. Three days later, Dihr repeated beating him. Josef was left completely disabled by his treatment at the hands of the Gestapo. He gave his evidence to the denazification tribunal in a wheelchair. Johannes Hottger, a merchant from Cologne, was arrested by Dihr in January 1935, and then transported to Krefeld. He claimed Dihr hit him with a baton several times during his interrogation. A total of fifteen witnesses gave evidence concerning Dihr's extremely brutal and violent interrogation methods. On 27 May 1949, Dihr was sentenced to two years and seven months in prison for what the judge described as his 'rude and grave assaults', but his previous detention in an internment camp was deducted from this sentence. On 13 June 1950, Otto Dihr was released from a prison in Münster. The senior prosecutor who sanctioned his release noted that 'he should be exempted from his last three months in prison, because he is a widower and has a little daughter'.[16] He was then classed as 'Exonerated' and received his full occupational pension.

The courts in the West German zones of occupation convicted a total of only 5,228 defendants of war crimes between 1945 and 1950. Between 1956 and 1981 an average of just twenty-four people were convicted for war crimes per year. Between 1945 and 1997, only 1,878 people ever faced trial in West German courts for crimes committed in the Nazi era. Of these, only 14 were given death sentences, and 150 were given life imprisonment. By 1948, in the British zone of occupation, the authority for issuing denazification certificates was devolved to German officials.

It was common knowledge in Germany that the Gestapo had relied heavily on denunciations from the public to carry out its work. Free of Nazi repression, victims called for denouncers to be punished, as 'indirect perpetrators', for their 'crimes against humanity'. It was decided denouncers should be prosecuted. Between 1945 and 1964, there were 7,674 cases of suspected denunciations in West Germany, with 603 convictions. The bulk of these took place during the period before the creation of the Federal German Republic. Only one person was sentenced to life imprisonment, 566 received a prison sentence, 36 were fined and 6,992 cases ended with no conviction.[17] Cases continued to be brought against people who had denounced fellow citizens to the Gestapo until the mid-1960s.

Sentences varied widely. Those denunciations that led to executions stood the best chance of securing a conviction. These cases proceeded on the principle that the average citizen in Hitler's Germany knew that severe punishments would follow a denouncement to the Gestapo. One of the most high-profile early cases concerned Helene Schwärzel, who had denounced Dr Karl Gördeler, the former mayor of Leipzig, who was a central figure in the July 1944 bomb plot to kill Hitler. He was executed for high treason by the notorious 'People's Court' on 2 February 1945. It was Schwärzel who reported Gördeler to the authorities. She received a substantial monetary reward and public acclaim for doing so. On 14 November 1946, she was sentenced to fifteen years' imprisonment by a jury court on the grounds that her denunciation led directly to Gördeler's death. This verdict was later overturned by the appeal court, which ruled it had not been conclusively proven that Schwärzel had acted out of political loyalty to the Nazi regime when she denounced Gördeler. A second trial was ordered. In this trial, the prosecution changed its line of attack by characterising Schwärzel's motives as purely selfish and personal. It was suggested she had denounced Gördeler because she craved admiration, and hoped her denunciation would make her popular with the general public. She was sentenced to six years in prison at the end of her second trial on 1 November 1947. This verdict was considered far too lenient. A further appeal was lodged, this time by the public prosecutor. Schwärzel's original fifteen-year sentence was reinstated. This high-profile case brought the issue of denunciation to the forefront of public debate and opened the way to further prosecutions.[18]

A case heard by the Siegen regional court was against a man who had denounced a work colleague to the Gestapo for telling political jokes. During the latter stages of the war, the Gestapo became harsher in the way it dealt with allegations that it had previously treated as trivial. This denouncement had been made out of pure spite, without any consideration of what the consequences might be. The denounced man was put on trial in the 'People's Court' for 'undermining the war effort' on 10 March 1944, sentenced to death and then executed by guillotine. In the judgment of this case, the denouncement was described as 'reprehensible' as the denouncer knew that by reporting the man's harmless jokes to the Gestapo his colleague was likely to suffer imprisonment at the very least. The court judged his actions as a 'crime against humanity' which caused inhumane suffering to another human being. He was sentenced to five years' imprisonment.[19]

Another case took place in the Hamburg regional court in May 1948. The two defendants were a father and his sister. The father had a Jewish wife. According to the man's account, the couple had been in conflict for several years and he had already instituted divorce proceedings against her. His sister, who lived with the couple, said her sister-in-law was extremely argument-ative. The wife was seemingly disrupting family harmony all the time. In early 1944, the Jewish woman reportedly said during a conversation in the family home that 'the day of vengeance of the Jews will come soon' and that children killed in air raids 'were murdered by Hitler'. The husband passed on this infor-mation to the Gestapo. This was to have far-reaching consequences for his wife. The Jewish woman was arrested, sent to Auschwitz and died there at the end of October 1944. The court charged the husband and his sister with a crime against humanity. The prosecution claimed their denunciations were undertaken purely for the purpose of persecution and with the clear knowledge of the very serious consequences that would undoubtedly follow. They had denounced a Jewish woman to the Gestapo to resolve a minor domestic conflict for purely vengeful motives. The husband was sentenced to six months in prison and the sister-in-law to eight months. A court of appeal upheld these sentences on 9 November 1948.[20]

The widow of a man who had been executed for 'under-mining the war effort' on 5 January 1944 made a complaint against the two men who had denounced her husband. They denounced the man to the Gestapo after they heard him saying, 'Hitler, Göring and Goebbels should be chopped into pieces for all the disaster they have brought to the people.' The case was heard by a denazification court in Frankfurt am Main. In the judgment, delivered on 10 March 1947, one of the defend-ants was sentenced to four years in a labour camp, the other given six months in prison for causing the arrest and murder of an opponent of National Socialism in the full knowledge that their denouncement was likely to lead to imprisonment and death.[21]

There was also a denazification process in communist East Germany. The DDR claimed it enacted a more comprehensive purging of Nazis than occurred in West Germany. During the era of the Cold War this was thought to be self-serving East

German communist propaganda. It turns out that these claims were largely true. In the DDR anyone tainted by any Nazi Party association was removed from employment. Most former Nazis who remained in East Germany were tracked down and brought to justice. It is also a complete myth to believe that the notorious East German secret police, the *Stasi*, was staffed by former Gestapo officers. It's hard to find many *Stasi* officers who ever worked for the Gestapo. Former Nazi Party members did not occupy key positions in the post-war East German judiciary either. In 1950, of the 1,000 East German judges, only one had been a former member of the Nazi Party. Just 3 per cent of prison officials had been former members of the Nazi Party by 1947.

The most high-profile trials of Nazi perpetrators in East Germany were the ten 'Waldheim Trials', which took place between April and July of 1950. All ninety-one defendants were defined as having committed 'homicidal crimes' while serving Hitler's regime and all were found guilty. A total of twenty-four were sentenced to death, and seventeen were executed, another thirty-one were given life sentences and the remaining thirty-six were given lengthy prison sentences. Only five of those convicted in these trials remained in prison by the end of 1957.[22] Among those convicted of war crimes in East Germany were former judges, Gestapo officers, denouncers, informers, concentration camp staff and those who had participated in the murderous *Einsatzgruppen* killings in the Soviet Union. There were a total of 4,000 convictions in the DDR for war crimes in 1950 in fast-track trials. After these major trials were over, the pursuit of war criminals in East Germany was scaled down.

The DDR government made great propaganda capital out of the fact it paid additional welfare and pension benefits to those who had been victims of Gestapo terror, whereas in West Germany former members of the resistance to Hitler were generally ostracised and found it difficult to gain employment. The DDR frequently published damaging allegations of the extent to which West German society remained tainted by Nazism. In 1965, the National Front of the DDR published a book known as the Brown Book: *War and Nazi War Criminals in West Germany: State, Economy, Administration, Justice, Science*. It named and shamed 1,800 former leading Nazis who still held key positions in West Germany. The list included 15 government ministers, 100 generals and admirals, 828 senior judges and public prosecutors, 245 members of the foreign and diplomatic service, and 297 senior police officials, including former SS, SD, Kripo and Gestapo officers. A West German government statement at the time of its publication described the 'Brown Book' as 'pure falsification' and copies of it were seized by the West German police at the 1967 Frankfurt Book Fair.[23] The book was not merely true, but it seriously underestimated the number of former Nazis who had retained prominent positions in West Germany.[24]

The establishment of the West German Federal Republic in 1949 led to a number of important changes in the treatment of former Nazi perpetrators. The desire of the Western Allies to rehabilitate West Germany as a bulwark against Soviet communism led to a noticeable softening of attitudes towards the treatment of Nazi war criminals. Blame was placed on 'Hitler and his cronies' for the German tragedy and the roles of everyone else were diminished. Under West German law, only individuals could be charged for murder, not organisations. This seemingly ruled out a full-scale trial of the Gestapo.

In 1949, General John McCloy, the US High Commissioner responsible for convicted German war criminals, formed a commission to review the original sentences in all the major war crimes trials. On 31 January 1951, McCloy announced a huge reduction of sentences in fifty-two cases, with the result that thirty-two were released immediately. He reduced seventeen of the twenty life sentences, and commuted ten of the outstanding fifteen death sentences to prison terms. Of an original figure of 800 death sentences for war criminals, 300 of those were commuted to life in prison. Death sentences were only upheld against SS Main Office head Oswald Pohl, and four of those convicted at the *Einsatzgruppen* trial: Paul Blobel, Werner Braune, Erich Naumann and the notorious and unrepentant SS officer Otto Ohlendorf. These five, executed on 7 June 1951, were the last war criminals executed by the West German Federal Republic.[25] By 1955, only eighty people who had been sentenced for war crimes and crimes against humanity remained in prison.

On 31 December 1949, an 'Immunity Law' was passed by the West German government. It gave a blanket amnesty to all Nazi crimes for which the punishment would have resulted in six months' imprisonment or less. Under Article 131 of the Basic Law of the FDR any person who had worked for the public services during the Nazi period could apply for 'professional rehabilitation'. It has been estimated that just 55,000 people had lost their jobs due to their affiliation to the Nazi regime. Only those who had been convicted of a 'serious' war crime were excluded from the opportunity of rehabilitation.

Article 131 was supposed to exclude Gestapo officers, and former members of the Waffen SS, but if an individual could prove they joined the police before 1933 and then transferred into the Gestapo, they could apply for rehabilitation. Former Gestapo officers seized on this legal loophole. Special welfare benefits were offered, while final decisions were arrived at in individual cases. It's been estimated that around 50 per cent of former Gestapo officers were redeployed to civil service posts. Only eight members of Gestapo Office IV in the Berlin HQ were appointed to important civil services posts. The vast majority of former high-ranking Gestapo officials with law degrees resumed their careers as private practice lawyers. Special quotas were even applied to government posts and in the private sector, which in effect operated a system of positive discrimination towards 'rehabilitated' individuals. Even Gestapo officers who were not re-employed encountered little difficulty having their generous occupational pensions restored.[26]

A typical example was Karl Löffler, former head of the 'Jewish Desk' at the Cologne Gestapo. He was responsible for organising the deportations of the Jews of Cologne to the Nazi death camps during the war. Using personal testimonials from a range of people he had interrogated, including priests, socialists and Jews, Löffler was able to get his denazification status reduced from 'Minor Offender' to 'Exonerated'. His Nazi past had magically disappeared. This meant Löffler could regain his generous occupational final salary pension. He originally received a pension in 1950 that did not take account of his time as head of the 'Jewish Desk' in Cologne. He complained that it was during this period he was receiving his highest salary, and mounted a five-year campaign of lobbying to have his fully enhanced pension restored. In 1956, the state government in North-Rhine Westphalia granted Löffler his full pension.[27]

On 1 January 1950, German courts were given complete autonomy to pursue war crimes trials. They were hardly overworked. Between 1951 and 1955, West German courts convicted a total of just 636 Nazi war criminals.[28] The very few high-profile cases that came to court in the 1950s involving Gestapo officers resulted in extraordinarily mild sentences. Kurt Lindow, who had been the head of Department IV-A in the Berlin HQ, which dealt with communists, was arrested in 1950 for his involvement in the murder of Soviet POWs, but he was acquitted at his subsequent trial in Frankfurt am Main due to lack of evidence.[29]

There were two high-profile cases involving Gestapo officers in 1954. The first took place in Cologne. Over a hundred Gestapo officers were originally investigated by the public prosecutor. In the end, only three individuals faced trial: Dr Emanuel Schäfer, Franz Sprinz and Kurt Matschke. Of the 13,500 Jews who were deported from Cologne, only 600 survived, but this trial lasted just four days and the sentences were very lenient.

Schäfer served nearly seven years in prison. Sprinz was given three years and Matschke two. The time they spent in prison prior to the trial was deducted from their sentences.[30]

The second case took place in Darmstadt and produced an even more bewildering outcome. It involved two Gestapo officers: Waldemar Eisfeld and Heinrich Lorenz. They were charged with organising the deportations of thousands of Jews from Thuringia to the death camps. Witnesses testified about the brutality Eissfeld had inflicted on Jews during his interrogations. The judge concluded that the accusations of brutality fell outside the statute of limitations and this charge was dropped. He then acquitted both men of all charges, on the grounds that they did not know what the fate of the Jews would be when they ordered their transportation.[31] These two men showed precious little remorse and admitted no responsibility throughout the trial.

On 5 October 1955, Bruno Streckenbach, chief of Department I of the RHSA, who issued orders to the *Einsatzgruppen* in the Soviet Union for the 'Final Solution', returned to West Germany, due to an amnesty awarded to former German POWs imprisoned in the Soviet Union. At the *Einsatzgruppen* trial in 1948, it was presumed that Streckenbach had been captured by the Red Army and executed. His return presented the West German authorities with a huge dilemma. No one doubted he was a major war criminal, but the West German judiciary showed little desire to mount a major war crimes trial involving such a high-profile figure. There were two criminal allegations outstanding, these being related to severe beatings Streckenbach had inflicted against communists during Gestapo interrogations while he was chief of the Hamburg Gestapo. Both charges were dropped due to statute-of-limitation laws. The Hamburg state prosecutor then concluded that no evidence had emerged to show that Streckenbach had committed any war crimes inside Nazi Germany. As for the mass murder of Jews in the Soviet Union, the state prosecutor argued that Streckenbach had already served a sentence for this. In September 1956, the investigation against Streckenbach was suspended and was never revived.[32]

By the late 1950s, there was a growing realisation among the thirteen West German states that a co-ordinated approach was required to successfully prosecute Nazi war criminals. This resulted in the creation on 1 December 1958 of 'The Central Office of the State Administrations Judicial Authorities for the Investigation of National Socialist Crimes', based in Ludwigsburg.[33] The Central Office, staffed primarily by energetic young lawyers and archivists, was designed to assist in the prosecution of war crimes by collecting evidence against alleged Nazi perpetrators. It created a huge archive. It now contains 1.6 million documents from the Nazi era and is still in operation.[34]

The Central Office was initially given the task of investigating all actions by Nazi perpetrators outside Germany. This was later amended so that crimes committed by individuals inside Nazi Germany could be prosecuted.[35] Even when enough evidence was assembled to mount a trial, the authenticity of the surviving evidence was questioned by skilled defence lawyers. Most convictions rested primarily on witness evidence given by individuals describing events which occurred many years before. These recollections often lacked the necessary detail to gain convictions. The accused often co-ordinated their defence, and gave what seemed the most reliable version of events.

By 1960 it was clear that the government of Konrad Adenauer wanted to avoid high-profile war crimes trials on the grounds they damaged the current glowing economic and political reputation of democratic West Germany on the international stage. Subtle legal amendments were used by the West German government to restrict prosecutions of Nazi war criminals during the 1960s. A West German law of March 1960 placed a limitation of fifteen years, dating from 1 January 1950, on all crimes, except those defined as 'wilful murder'. This meant that by 1965 it would become impossible to prosecute any crimes from the

Nazi era. The most controversial legal manoeuvre to make prosecuting Nazi war criminals even more difficult involved a minor amendment to Article 50, paragraph 2, of the West German Penal Code, called 'The Introductory Act to Regulatory Offences of 1968'.[36] This decreed that if it could be proved that an individual participated in a murder due to clear base motives such as delight in murder, racial hatred or for revenge they could be charged, but it held that those defined as 'accomplices' to crimes should be punished more leniently by judges when deciding sentences. This legal amendment was supposedly not aimed at war crimes, but wily defence lawyers for war criminals invoked it to halt or suspend prosecutions. On 20 May 1969, the West German Federal Court of Justice ruled that in future war crimes trials it needed to be proved that individuals acted from 'personal murderous motives' in order for maximum sentences to be imposed. Otherwise, they had to be treated as 'accomplices' to whoever issued orders to them.[37]

Given the increasing legal restrictions on bringing war criminals to trial in West Germany, it is hardly surprising that the most sensational trial of a leading Nazi war criminal after 1948 did not take place in West or East Germany. It took place in Israel. On 11 May 1960, an eight-man team of Israeli Secret Service agents tracked down and captured the no. 1 Nazi Gestapo war criminal still at large, Adolf Eichmann, who was living in a house in a suburb of Buenos Aires, Argentina. He was flown to Israel to face justice.

The sensational trial of Adolf Eichmann began in Jerusalem on 11 April 1961. The transcript of the proceedings runs to 3,500 pages. He was the most high-ranking Gestapo administrative official to face trial since the Nuremberg trials. His line managers were Heinrich Müller, the head of the Gestapo, and Heinrich Himmler, chief of the SS. During the trial, Eichmann claimed he was just a bureaucratic cipher following orders. The proceedings received huge media coverage. The trial was broadcast on TV around the world. A total of 112 witnesses gave evidence, including numerous Holocaust survivors. Eichmann had the appearance of a very 'ordinary' and rather dull administrator. He spoke in a flat, low, monotone voice, without any intonation. He answered questions from the prosecution in a matter-of-fact manner. In describing his domestic life, and his work at Gestapo HQ, he seemed like a solid member of the middle classes. He even brought his own sandwiches to work for lunch, enjoyed playing with his children at home in the evenings and looked forward to family summer holidays. He did not appear violent in any way. This proved extremely disconcerting for TV viewers. He freely admitted he organised the deportation of the Jews, but did not feel any personal responsibility for the consequences of these actions. He kept repeating it was his superiors who were the real criminals. Jewish writer Hannah Arendt memorably summed up Adolf Eichmann's behaviour during his trial as representing the 'banality of evil'. In the judgment, delivered on 12 December 1961, he was found guilty of organising the transportation of the Jews and for the awful conditions they endured during their journey to oblivion. Two days later, the judge passed a sentence of death.[38] He was hanged at midnight on 31 May 1962.

The Eichmann Trial provided a much-needed stimulus to a small group of West German prosecutors who were determined to bring Nazi war criminals to justice. This led to the Frankfurt Auschwitz trial, which took place between 20 December 1963 and 19 August 1965. It was the most high-profile war crimes trial ever undertaken in West Germany. A total of 359 witnesses gave evidence, including 248 Auschwitz survivors. The trial lasted for 183 days and received extensive media coverage. The twenty-two defendants were charged under West German law for murder and other serious crimes committed while working at the infamous Auschwitz-Birkenau concentration camp. Although 7,000 SS personnel had worked there at one time or another, but only 63 of them ever faced trial after 1945.

The trial came about largely through the dogged and brave

determination of the radical lawyer Fritz Bauer, who was born on 16 July 1903 to Jewish parents. During the Weimar period, Bauer was an active member of the socialist SPD and a practising lawyer. In 1933 he was arrested by the Gestapo and sent to Heuberg concentration camp. After his release in 1935, he went into exile in Denmark, and survived the Holocaust. He returned to West Germany after the war and became a leading prosecutor in the state of Hesse, of which Frankfurt am Main is the capital. It was Bauer who discovered evidence that Eichmann was living in Argentina. He pressed the West German authorities to take action to bring him to justice. When he became convinced this would not happen, he supplied the Israeli secret service Mossad with this information, which led directly to the capture of Eichmann.

Bauer's determination to hunt down Nazi war criminals made him a controversial figure within West German legal circles, as so many judges and lawyers were tainted by their association with the National Socialist criminal justice system. One of the key defendants in the Auschwitz trial was the notorious Gestapo officer Wilhelm Boger. Having joined the Nazi Party in 1929, in 1933 he became an officer in the political police and was then transferred into the Gestapo. In 1936 he was charged with mistreating prisoners during interrogations, and served a brief prison sentence for his behaviour. This did not hamper his career. In 1937, Boger was appointed as a police commissioner in Kripo. In 1942, he was sent to run the 'political department' in Auschwitz on behalf of the RSHA. His main task in the camp was keeping files on political prisoners and conducting interrogations. Frau Braun, a prosecution witnesses at the trial, worked as a clerical worker in Boger's office in Auschwitz. She described his torture techniques in graphic detail:

A prisoner would be brought in for 'questioning', stripped naked and handcuffed on to a metre-long iron bar that was linked by chains from the ceiling . . . A guard at one side would shove

him – or her – off in a slow arc, while Boger would ask questions, at first quietly, then barking them out, or at least bellowing.
At each return [as the prisoner swung around on the bar],
another guard, armed with a crow bar, would smash the victim
across the buttocks. As the swinging went on, and the wailing
victim fainted, was then revived, only to faint howling again,
the blows continued – until only a mass of bleeding pulp hung
before their eyes. Most perished from this ordeal, some sooner,
some later; in the end a sack of bones and flayed flesh and fat
was swept along the shambles of that concrete floor and dragged
away.[39]

Bauer's meticulous and tenacious prosecution managed to
secure six life sentences, including that of Wilhelm Boger, and
the maximum prison terms available in all the other cases. Bauer
complained that West German media coverage of the trial
depicted the accused as merely following the orders of a Nazi
regime that appeared to be an alien group who had landed in
Germany and taken the German people prisoner. In reality,
Bauer claimed, Hitler's regime had enjoyed widespread popular
support and Gestapo officers such as Boger had been the norm,
not the exception.[40]

The Frankfurt Auschwitz Trial sparked a political debate
within West Germany as to why so many leading Nazi war
criminals still remained at large. In February 1963, the chief
prosecutor of the Supreme Court in Berlin began a major
investigation into the activities of the Reich Main Security
Office (RSHA) in which the Gestapo, the SD and the SS had
all been located. Up to this point, only four former members
of the RSHA had ever been convicted of war crimes by West
German courts.

It was decided to mount several major trials to deal with
leading figures in Heinrich Himmler's RSHA. Prosecutors identified 7,000 potential suspects, but then focused on 3,000
individuals who held leading roles in the RSHA during the

Nazi era. In the end, only one major trial was ever undertaken in the Berlin District Court, in 1969. The leading defendant was Otto Bovensiepen, head of the Berlin Gestapo, who had organised the deportation of 40,000 Jews from the capital between 1941 and 1943.

Bovensiepen was born in Duisburg on 8 July 1905. He joined the Nazi Party in 1925, completed a law degree at the University of Bonn in 1933, and then joined the political department of what became the Gestapo in Düsseldorf. He held leading roles in Gestapo offices in Dortmund, Köslin, Bielefeld and Halle before taking up the post of the head of Berlin's Gestapo. He played a leading role in tracking down communist resistance groups in the city, and was well known for his encouragement of the notorious 'enhanced interrogations' to break communist resistance groups. In 1944, he became the head of the security police in Nazi-occupied Denmark under Dr Werner Best. The details of how he conducted his interrogations have survived. He admitted during an Allied interrogation that he had ordered 'the application of torture in certain cases' involving figures who were hostile to Nazi rule in Denmark, in order to 'get a confession out of a prisoner if a speedy clarification of a matter was necessary'.[41] In September 1948, he was sentenced to death during a Danish war crimes trial. In 1951 he was released from prison as part of a general amnesty on war criminals and returned to West Germany. He gained a highly paid job in a leading West German insurance company and rose to the post of Managing Director.

The trial of Otto Bovensiepen and two other key defendants began in December 1969.[42] During the proceedings, Bovensiepen suffered a heart attack. He was then declared 'unfit to face trial' by a number of doctors in 1970. The trial proceedings were promptly suspended on 19 November 1971. Trial suspensions due to ill health were rarely awarded to those accused of murders in ordinary criminal trials. Once again, a Nazi war criminal received special treatment. The trial against Bovensiepen was never resumed. He lived an affluent lifestyle for another eight years before his death in 1979.

One leading Gestapo official who had managed to escape justice in post-war West Germany was Dr Werner Best. He played the role of professional bureaucrat with consummate skill while he worked for the Gestapo. Best was a key figure in the recruitment of all the leading personnel who carried out the Holocaust and the mass murders of the *Einsatzgruppen*. He considered the murder of the Jews as 'historically necessary'. He believed the biological racism of the Nazi regime was 'rational and logical'. In 1941, he wrote a book praising the methods of the Gestapo called *Die Deutsche Polizei* (The German Police) in which he depicted the Gestapo as staffed by professional policemen who always treated suspects with the utmost respect and dignity. Best was sentenced to death by a Danish war crimes trial in 1948, due to his role as governor of Denmark during the Nazi occupation. The sentence was never carried out. He was released in 1951 and returned to West Germany. In 1958, a denazification tribunal ordered him to pay a fine of 70,000 marks, due to his activities as a leading Gestapo official. By then he was working as a highly paid legal adviser for the leading West German company Stinnes.[43]

In March 1969, police raided Werner Best's lavish apartment in the city of Mülheim in the Ruhr and brought him to Berlin for detailed questioning. The Berlin prosecutor had assembled a huge amount of incriminating evidence against him, and was very confident of a guilty verdict at trial. Using all of his many powerful political and legal contacts at the top of West German society, Best was advised to claim that he was too ill, too old and too frail to face a lengthy and emotionally taxing war crimes trial. In August 1972, the West German authorities adjourned the case. The trial never took place.[44]

On 23 June 1989, Dr Werner Best died, having never paid for his extensive crimes against humanity during the Nazi era.

Nor did the Gestapo.

Notes

Introduction

1. This story is based on the following accounts: D. Bracher (ed.), *The Conscience in Revolt Portraits of German Resistance, 1933–1945*, Mainz; Hase and Koehler, 1994, pp. 320–322; D. Stroud (ed.), *Preaching in Hitler's Shadow*, Michigan, Eerdmans Publishing, 2013, pp. 94–105; quote from Alfred Leikam in R. Wentorf and P. Schneider, *Witness of Buchenwald*, Vancouver, Regent, 2008, p. 20.
2. H. Arendt, *The Origins of Totalitarianism*, London, André Deutsch, 1951, pp. 434–435.
3. The classic expression of this view is the 1961 bestseller by William Shirer, *The Rise and Fall of the Third Reich*. See also E. Bramstead, *Dictatorship and Political Police: The Technique of Control by Fear*, New York, Oxford University Press, 1945.
4. The most famous biography was A. Bullock, *Hitler: A Study in Tyranny*, London, Penguin, 1952. The emphasis Bullock placed on Hitler being more interested in power than his ideology has now been comprehensively rejected by modern scholars on the Third Reich.
5. See J. Delarue, *The Gestapo: A History of Horror* New York, Viking Press, 1962.
6. See *The Trials of the Major War Criminals before the International Military Tribunal*, (IMT) 42 vols, Washington, DC, Government Printing House, 1947–1949.
7. Delarue, *The Gestapo*, p. ix.
8. See M. Broszat, *The Hitler State: The Foundations and Development of the Internal Structure of the Third Reich*, London, Longman, 1981.
9. This work was brought together in six volumes. See M. Broszat et al. (eds), *Bayern in der NS-Zeit*, 6 vols, Munich, Oldenbourg, 1977–1983.
10. See R. Mann, *Protest and Kontrolle im Dritten Reich: Nationalsozialisctische Herrschaft im Alltag einer rheinischen Großstadt*, Frankfurt am Main, Campus Verlag, 1987. Sarah Gordon looked at the Gestapo files just related to Jewish 'race defilement' in the city of Düsseldorf, but she did not go into detail on individual cases. See S. Gordon, *Hitler, Germans and the Jewish Question*, Princeton, NJ, Princeton University Press, 1984. Joshi Vandana looked at cases involving female denouncers in Düsseldorf city too. See J. Vandana, *Gender and Power in the Third Reich: Female Denouncers and the Gestapo, 1933–1945*, Basingstoke, Palgrave Macmillan, 2003.

11. See R. Gellately, *The Gestapo and German Society: Enforcing Racial Policy, 1933–1945*, Oxford, Clarendon Press, 1990.

12. The trend towards examining denunciations is illustrated in the following works: R. Gellately, 'Denunciations and Nazi Germany: New Insights and Methodological Problems', *Historical Social Research*, Vol. 22 (1997), pp. 228–239; R. Gellately and S. Fitzpatrick, *Accusatory Practices: Denunciations in Modern European History, 1789–1989*, Chicago, IL, University of Chicago Press, 1997; R. Gellately, *Backing Hitler: Power and Consent in Nazi Germany*, Oxford, Oxford University Press, 2001; B. Frommer, 'Denunciations and Fraternisers: Gender Collaborations and Revolution on Bohemia and Moravia during World War II and After', in N. Wingfield and M. Bucur (eds), *Gender and War in Twentieth-Century Eastern Europe*, Indiana, IL, Indiana University Press, 2006, pp. 111–132.

13. See E. Johnson, *The Nazi Terror: The Gestapo, Jews and Ordinary Germans*, London, John Murray, 1999. See also E. Johnson and K.-H. Reuband, *What We Knew: Terror, Mass Murder and Everyday Life in Nazi Germany*, London, John Murray, 2005; E. Johnson, 'German Women and Nazi Justice: Their Role in the Process from Denunciation to Death', *Historical Research*, Vol. 20 (1995), pp. 33–69.

14. See F. McDonough, *Sophie Scholl: The Real Story of the Woman Who Defied Hitler*, Stroud, History Press, 2010.

15. Due to German privacy laws, the names of private individuals contained in Gestapo files, except those of Nazi officials, must be changed. All the other details contained in these cases remain identical to what actually happened.

Chapter 1

1. C. Walton-Kerr, *Gestapo: The History of the German Secret Police*, London, Senate, 1996, pp. 15–30.

2. Ibid. pp. 32–33.

3. W. Stieber, *The Chancellor's Spy: The Revelations of the Chief of Bismarck's Secret Service*, New York, Grove Press, 1980, pp. 25–38.

4. C. Graf, 'The Genesis of the Gestapo', *Journal of Contemporary History*, Vol. 22 (1987), p. 422.

5. C. Dams, and M. Stolle, *The Gestapo: Power and Terror in the Third Reich*, Oxford, Oxford University Press, 2014, p. 2.

6. Delarue, *The Gestapo*, p. 32.

7. Gellately, *The Gestapo and German Society*, p. 25.

8. Quoted in L. Machtan, *The Hidden Hitler*, Oxford, Perseus Press, p. 196.

9. Ibid., p. 68.

10. M. Williams, *Reinhard Heydrich: The Biography – Volume 1: The Road to War*, Church Stretton, Ulrich, 2001, pp. 22–30.

11. Walton-Kerr, *Gestapo*, p. 97.

12. Ibid., p. 101.

13. Ibid., pp. 102–103.
14. Ibid., pp. 181–230.
15. Dams and Stolle, *The Gestapo*, p. 5.
16. Avalon Project, Yale University. Online archive of Nuremberg Trial Proceedings of the International Military Tribunal at Nuremberg (hereafter AP-IMT) Affadavit of Rudolf Diels.
17. R. J. Evans, *The Coming of the Third Reich*, London, Penguin, 2004, p. 332.
18. Ibid., p. 34. Göring denied he ever gave the SA or the police an order to kill people. See AP-IMT. Göring Testimony, 18 March 1946.
19. N. Wachsmann, 'The Dynamics of Destruction: The Development of the Concentration Camps, 1933–1945', in J. Caplan and N. Wachsmann (eds), *Concentration Camps in Germany: The New Histories*, Abingdon, Routledge, pp. 18–19.
20. AP-IMT. Affadavit of Rudolf Diels.
21. Quoted in M. Wildt, *An Uncompromising Generation: The Leadership of the Reich Security Main Office*, Madison, WI, University of Wisconsin Press, 2009, p. 89.
22. AP-IMT. Werner Schäfer Testimony, 13 April 1946.
23. Ibid.
24. Delarue, *The Gestapo*, pp. 35–36.
25. Wachsmann, *Hitler's Prisons*, p. 166.
26. W. Shirer, *Rise and Fall of the Third Reich*, London, Folio, 2004, p. 256. A recent detailed study has produced new evidence which indicates Nazi involvement in the Reichstag fire, which Shirer argued was clear. See B. Hett, *Burning the Reichstag: An Investigation into the Third Reich's Enduring Mystery*, Oxford, Oxford University Press, 2014.
27. Delarue, *The Gestapo*, p. 34.
28. Gellately, *Gestapo and German Society*, pp. 27–28.
29. The term Gestapo is formed from letters highlighted in the title: GEheime STAatsPOlizei (Secret State Police).
30. Dams and Stolle, *The Gestapo*, p. 7.
31. Delarue, *The Gestapo*, pp. 57–58.
32. Quoted in G. Bowder, *Foundations of the Nazi Police State: The Formation of Sipo and S.D.*, Lexington, KY University Press of Kentucky, 2004, pp. 88–89.
33. Ibid., p. 117.
34. This interpretation features heavily in many general histories of the Third Reich and in some studies of the Gestapo. See, for example, Delarue, *The Gestapo*, pp. 57–72.
35. Quoted in Delarue, *The Gestapo*, p. 106.
36. Ibid., p. 105.
37. Quoted in Shirer, *Third Reich*, p. 260.
38. R.J. Evans, *The Third Reich in Power*, London, Penguin, 2006, p. 24.
39. See R. Diels, *Lucifer ante Portas: Es spricht der erste Chef der Gestapo*, Stuttgart, Deutche Verlags-Antsalt, 1950. This is a neglected, but important memoir on

the early development of the Gestapo, though it must be considered alongside other evidence.

40. Bowder, *Foundations of the Nazi Police State*, p. 127.
41. L. Goldensohn, *The Nuremberg Interviews: Conversations with Defendants and Witnesses*, London, Pimlico, p. 207.
42. Walton-Kerr, *Gestapo*, p. 123.
43. Bowder, *Foundations of the Nazi Police State*, p. 140.
44. Goldensohn, *The Nuremberg Interviews*, p. 207.
45. Quoted in Shirer, *Third Reich*, pp. 270–271.
46. Bowder, *Foundations of the Nazi Police State*, p. 141.
47. Shirer, *Third Reich*, p. 273.
48. Evans, *Third Reich in Power*, p. 26.
49. Ibid., pp. 30–31.
50. Delarue, *The Gestapo*, p. 113.
51. Ibid., pp. 114–117.
52. Shirer, *Third Reich*, p. 279.
53. Quoted in E. Crankshaw, *Gestapo: The Instrument of Terror*, London, Wren's Park, 2002, p. 84.
54. Evans, *Third Reich in Power*, pp. 33–34.
55. Delarue, *The Gestapo*, p. 123.
56. Evans, *Third Reich in Power*, p. 40.
57. Shirer, *Third Reich*, pp. 278–279.
58. Quoted in Wildt, *Uncompromising Generation*, p. 133.
59. Delarue, *The Gestapo*, p. 129.
60. Bowder, *Foundations of the Nazi Police State*, pp. 154–158.
61. Ibid., pp. 163–186.
62. C. Hammer (translator), *The Gestapo and SS Manual*, Boulder, CO Paladin Press, p. 61.
63. Wildt, *Uncompromising Generation*, pp. 134–136.
64. Delarue, *The Gestapo*, pp. 136–137.
65. Wildt, *Uncompromising Generation*, p. 9.
66. Delarue, *The Gestapo*, p. 139.
67. Quoted in Bowder, *Foundations of the Nazi Police State*, p. 229.

Chapter 2

1. Gellately, *Gestapo and German Society*, p. 44.
2. Ibid., p. 45.
3. Johnson, *Nazi Terror*, p. 47.
4. AP-IMT. Statement of Dr Merkel, defence counsel for Gestapo, 19 August 1946.
5. Gellately, *Gestapo and German Society*, p. 63.
6. *Gestapo and SS Manual*, pp. 28–29.
7. Dams and Stolle, *The Gestapo*, p. 45.

8. C. Whiting, *The Search for 'Gestapo Müller': The Man Without a Shadow*, Barnsley, Leo Cooper, 2001, pp. 39–52.

9. R. Butler, *An Illustrated History of the Gestapo*, Osceolo, WI, Worldwright Books, pp. 71–72.

10. M. Burleigh, *The Third Reich: A New History*, London, Macmillan, 2000, p. 178.

11. Gellately, *Gestapo and German Society*, p. 56.

12. Dams and Stolle, *The Gestapo*, pp. 42–43.

13. Wildt, *Uncompromising Generation*, p. 189.

14. Dams and Stolle, *The Gestapo*, pp. 42–43.

15. Ibid., p. 42.

16. Butler, *The Gestapo*, p. 79.

17. Wildt, *Uncompromising Generation*, p. 196.

18. Ibid., pp. 191–192.

19. Ibid., p. 203.

20. Johnson, *Nazi Terror*, pp. 53–56.

21. Ibid., p. 32.

22. In the UK this is similar to A/S levels or in the USA similar to the High School Leaving Certificate.

23. Dams and Stolle, *The Gestapo*, p. 46.

24. Gellately, *Gestapo and German Society*, p. 53.

25. Ibid., pp. 53–54.

26. Johnson, *Nazi Terror*, p. 47.

27. Ibid., pp. 59–65.

28. Gellately, *Gestapo and German Society*, pp. 58–59.

29. Dams and Stolle, *The Gestapo*, p. 51.

30. *Gestapo and SS Manual*, p. 91.

31. Ibid., p. 87.

32. Wachsmann, 'The Dynamics of Destruction', p. 21.

33. Quoted in N. Wachsmann, *Hitler's Prisons: Legal Terror in Nazi Germany*, London, Yale University Press, 2004, p. 179.

34. AP-IMT. Circular on regulations for arresting suspects by the Gestapo, 25 January 1938.

35. For a detailed discussion on how Gestapo cases usually developed, see Johnson, *Nazi Terror*, pp. 29–46.

36. AP-IMT. Letter from Franz Gürtner, Reich Minister of Justice to Wilhelm Frick, Minister of the Interior, 14 May 1935.

37. D. Dejali, *Torture and Democracy*, Princeton, NJ, Princeton University Press, p. 96.

38. Crankshaw, *Gestapo*, pp. 128–129.

39. Quoted in S. Brysac, *Resisting Hitler: Mildred Harnack and the Red Orchestra*, Oxford, Oxford University Press, 2000, p. 341.

40. Bowder, *The Nazi Police State*, pp. 234–235.

Chapter 3

1. Quoted in M. Oakshott (ed.), *The Social and Political Doctrine of Contemporary Europe*, Cambridge, Cambridge University Press, 1953, pp. 192–193.

2. J. Conway, *The Nazi Persecution of the Churches, 1933–1945*, Vancouver, Regent, 1968, p. 232.

3. Johnson, *Nazi Terror*, pp. 228–229.

4. Quoted in Conway, *Nazi Persecution of the Churches*, p. 15.

5. Goebbels Diary, 29 December 1939: quoted in F. Taylor (ed.), *The Goebbels Diaries, 1939–1941*, London, Hamish Hamilton, p. 77.

6. Conway, *Nazi Persecution of the Churches*, p. 20.

7. Pacelli would later become Pope Pius VII.

8. Conway, *Nazi Persecution of the Churches*, p. 287.

9. H. Himmler in *Die Schutzstaffel als antibolschewistische Kampforganisation*, Munich, F. Eher Nachtführung, 1936, p. 27. See also Conway, *Nazi Persecution of the Churches*, p. 363.

10. According to H. Mohr, the figure was 260. See H. Mohr, *Katholische Orden und Deutscher Imperialismus*, Berlin, Akademie Verlag, 1965, p. 135. Barrack 26 at Dachau just contained Catholic priests and Protestant pastors.

11. For a detailed analysis see M. Gross, *The War against Catholicism: Liberalism and the Anti-Catholic Imagination on Nineteenth-Century Germany*, Michigan, SOM, University of Michigan Press, 2004.

12. Quoted in Conway, *Nazi Persecution of the Churches*, p. 112.

13. This was known as the 'Aryan paragraph', which was really designed to remove all those Christians who were married to Jews or to remove assimilated Jews who had converted to Christianity.

14. Karl Barth was stripped of his Professorial chair in 1935 and fled into exile to Switzerland.

15. Shirer, *Rise and Fall of the Third Reich*, p. 296.

16. HStAD. RW 58/16977. Personal Details of Enke Hansse (born January 1896).

17. HStAD. RW 58/16977. Gestapo Case File on Enke Hansse.

18. Conway, *Nazi Persecution of the Churches*, p. 433.

19. Quoted in Holocaust Encyclopaedia, website of US Holocaust Museum, Washington, DC.

20. R. Rubenstein 'The Dean and the Chosen People', in *After Auschwitz: Radical Theology and Contemporary Judaism*, Indianapolis, IN, Bobbs-Merrill, 1966, pp. 46–58.

21. Quoted in Conway, *Nazi Persecution of the Churches*, pp. 264–265.

22. HStAD. RW 58/47308. Personal Details of Helmut Hesse (born May 1916).

23. Bracher (ed.), *The Conscience in Revolt*, p. 326.

24. HStAD. RW 58/47308. Gestapo Case File of Helmut Hesse.

25. HStAD. RW 58/1211. Personal Details of Wilhelm Kenath (born February 1896).

26. HStAD. RW 58/1211. Gestapo Case File of Wilhelm Kenath.

27. Quoted in S. Aronson, *The Beginnings of the German Gestapo: The Bavarian Model in* 1933, Jerusalem, Israel University Press, p. 40.
28. HStAD. RW 58/17253. Personal Details of Joseph Broch (born March 1907).
29. These were known as '*Fahrtenlieder* songs' and were used on hiking trips. Many ridiculed the Nazis.
30. HStAD. RW 58/17253. Gestapo Case File on Joseph Broch.
31. Evans, *The Third Reich in Power*, p. 244.
32. Conway, *Nazi Persecution of the Churches*, p. 90.
33. Bracher (ed.), *The Conscience in Revolt*, pp. 333–335, p. 319.
34. Evans, *The Third Reich in Power*, p. 245.
35. Bramstead, *Dictatorship and Political Police,* pp. 200–201.
36. This case is discussed in detail in Johnson, *Nazi Terror*, pp. 212–219. Johnson suggests cases such as this were rare, and he suggests that the priest was given very lenient treatment considering the widespread extent of his homosexual abuse.
37. Quoted in Conway, *Nazi Persecution of the Churches*, pp. 113–114.
38. Bracher (ed.), *The Conscience in Revolt*, pp. 333–335.
39. 'Transcript of Trial of Rupert Mayer', in J. Donohue, *Hitler's Conservative Opponents in Bavaria*, Leiden, Brill, 1961, pp. 230–245.
40. Bracher (ed.), *The Conscience in Revolt*, pp. 333–335.
41. *Mit Brennender Sorge* ('With Burning Anxiety'), Vatican, Rome, 14 March 1937.
42. Conway, *Nazi Persecution of the Churches*, p. 166.
43. Clemens von Galen speech, 9 March 1936.
44. Anonymous, *The Persecution of the Catholic Church in the Third Reich: Facts and Documents*, London, Pelican, 2003, p. 19.
45. Conway, *Nazi Persecution of the Churches*, pp. 168–173.
46. *The Persecution of the Catholic Church in the Third Reich*, p. 45.
47. Conway, *Nazi Persecution of the Churches*, p. 279.
48. Ibid., p. 167.
49. Ibid., p. 234.
50. Gestapo Report, March 1943. Quoted as Document 3.15 in M. Housden, *Resistance and Conformity in the Third Reich*, Abingdon, Routledge, 1997, pp. 46–67.
51. Conway, *Nazi Persecution of the Churches*, pp. 235–236.
52. Bracher (ed.), *The Conscience in Revolt*, pp. 339–340.
53. It was known as the T-4 Euthanasia Programme.
54. Sermon by Clemens von Galen, 3 August 1941.
55. The public hostility towards euthanasia forced Hitler to halt the programme within Germany's borders on 28 August 1941. Thereafter it was carried out in absolute secrecy, and mostly in the extermination centres in Poland.
56. A. Ebbinghaus (ed.), *Opfer und Täterinnen: Frauenbiographien des Nationalsozialismus*, Nördlingen, Delphi Politik, 1987, pp. 237–238.
57. HStAD. RW 58/19795. Personal Details of Seline Winter (born March 1873).

58. See P. Demand, *Luisenkult*, Cologne, Böchlau, 2003.
59. Burleigh, *Third Reich*, pp. 196–197.
60. HStAD. RW 58/19795. Gestapo Case File of Seline Winter.
61. Quoted in Conway, *Nazi Persecution of the Churches*, p. 286.
62. They were also known in Germany as *Internationale Bibelforschergesellschaft* (IBV).
63. In Gestapo files the terms '*Erneste Bibelforscher*' (Earnest Bible Students) and the '*Bibelforscher-Vereingung-IBV*' (International Bible Students Association) are both used. The English term Jehovah's Witnesses is used here.
64. D. Garbe, *Between Resistance and Martyrdom; Jehovah's Witnesses and the Third Reich*, Wisconsin, WI, University of Wisconsin Press, 2008, p. 508.
65. Quoted in Conway, *Nazi Persecution of the Churches*, p. 197.
66. Johnson, *Nazi Terror*, p. 249.
67. The figures on how many Jehovah's Witnesses died in prisons and concentration camps are disputed. The figure of 1,200 was given in Detlef Garbe, *Jehovah's Witnesses and the Third Reich*. Richard Evans gives a lower figure of 950.
68. Evans, *Third Reich in Power*, p. 255.
69. Garbe, *Jehovah's Witnesses and the Third Reich*, p. 508.
70. Quoted in M. Reynard and S. Graffard, *The Jehovah's Witnesses and the Nazis: Persecution, Deportation and Murder, 1933–1945*, New York, Cooper Square Press, 2001, p. 75.
71. HStAD. RW 58/17508. Personal Details of Wilhelm Gerres (born November 1901).
72. This declaration was required to be signed by all Jehovah's Witnesses before they were allowed to be released from prison. The translation quoted here comes from M. Penton, *Jehovah's Witnesses and the Third Reich: Sectarian Politics under Persecution*, Toronto, University of Toronto Press, 2004, p. 362.
73. *Preussische Landeszeitung*, 14 February 1937.
74. See Penton, *Jehovah's Witnesses*, p. 188.
75. HStAD. RW 58/17508. Gestapo Case File of Wilhelm Gerres.
76. Johnson, *Nazi Terror*, p. 244.
77. Ibid., p. 71.
78. HStAD. RW 58/1142. Personal Details of Heinrich Winten (born May 1905).
79. HStAD. RW 58/1142. Gestapo Case File of Heinrich Winten.
80. HStAD. RW 58/15472. Personal Details of Paul Schlemann (born February 1882).
81. HStAD. RW 58/15472. Gestapo Case File of Paul Schlemann.
82. Quoted in E. Kogon, *The Theory and Practice of Hell: The German Concentration Camps and the System Behind Them*, New York, Berkley Books, 1964, p. 43.
83. Quoted in Johnson, *Nazi Terror*, p. 241.
84. Reynard and Graffard, *The Jehovah's Witnesses and the Nazis*, p. 76.

Chapter 4

1. Quoted in J. Noakes and G. Pridham (eds), *Nazism 1919–1945 – Volume 4: The German Home Front in World War II: A Documentary Reader*, Exeter, Exeter University Press, 1998, p. 588 (hereafter *Nazism: A Documentary Reader*, followed by volume number and page number).

2. A. Merson, *Communist Resistance in Nazi Germany*, London, Lawrence and Wishart, 1985, p. 55.

3. Johnson, *Nazi Terror*, p. 162.

4. Merson, *Communist Resistance*, pp. 13–15.

5. E. Weitz, *Creating German Communism, 1890–1990: From Popular Protest to the Socialist State*, Princeton, NJ, Princeton University Press, 1997 p. 189.

6. Gordon, *Hitler, Germans and the Jewish Question*, p. 20.

7. L. Peterson, *German Communism: Workers' Protest and Labour Unions – The Politics of the United Front in Rhineland-Westphalia*, Amsterdam, Kluwer Academic Publishers, 1993 p. 258.

8. Burleigh, *Third Reich*, pp. 666–667.

9. In German: *Roter Frontkämpferbund* – RFB.

10. In German: *Revolutionäire Gewerkschaftsoppostion* – RGO.

11. Merson, *Communist Resistance*, pp. 91–92.

12. Ibid., p. 27.

13. Ibid., p. 34.

14. Ibid., p. 120.

15. Dams and Stolle, *The Gestapo*, p. 97.

16. Merson, *Communist Resistance*, p. 41.

17. Johnson, *Nazi Terror*, pp. 172–173.

18. Quoted in D. Peukert, *Inside Nazi Germany: Conformity, Opposition and Racism in Everyday Life*, London, Batsford, 1987, pp. 122–123.

19. Ibid., p. 105.

20. J. Herf, *The Nazi Past in the Two Germanys*, Cambridge, MA, Harvard University Press, 1997, p. 13.

21. J.-M. Palmier, *Weimar in Exile: The Anti-Fascist Emigration in Europe and America*, London, Verso, 2006, p. 172.

22. C. Epstein, *The Last Revolutionaries: German Communists and their Century*, Cambridge, MA, Harvard University Press, p. 54.

23. HStAD. RW 58/288. Personal Details of Luise Vögler (born November 1904).

24. It is now called Luhansk.

25. HStAD. RW 58/288. Gestapo Case File of Luise Vögler.

26. O. Figes, *The Whisperers: Private Life in the Soviet Union*, London, Penguin, pp. 171–172.

27. The Gestapo gave the group the nickname 'The Red Orchestra' and accused them of passing on intelligence information to the Soviet Union. In the summer of 1942 all the leading members of the group were tracked down by the Gestapo. It has never been fully established they did pass on secrets.

Nevertheless, the members of the group were charged with 'high treason'. Most were either tortured, executed or faced lengthy prison sentences.

28. Quoted in Bracher (ed.), *Conscience in Revolt*, p. 304.
29. Merson, *Communist Resistance*, p. 182.
30. Ibid., p. 139.
31. Report of the State Police Office, Darmstadt, 21 April 1937. Quoted in T. Mason, *Arbeiterklasse und Volksgemeinschaft*, Berlin, Opalden 1975, pp. 315–316.
32. Peukert, *Inside Nazi Germany*, pp. 124–125.
33. Merson, *Communist Resistance*, p. 183.
34. Ibid., p. 187.
35. SOPADE Report, July 1938. Quoted in *Nazism: A Documentary Reader*, Vol. 2, p. 387.
36. HStAD. RW 58/17801. Personal Details of Karoline Krupp (born June 1905).
37. HStAD. RW 58/17801. The Gestapo file of Karoline Krupp.
38. HStAD. RW 58/1959. Personal Details of Peter Penk (born May 1915).
39. The city was called Münchengladbach in the Nazi era. It was renamed Mönchengladbach in 1960. It is called Münchengladbach here.
40. There are no details in Peter Penk's file about what punishment he received for this crime, if any.
41. HStAD. RW 58/1958 and RW 58/19428. Gestapo Case Files on Peter Penk.
42. Peukert, *Inside Nazi Germany*, p. 112.
43. R. Grunberger, *A Social History of the Third Reich*, London, Phoenix, 2005 edn, p. 257.
44. Gestapo Report, Düsseldorf, 1937. Quoted in *Nazism: A Documentary Reader*, Vol. 2, p. 398.
45. HStAD. RW 58/22533. Personal Details of Anton Kendricks (born 1887).
46. The Züblin Construction Company is still one of Germany's major building companies.
47. HStAD. RW 58/22533 and RW 58/55166. Gestapo Case Files of Anton Kendricks.
48. HStAD. RW 58/37523. Personal Details of Heinz Wasschermann (born December 1921).
49. HStAD. RW 58/37523 and RW 58/52505. Gestapo Case Files of Heinz Wasschermann.
50. Quoted in Merson, *Communist Resistance*, p. 213.
51. HStAD. RW 58/18552. Personal Details of Erich Weiss (born September 1900).
52. HStAD. RW 58/18552. Gestapo Case File of Erich Weiss.
53. HStAD. RW 58/1544. Personal Details of Aloys Vock (born June 1891).
54. HStAD. RW 58/1544. Gestapo Case File of Aloys Vock.
55. HStAD. RW 58/17606. Personal Details of Wilhelm Struck (born June 1905).
56. HStAD. RW 58/17606. Gestapo Case File of Wilhelm Struck.
57. HStAD. RW 58/17060. Personal Details of Friedrich Grossmann (born September 1899).

58. The old comrade is called Böhme in the Gestapo file.
59. HStAD. RW 58/17060. The Gestapo Case file of Friedrich Grossmann.
60. Gellately, *Gestapo and German Society*, p. 223.
61. Peukert, *Inside Nazi Germany*, p. 126.
62. The soldiers' wives were called 'Kriegsfrauen'.
63. Quoted in Gellately, *Gestapo and German Society*, p. 236.
64. J. Vandana, *Gender and Power in the Third Reich: Female Denouncers and the Gestapo, 1933–1945*, London, Palgrave, 2003, pp. 151–152.
65. U. Herbert, *Hitler's Foreign Workers: Enforced Labour in Germany under the Third Reich*, Cambridge, Cambridge University Press, p. 335.
66. Ibid., p. 129.
67. Ibid., p. 335.
68. HStAD. RW 58/9196. Personal Details of Hermann Haus (born September 1892).
69. The evidence suggests these two foreign workers were from Belgium.
70. HStAD. RW 58/9196. The Gestapo Case File of Hermann Haus. The Gestapo file RW 58/45278 contains identical details of the case.
71. These findings add further weight to the work of both Robert Gellately and Eric Johnson.
72. Gellately, *Gestapo and German Society*, p. 137.

Chapter 5

1. Gellately, *Gestapo and German Society*, p. 134.
2. Denouncement was a minority activity among the German population as a whole. Eric Johnson shows that in the city of Krefeld, with a population of 170,000, denouncers represented between just 1 and 2 per cent of the population. This figure holds true of other areas.
3. Gellately, *Gestapo and German Society*, p. 149.
4. Vandana, *Gender and Power in the Third Reich*, pp. 183–185.
5. In areas occupied by the Nazi regime during the Second World War, women made up the majority of denunciations, particularly in Czechoslovakia and certain areas of France. See B. Frommer, 'Denunciations and Fraternisers: Gender Collaboration and Revolution in Bohemia and Moravia during World War II and After', in N. Wingfield and M. Bucur (eds), *Gender and War in Twentieth-Century Eastern Europe*, Indiana, IL, Indiana University Press, 2006, p. 113.
6. Ibid., p. 146.
7. R. Grunberger, *A Social History of the Third Reich*, London, Phoenix, 2005 edn, p. 150.
8. Quoted in *Nazism: A Documentary Reader*, Vol. 2, p. 284.
9. Grunberger, *Social History of the Third Reich*, p. 146.
10. Ibid., p. 286.
11. Evans, *Third Reich in Power*, p. 115.
12. HStAD. RW 58/71336. Personal Details of Heinrich Veet (born August 1876).

13. The copper factory was called *Duisburger Kufternütte*.
14. HStAD. RW 58/71336. Gestapo Case File of Heinrich Veet.
15. Stockhouse, 'Gestapo Interrogations', p. 83.
16. Ibid., p. 80.
17. HStAD. RW 58/16829. Personal Details of Karl Vort (born 4 October 1904).
18. HStAD. RW 58/16829. Gestapo Case File of Karl Vort.
19. HStAD. RW 58/30555. Personal Details of Karl Feedler (born March 1903). He listed his religion as 'Catholic'.
20. HStAD. RW 58/30555. Gestapo Case File of Karl Feedler.
21. Grunberger, *Social History of the Third Reich*, p. 151.
22. Gellately, *Gestapo and German Society*, p. 148.
23. Vandana, *Gender and Power in the Third Reich*, p. 50.
24. Ibid., pp. 52–55.
25. Ibid., pp. 149–150.
26. Ibid., p. 80.
27. HStAD. RW 58/1098. Personal Details of Rosa Deeser (born October 1916). She listed her religion as 'Catholic'.
28. HStAD. RW 58/1098. Gestapo Case File of Rosa Deeser.
29. HStAD. RW 58/5186. Personal Details of Walter Remmer (born August 1913). He listed his religion as 'Protestant'.
30. HStAD. RW 58/5186. Gestapo Case File of Walter Remmer.
31. Johnson, *Nazi Terror*, p. 313.
32. *Nazism: A Documentary Reader*, Vol. 4, p. 122.
33. Ibid., p. 126.
34. Johnson, *Nazi Terror*, p. 323.
35. Gellately, *Gestapo and German Society*, p. 141.
36. *Nazism: A Documentary Reader*, Vol. 4, pp. 127–128.
37. R. Moorhouse, *Berlin at War: Life and Death in Hitler's Capital*, London, Vintage, 2010, p. 214.
38. Quoted in *Nazism: A Documentary Reader*, Vol. 4, p. 127.
39. For full details of this case see Johnson, *Nazi Terror*, pp. 329–331.
40. Robert Gellately, *Backing Hitler: Consent and Coercion in Nazi Germany*, Oxford, Oxford University Press, 2001, p. 196.
41. HStAD. RW 58/17801. Personal Details of Peter Holdenberg (born February 1875).
42. HStAD. RW 58/17801. Gestapo Case File of Peter Holdenberg.
43. Interview with Maria von Lingen. Quoted in Alison Owings, *Frauen: German Women Recall the Third Reich*, London, Penguin, 1993, pp. 122–123.
44. HStAD. RW 58/1183. Personal Details of Karl Kesler (born April 1904).
45. HStAD. RW 58/1183. Gestapo Case File of Karl Kesler.
46. Evans, *Third Reich in Power*, p. 103.
47. Quoted in *Nazism: A Documentary Reader*, Vol. 2, p. 286.
48. HStAD. RW 58/58532. Personal Details of Rudolf Henning (born April 1909). He listed his occupation as 'barber' and his religion as 'God Believer'.

This was a Nazi group that stood outside the main religious groups. He had formerly been a Catholic.

49. HStAD. RW 58/58532. Gestapo Case File of Rudolf Henning.
50. HStAD. RW 58/61051. Personal Details of Johann Konte (born February 1902). He listed his religion as 'Catholic'.
51. HStAD. RW 58/61051. Gestapo Case File of Johann Konte.
52. Delarue, *Nazi Terror*, pp. 86–87.
53. Called '*Winterhilfswerk*'. This annual and popular Nazi charity drive collected donations from the public and then distributed food hampers to the old and the poor at Christmas.
54. G. Quinn, *Hidden Beneath the Thorns: Growing Up Under Nazi Rule, A Memoir of Ingeborg Tismor*, New York, iUniverse, 2009, p. 54.
55. Gellately, *Backing Hitler*, p. 228.
56. Quoted in *Nazism: A Documentary Reader*, Vol. 2, p. 324.
57. It is now called Töniverst and is about five kilometres west of the Rhineland city of Krefeld.
58. HStAD. RW 58/17511. Personal Details of Johann Hack (born March 1888). He listed his religion as 'Catholic'.
59. HStAD. RW 58/17511. Gestapo Case File of Johann Hack.
60. HStAD. RW 58/18453. Personal Details of Adam Lipper (born July 1892). He listed his religion as 'Catholic'.
61. HStAD. RW 58/18453. Gestapo Case File of Adam Lipper.
62. Quoted in *Nazism: A Documentary Reader*, Vol. 4, p. 545.
63. Gellately, *Backing Hitler*, p. 228.
64. This case is examined in Johnson, *Nazi Terror*, pp. 309–312.
65. Gellately, *Backing Hitler*, p. 227.
66. N. Stargardt, *Witnesses of War: Children's Lives under the Nazis*, London, Pimlico, p. 237.
67. HStAD. RW 58/21829. Personal Details of Walter Needen (born August 1903). He listed his religion as 'Protestant'.
68. HStAD. RW 58/21829. The Gestapo Case File of Walter Needen.
69. Gellately, *Backing Hitler*, p. 201.
70. This view is most forcibly and successfully advanced by Robert Gellately.
71. Evans, *Third Reich in Power*, p. 104.
72. Quoted in Gellately, *Gestapo and German Society*, p. 142.

Chapter 6

1. Quoted in Wildt, *Uncompromising Generation*, p. 149.
2. Quoted in Peukert, *Inside Nazi Germany*, p. 221.
3. *Nazism: A Documentary Reader*, Vol. 2, p. 264.
4. Evans, *Third Reich in Power*, pp. 507–554.
5. Interview with Greta. Quoted in B. Engelmann, *In Hitler's Germany*, New York, Pantheon Books, 1986 p. 39.

6. Evans, *Third Reich in Power*, pp. 507–508.
7. H. Biesold, *Eugenics and Deaf People in Nazi Germany*, Washington, DC, Gallaudet University Press, 1999 p. 5.
8. For a detailed discussion see Burleigh, *The Third Reich*, pp. 333–381.
9. R. Proctor, 'The Collaboration of Medicine and Nazism', in J. Michalcyzk (ed.), *Medicine, Ethics and the Third Reich: Historical and Contemporary Issues*, Kansas City, MO Sheed and Ward, 1994, p. 36.
10. Interview with Maria von Lingen. Quoted in Owings, *Frauen*, p. 133.
11. Burleigh, *The Third Reich*, p. 371.
12. Quoted in Evans, *Third Reich in Power*, p. 510.
13. Quoted in Peukert, *Inside Nazi Germany*, pp. 212–213.
14. G. Lewy, *The Nazi Persecution of the Gypsies*, Oxford, Oxford University Press, 2000, pp. 40–41.
15. *Nazism: A Documentary Reader*, Vol. 2, p. 265.
16. For a detailed analysis see L. Pine 'Hashude: The Imprisonment of "Asocial" Families in the Third Reich', *German History*, Vol. 13, no. 2 (1995), pp. 182–197.
17. Wachsmann, *Hitler's Prisons*, pp. 140–143.
18. *Nazism: A Documentary Reader*, Vol. 4, p. 136.
19. Gellately, *Backing Hitler*, p. 95.
20. Quoted in Wachsmann, *Hitler's Prisons*, p. 137.
21. Ibid., p. 132.
22. Gellately, *Backing Hitler*, p. 96.
23. Peukert, *Inside Nazi Germany*, p. 226.
24. *Nazism: A Documentary Reader*, Vol. 4, p. 136.
25. Ibid., p. 135.
26. Wachsmann, *Hitler's Prisons*, pp. 154–156.
27. Ibid., p. 218.
28. Ibid., p. 288.
29. For an in-depth analysis see N. Wachsmann, 'From Indefinite Confinement to Extermination: Habitual Criminals and the Third Reich', in R. Gellately and N. Stoltzfus (eds), *Social Outsiders in Nazi Germany*, Princeton, Princeton University Press, 2001, pp. 165–191.
30. Lewy, *Nazi Persecution of the Gypsies*, p. 29.
31. Gellately, *Backing Hitler*, p. 99.
32. *Nazism: A Documentary Reader*, Vol. 4, p. 135.
33. Nicholas Stargardt, *Witnesses of War: Children's Lives under the Nazis*, London, Pimlico, p. 62.
34. Ibid., p. 60.
35. Ibid., p. 64.
36. Quoted in *Nazism: A Documentary Reader*, Vol. 4, p. 452.
37. Ibid., p. 450.
38. Quoted in Peukert, *Inside Nazi Germany*, p. 160.
39. Ibid., pp. 162–165.
40. *Nazism: A Documentary Reader*, Vol. 4, p. 455.

41. Peukert, *Inside Nazi Germany*, p. 161.
42. Johnson, *Nazi Terror*, p. 276.
43. Quoted in Peukert, *Inside Nazi Germany*, p. 166.
44. See A. Time, 'The Ambivalent Outsider: Prostitutes, Promiscuity and VD in Nazi Berlin', in Gellately and Stoltzfus (eds), *Social Outsiders*, pp. 192–211.
45. Gellately, *Backing Hitler*, p. 111.
46. L. Pine, *Hitler's 'National Community': Society and Culture in Nazi Germany*, London, Bloomsbury, 2011, pp. 144–148.
47. Gestapo Case File. Quoted in Ebbinghaus (ed.), *Opfer und Tatterinnen*, p. 91.
48. Gellately, *Backing Hitler*, p. 112.
49. N. Herbermann et al., *The Blessed Abyss: Inmate #6582 in Ravensbrück Concentration Camp for Women*, Detroit, Wayne State University Press, pp. 32–34.
50. Homosexual laws stayed in force in West Germany until 1969 and in Britain until 1967.
51. Evans, *Third Reich in Power*, p. 530.
52. R. Plant, *The Pink Triangle: The Nazi War against Homosexuals*, Edinburgh, Mainstream, 1987, p. 89.
53. Ibid., p. 50.
54. *Nazism: A Documentary Reader*, Vol. 4, p. 390.
55. For details see Johnson, *Nazi Terror*, pp. 292–294.
56. Quoted in G. Beck, *An Underground Life*, Wisconsin, University of Wisconsin Press, 1999, pp. 22–24.
57. Plant, *The Pink Triangle*, pp. 133–136.
58. Ibid., p. 163.
59. Quoted in Pine, 'National Community', p. 143.
60. Plant, *The Pink Triangle*, p. 164.
61. Ibid., pp. 176–178.
62. *Neues Volk, September 1937*, pp. 21–27.
63. Nicholas Stargardt, *Witnesses of War*, p. 75.
64. Lewy, *Nazi Persecution of the Gypsies*, pp. 38–43.
65. Ibid., p. 50.
66. Ibid., p. 28.
67. Ibid., p. 67.
68. Ibid., p. 137.
69. Ibid., p. 140.
70. Ibid., p. 141.
71. Quoted in Peukert, *Inside Nazi Germany*, p. 216.
72. Lewy, *Nazi Persecution of the Gypsies*, p. 144.
73. Ibid., p. 189.
74. Interview with Hilda. Quoted in Dan Bar-On, *Legacy of Silence: Encounters with Children of the Third Reich*, Cambridge, MA, Harvard University Press, 1989, p. 103.

Chapter 7

1. In 1933 Breslau was a German city in Lower Silesia. It is now called Wroclaw and is in Poland.
2. Yad Vashem Archive, Tel Aviv, 033/72, Ludwig Förder Testimony, March 1933.
3. Gordon, *Hitler, Germans and the Jewish Question*, p. 119.
4. Interview by author with Claus Moser, London, 3 August 2009.
5. Interview with Klaus Scheurenberg. Quoted in J. Steinhoff, P. Pechel and D. Showalter (eds), *Voices from the Third Reich: An Oral History*, Washington, DC, Da Capo Press, 1994, p. 53.
6. Gordon, *Hitler, Germans and the Jewish Question*, pp. 7–49.
7. Interview with Ursula Meyer-Semlies. Quoted in Owings, *Frauen*, p. 55.
8. Interview with Ellen Frey. Quoted in Owings, *Frauen*, p. 174.
9. Interview with Erna Tiertz. Quoted in Owings, *Frauen*, p. 280.
10. Quoted in Burleigh, *Third Reich*, p. 316.
11. Interview with Arnold Biegeleisen. Quoted in *Voices from the Third Reich*, p. 44.
12. *Jüdische Rundschau*, 4 April 1933.
13. Burleigh, *Third Reich*, p. 288.
14. Gellately, *Backing Hitler*, p. 133.
15. Interview by author with Claus Moser, London, 3 August 2009.
16. Beck, *An Underground Life*, 1999, p. 17.
17. Johnson, *Nazi Terror*, p. 96.
18. Ibid., pp. 101–102.
19. The term 'Aryan' was used by the Nazis to define someone 'racially pure'.
20. *The Times*, 8 November 1935.
21. Johnson, *Nazi Terror*, p. 106.
22. Interview by author with Cecile Lowenthal Hensel, Berlin, 4 September 2009.
23. Interview with Dorothea Schlosser. Quoted in *Voices of the Third Reich*, p. 45.
24. Interview by author with Claus Moser, London, 3 August 2009.
25. Quoted in C. Rittner and J. Roth, *Different Voices: Women and the Holocaust*, New York, Paragon House, 1993, p. 199.
26. I place 'race defilement' in inverted commas to emphasise it was a Nazi construct.
27. See P. Szobar, 'Telling Sexual Stories in Nazi Courts of Law: Race Defilement in Germany, 1933 to 1945', in D. Herzog (ed.), *Sexuality and German Fascism*, London, Berghahn, pp. 133–163.
28. *Nazism: A Documentary Reader*, Vol. 2, p. 346.
29. Gellately, *Backing Hitler*, pp. 134–135.
30. Gordon, *Hitler, Germans and the Jewish Question*, p. 213.
31. *Nazism: A Documentary Reader*, Vol. 2, pp. 346–347.
32. Vandana, *Gender and Power in the Third Reich*, p. 123.

33. Johnson, *Nazi Terror*, pp. 111–114.
34. HStAD. RW 58/8869. Personal Details of Dr Siegfried Kleff (born December 1882).
35. HStAD. RW 58/8869. Gestapo Case File of Dr Siegfried Kleff.
36. HStAD. RW 58/1252. Personal Details of Dr Michael Steinbeck (born August 1880).
37. HStAD. RW 58/1252. Gestapo Case File of Dr Michael Steinbeck.
38. HStAD. RW 58/55406. Personal Details of Josef Kahn (born September 1886).
39. HStAD. RW 58/55406. Gestapo Case File of Josef Kahn.
40. Quoted in Evans, *Third Reich in Power*, pp. 582–583.
41. Gellately, *Backing Hitler*, pp. 126–127.
42. Bundesarchiv, Berlin, Teletyped message by Heydrich, 10 November 1938.
43. SOPADE Report, November 1938. Quoted in Peukert, *Inside Nazi Germany*, p. 58.
44. HStAD. RW 58/64364, Personal Details of Leopold Funk (born March 1879).
45. HStAD. RW 58/64364. Gestapo Case File of Leopold Funk.
46. SOPADE Report, December 1938. Quoted in Peukert, *Inside Nazi Germany*, p. 59.
47. Quoted in Beck, *An Underground Life*, pp. 38–39.
48. Johnson, *Nazi Terror*, p. 292.
49. Gordon, *Hitler, Germans and the Jewish Question*, p. 188.
50. Johnson, *Nazi Terror*, p. 431.
51. Quoted in Vandana, *Gender and Power in the Third Reich*, p. 136.
52. Johnson, *Nazi Terror*, p. 292.
53. Gellately, *Backing Hitler*, p. 129.
54. Quoted in Burleigh, *Third Reich*, p. 300.
55. Testimony of Valerie Wolfenstein. Quoted in E. Boehm, *We Survived: Fourteen Histories of the Hidden and Hunted in Nazi Germany*, Boulder, CO, Westview, 2003 edn, p. 81.
56. Johnson, *Nazi Terror*, p. 398.
57. Gellately, *The Gestapo and German Society*, p. 212.
58. Testimony of Rolf Joseph. Quoted in Boehm, *We Survived*, p. 153.
59. Ibid., p. 155. Rolf Joseph was able to escape from a concentration camp and amazingly was never transported to Poland and survived the war.
60. HStAD. RW 58/4186. Personal Details of [Sara] Martha Peet (born May 1892).
61. HStAD. RW 58/4186. The Gestapo Case File of [Sara] Martha Peet.
62. Quoted in Gordon, *Hitler, Germans and the Jewish Question*, p. 189.
63. Ibid., p. 193.
64. Johnson, *Nazi Terror*, pp. 414–415.
65. Gellately, *Gestapo and German Society*, p. 191.
66. Johnson, *Nazi Terror*, pp. 422–426.
67. Gellately, *Backing Hitler*, pp. 144–145. The fate of the denouncers in this case are discussed in Chapter 8.

68. HStAD. RW 58/52490. Personal Details of Helene Krabs (born September 1906).

69. HStAD. RW 58/52490. The Gestapo Case File of Helene Krabs.

Chapter 8

1. Whiting, *The Search for Gestapo Muller*, pp. 11–35.

2. P. Longerich, *Heinrich Himmler: A Life*, Oxford, Oxford University Press, pp. 734–736.

3. AP-IMT. The Indictment against the Gestapo. Presented by Colonel Robert Storey, 20 December 1945 and 2 January 1946.

4. AP-IMT. Testimony of Dr Werner Best, 31 July 1946, 1 August 1946.

5. AP-IMT. Testimony of Karl-Heinz Hoffmann, 1 August 1946.

6. Ibid.

7. AP-IMT. Closing Speech for the Defence Counsel of the Gestapo, Dr Rudolf Merkel, 23 August 1946.

8. AP-IMT. The Nuremberg Judgment, 30 September 1946 and 1 October 1946.

9. For a detailed analysis see G. Steinacher, *Nazis on the Run: How Hitler's Henchmen Fled Justice*, Oxford, Oxford University Press, 2011.

10. Wildt, *Uncompromising Generation*, pp. 371–377.

11. Johnson, *Nazi Terror*, p. 479.

12. Gordon, *Hitler, Germans and the Jewish Question*, pp. 197–209.

13. Wildt, *Uncompromising Generation*, p. 375.

14. Wachsmann, *Hitler's Prisons*, pp. 342–347.

15. This individual came to my attention due to Eric Johnson's book on Nazi terror and so I decided to look at the case files on him in more detail. See also Johnson, *Nazi Terror*, pp. 240–241, 249, 244–247, 292, for cases that Dihr was involved in during the Nazi period.

16. HStAD. Rep. 8, no. 10. File on Otto Dihr.

17. A. Szanajanda, *Indirect Perpetrators: The Persecution of Informers in Germany, 1945–1965*, Plymouth, Lexington Books, 2010, p. 289.

18. Ibid., pp. 55–60.

19. Ibid., pp. 114–115.

20. Ibid., pp. 135–137.

21. Ibid., p. 43.

22. The East German trials can be found in English translations in DDR-Justiz und NS-Verbrechen, 14 vols, Amsterdam, University of Amsterdam Press, 2012.

23. On 26 October 1965 the West German Justice Minister presented a report to the German Bundestag which argued that the government had pursued Nazi war criminals since 1945. He mentioned that 61,761 people had been investigated, and 6,115 were convicted. The majority of these investigations had been undertaken during the period of the Allied occupation.

24. See *National Front des Demokratischen Deutschland*, Germany (East), *Staatliche Archivverwaltung Dokumentationszentrum*, Berlin, Zeit im Bild, 1965.
25. Wildt, *Uncompromising Generation*, p. 376.
26. Dams and Stolle, *The Gestapo*, p. 175.
27. For full details see Johnson, *Nazi Terror*, pp. 463–487.
28. Wachsmann, *Hitler's Prisons*, p. 344.
29. Wildt, *Uncompromising Generation*, p. 406.
30. Johnson, *Nazi Terror*, pp. 3–8.
31. *American Jewish Yearbook*, Vol. 56 (1955), p. 379.
32. Wildt, *Uncompromising Generation*, pp. 404–405.
33. In German it was known as *Zentral Stelle der Landesjustizverwaltungen zur Aufklärung Nationalsozialistischer Verbrechen*.
34. See Bundesarchiv catalogue, Records of the Central Office of the Judicial Authorities of the Federal States for the Investigation of National Socialist Crimes, for details of what is contained in the files.
35. This stipulation was progressively modified so that it could examine events that occurred inside Germany.
36. *Einführungsgesetz zum Ordungswidrigkeitengesetz*.
37. Wildt, *Uncompromising Generation*, pp. 414–416.
38. This analysis draws on the following: D. Cesarani, *Eichmann: His Life and Crimes*, London, Vintage, 2004; D. Lipstadt, *The Eichmann Trial*, New York, Random House; H. Arendt, *Eichmann in Jerusalem: A Report on the Banality of Evil*, New York, Penguin, 1963.
39. Testimony of Frau Braun at the Auschwitz Trial. Quoted in J. Kessler, 'The Boger Swing: Frau Braun and the Tiger of Auschwitz', *California Literary Review*, 26 March 2007, Callitreview.com.
40. This analysis of the Frankfurt Auschwitz Trials draws on D. Pendas, *The Frankfurt Auschwitz Trial*, 1963–1965, Cambridge, UK, Cambridge University Press, 2010.
41. Interrogation Transcript of Otto Bovensiepen, 20 August 1945. Quoted in: Cornell University online archive: http://ebooks.library.cornell.
42. The transcript of the trial of Bovensiepen can be found in Yad Vashem online archive, File number 58/3756400.
43. For a detailed examination of Best's life see U. Herbert, *Best*, Bonn, 1996.
44. Dams and Stolle, *The Gestapo*, pp. 170–171.

Glossary of German Terms and Organisations

Abitur The school-leaving certificate which was required for university entrance.

Asocial A person classed as anti-social and racially inferior.

Bekennende Kirche The Confessing Church. A group of Protestant pastors who defended Lutheran principles.

Führer Leader.

Gauleiter Regional Nazi leader.

Gestapo Secret state police.

Gestapa The administrative office that underpinned the activities of the Gestapo.

Jude Jew.

KPD German Communist Party.

Kripo The criminal detective branch of the criminal police force.

Luftwaffe Air Force.

NSDAP Nazi Party.

Orpo Uniformed ordinary German police force.

Reichskristallnacht Night of the Broken Glass (9–10 November 1938). The night of a major attack on the Jewish community inside Germany.

Reichstag German Parliament.

RSHA The Reich Security Main Office (established 1939) (*Reichssicherheitshauptamt*).

SA Nazi storm troopers (*Sturmabteilung*).

Schutzhaft Protective custody. This was a regulation that allowed the Gestapo to arrest people and hold them in prison or a concentration camp without trial.

SD The intelligence wing of the SS (*Sicherheitsdienst*).

Sipo The Department that controlled the Gestapo and Kripo between 1936 and 1939.

SPD Social Democratic Party.

Spruchkammer The special denazification courts established by the Allies during the occupation of Germany after the Second World War.

Sopade The secret reports of the exiled Social Democratic Party on German public opinion during the Nazi era.

SS (Schutzstaffel) Hitler's personal elite bodyguard. Led by Heinrich Himmler, it became the most powerful Nazi organisation within the German state.

Volksgemeinschaft The National Community. The term used to stress a kind of classless ethnic solidarity.

Volksgenossen National Comrade. Term used to describe a racially sound and loyal member of Hitler's Germany.

Wehrmacht German Army.

Sources and Bibliography

Archives

Nordrhein-Westfälisches Hauptstaatsarchiv, Düsseldorf (HStAD).
  This archive is now based in Duisburg.
RW-58 Gestapo-Personalakten (cited as RW-58 followed by case
  file number).
Avalon Project. Yale University (AP).
Online archive of the Nuremberg Trial Proceedings (cited as
  AP-IMT, followed by name and date)
Bundesarchiv Berlin (BA).
Photograph Archive.

Institut für Zeitgeschichte, Munich [IfZ]

Files on Rupert Mayer
(Material related to the prosecution of Nazi war criminals at
  the Nuremberg Trials)

Staatsarchiv Munich [SM]
Polizeidirektion München Files
Museum of Resistance, Berlin [MR]

Wiener Library, London

Eyewitness reports of Jewish persecution

Newspapers and Periodicals

Der Angriff
Der Stürmer
Jüdische Rundschau
Völkischer Beobachter

Interviews

Lord Claus Moser
Cecile Lowenthal-Hensel

Books

(The place of publication is London, UK, for all titles followed by publisher, name and year. For all other titles, the place of publication, publisher and year of publication is cited.)

Adler, H., *Der verwaltete Mensch: Studien zur Deportation der Juden aus Deutschland* (Tübingen, Mohr-Verlag, 1974).
Adorno, T. et al., *The Authoritarian Personality* (Harper, 1950).
Allen, W., *The Nazi Seizure of Power: The Experience of a Single German Town, 1922–1945* (New York, 1984).
Aly, G., *Aktion T4 1939–1945: Die 'Euthanasie'-Zentrale in der Tiergartenstrasse 4* (Berlin, Rotbuch 1989).
Aly, G., *'Final Solution': Nazi Population Policy and the Murder of the European Jews* (Arnold, 1999).
Aly, G., *Hitler's Beneficiaries: Plunder, Racial War and the Nazi Welfare State* (Henry Holt, 2007).
Aly, G., Chroust, P. and Pross, C., *Cleansing the Fatherland: Nazi Medicine and Racial Hygiene* (Baltimore, BD, Johns Hopkins University Press, 1994).
Anonymous, *The Persecution of the Catholic Church in the Third Reich: Facts and Documents* (Pelican, 2003).
Arad, Y., Krakowski, S. and Spector, S. (eds), *The Einsatzgruppen*

Reports: Selections from the Dispatches of the Nazi Death Squads (Washington, DC, US Holocaust Museum, 1990).

Arendt, H., *The Origins of Totalitarianism* (Andre Deutsch, 1951).

Arendt, H., *Eichmann in Jerusalem: A Report on the Banality of Evil* (Penguin, 1994).

Arendt, H., *Eichmann and the Holocaust* (Penguin, 2006).

Aronson, S., *The Beginnings of the German Gestapo: The Bavarian Model in* 1933 (Jerusalem, Israel Universities Press, 1970).

Ayçoberry, P., *The Social History of the Third Reich, 1933–1945* (New York, The New Press, 1999).

Bajohr, F., *'Aryanisation' in Hamburg: The Economic Exclusion of the Jews and the Confiscation of their Property in Nazi Germany* (Berghahn, 2002).

Baldwin, P. (ed.), *Reworking the Past: Hitler, the Holocaust and the Historians' Debate* (Beacon Press, 1990).

Bankier, D., *The Germans and the Final Solution: Public Opinion under Nazism* (Blackwell, 1996).

Bankier, D. (ed.), *Probing the Depths of German Anti-Semitism: German Society and the Persecution of the Jews, 1933–1941* (Berghahn, 2000).

Baranowsky, S., *The Confessing Church: Conservative Elites and the Nazi Elite* (Lewiston, NY, Edward Mellen Press, 1986).

Barkai, A., *From Boycott to Annihilation: The Economic Struggle of German Jews, 1933–1943* (Harrisburg, PA, Brandeis University Press, 1990).

Barnett, V., *For the Soul of the People: Protestant Protest against Hitler* (Oxford, Oxford University Press, 1992).

Barnett, V., *Bystanders: Conscience and Complicity during the Holocaust* (Westport, CT, Greenwood Press, 2000).

Bar-On, D., *Legacy of Silence: Encounters with Children of the Third Reich* (Cambridge, MA, Harvard University Press, 1989).

Bartov, O. (ed.), *The Holocaust: Origins, Implementation, Aftermath* (Routledge, 2000).

Bauer, Y., *The Holocaust in Historical Perspective* (Seattle, University of Washington Press, 1978).

Baumann, Z., *Modernity and the Holocaust* (Polity Press, 2000).

Baynes, N. (ed.), *The Speeches of Adolf Hitler* (Oxford, Oxford University Press, 1942).

Beck, G., *An Underground Life: Memoirs of a Gay Jew in Berlin* (Madison, WI, University of Wisconsin Press, 1999).

Beevor, A., *Berlin: The Downfall 1945* (Penguin, 2007).

Berenbaum, M. (ed.), *A Mosaic of Victims: Non-Jews Persecuted and Murdered by the Nazis* (New York, New York Press, 1992).

Bergen, D., *Twisted Cross: The German Christian Movement in the Third Reich* (Chapel Hill, NC, University of North Carolina Press, 1996).

Berkley, G., *Hitler's Gift: The Story of Theresienstadt* (Boston, Mass, Branden Publishing, 2002).

Bernadotte, Count F., *The Curtain Falls: The Last Days of the Third Reich* (New York, Knopf, 1946).

Bernstein, R., *Hannah Arendt and the Jewish Question* (Polity Press, 1996).

Berschel, H., *Bürokratie und Terror: Das Judenreferat der Gestapo Düsseldorf, 1935–1945* (Essen, Klartext Verlag, 2001).

Bessel, R., *Political Violence and the Rise of Nazism: The Stormtroopers in Eastern Germany, 1925–1934* (New Haven, CT, Yale University Press, 1984).

Bessel, R. (ed.), *Life in the Third Reich* (Oxford, Oxford University Press, 1987).

Best, W., *Die Deutsche Polizei* (Darmstadt, L.C. Wittlich Verlag, 1941).

Bielenburg, C., *The Past is Myself* (Corgi, 1984).

Biesold, H., *Eugenics and Deaf People in Nazi Germany* (Washington, DC, Gallaudet University Press, 1999).

Black, P., *Ernst Kaltenbrunner: Ideological Soldier of the Third Reich* (Princeton, NJ, Princeton University Press, 1984).

Blass, T., *The Man Who Shocked the World: The Life and Legacy of Stanley Milgram* (Oxford, Perseus Press, 2004).

Bloxham, D., *Genocide on Trial: War Crimes Trials and the Formation of Holocaust History and Memory* (Oxford, Oxford University Press, 2001).

Bluel, H., *Strength through Joy: Sex and Society in Nazi Germany* (Secker & Warburg, 1973).

Boehm, E., *We Survived: Fourteen Histories of the Hidden and Hunted of Nazi Germany* (Boulder, CO, Westview Press, 2004).

Bosworth, R., *Explaining Auschwitz and Hiroshima: History Writing and the Second World War 1945–90* (Routledge, 1993).

Bowder, G., *The Foundation of the Nazi Police State: The Formation of Sipo and S.D.* (Lexington, KY, University of Kentucky Press, 1990).

Bowder, G., *Hitler's Enforcers: The Gestapo and S.S. Security Service in the Nazi Revolution* (New York, Oxford University Press, 1996).

Bracher, K., *The German Dictatorship: The Origins, Structures, and Effects of National Socialism* (Pelican, 1973).

Bramstead, E., *Dictatorship and Political Police: The Technique of Control by Fear* (New York, Oxford University Press, 1945).

Breitman, R., *The Architect of Genocide: Himmler and the Final Solution* (Grafton, 1992).

Breyvogel, W. (ed.), *Piraten, Swings und Junge Garde: Jugendwiderstand im Nationalsozialismus* (Bonn, Dietz, 1991).

Bridenthal, R., Grossmann, A. and Kaplan, M. (eds), *When Biology Became Destiny: Women in Weimar and Nazi Germany* (New York, Monthly Review Press, 1984).

Broszat, M., *The Hitler State: The Foundation and Development of the Internal Structure of the Third Reich* (Longman, 1981).

Broszat, M. (ed.), *Kommandant in Auschwitz: Autobiographische Aufzeichnungen des Rudolf Höss* (Stuttgart, Deutche Verlags-Anstalt, 1958).

Broszat, M. et al. (eds), *Bayern in der NS-Zeit*, 6 vols (Munich, Oldenbourg, 1977–1983).

Browning, C., *Fateful Months: Essays on the Emergence of the Final Solution* (Holmes & Meier, 1985).

Browning, C., *The Path to Genocide: Essays on Launching the Final Solution* (Cambridge, Cambridge University Press, 1995).

Browning, C., *Ordinary Men: Reserve Police Battalion 101 and the Final Solution in Poland* (Penguin, 2001).

Browning, C., *The Origins of the Final Solution: The Evolution of Jewish Policy 1939–1942* (Heinemann, 2004).

Brustein, W., *Roots of Hate: Anti-Semitism in Europe before the Holocaust* (Cambridge, Cambridge University Press, 2003).

Brysac, S., *Resisting Hitler: Mildred Harnack and the Red Orchestra* (Oxford, Oxford University Press, 2000).

Bullock, A., *Hitler: A Study in Tyranny* (Penguin, 1952).

Burleigh, M., *Death and Deliverance: 'Euthanasia' in Germany 1900–1945* (Cambridge, Cambridge University Press, 1994).

Burleigh, M., *Ethics and Extermination: Reflections on Nazi Genocide* (Cambridge, Cambridge University Press, 1997).

Burleigh, M., *The Third Reich: A New History* (Macmillan, 2000).

Burleigh, M. and Wippermann, W., *The Racial State: Germany 1933–1945* (Cambridge, Cambridge University Press, 1991).

Burrin, P., *Hitler and the Jews: The Genesis of the Holocaust* (Arnold, 1994).

Burrin, P., *Nazi Anti-Semitism: From Prejudice to the Holocaust* (New York, The New Press, 2005).

Caplan, J., *Government without Administration: State and Civil Service in Weimar and Nazi Germany* (Oxford, Oxford University Press, 1989).

Cesarani, D., *Eichmann: His Life and Crimes* (Heinemann, 2004).

Cesarani, D., *Becoming Eichmann: Rethinking the Life, Crimes and Trial of a Desk Murderer* Washington, DC (Da Capo Press, 2006).

Cesarani, D. (ed.), *The Final Solution: Origins and Implementation* (Routledge, 1994).

Childers, T., *The Nazi Voter: The Social Foundations of Fascism in Germany, 1919–1933* (Chapel Hill, NC, University of North Carolina Press, 1983).

Childers, T. and Caplan, J. (eds), *Re-Evaluating the Third Reich* (Holmes and Meier, 1993).

Choumov, P., Kogon, E., Langbein, H. and Ruckerl, A. (eds),

Nazi Mass Murder: A Documentary History (New Haven, CT, Yale University Press, 1994).

Cohen, E., *Human Behaviour in the Concentration Camp* (Free Association Books, 1988).

Conway, J., *The Nazi Persecution of the Churches, 1933–1945* (New York, Basic Books, 1968).

Cornwell, J., *Hitler's Pope: The Secret History of Pius XII* (Penguin, 1999).

Cornwell, J., *Hitler's Scientists* (Viking, 2003).

Crankshaw, E., *Gestapo: Instrument of Tyranny* (Four Square, 1966).

Crew, D. (ed.), *Nazism and German Society 1933–1945* (Routledge, 1994).

Crowe, D. and Kolsti, J. (eds), *The Gypsies of Eastern Europe* (Sharpe, 1992).

Dams, C. and Stolle, M., *The Gestapo: Power and Terror in the Third Reich* (Oxford, Oxford University Press, 2014).

Dawidowicz, L., *The War against the Jews 1933–45* (Pelican, 1979).

Dawidowicz, L., *The Holocaust and the Historians* (Cambridge, Mass, Harvard University Press, 1981).

Dedencks, M., *Heydrich: The Face of Evil* (Greenhill, 2006).

Delarue, J., *The Gestapo: A History of Horror* (New York, Viking Press, 1962).

Deschner, G., *Heydrich: The Pursuit of Total Power* (Orbis, 1981).

Diels, R., *Lucifer ante portas: Es spricht der erste Chef der Gestapo* (Stuttgart, Deutsche Verlags-Anstalt, 1950).

Dunke, H., *Die KPD von 1933 bis 1945* (Cologne, Kiepenheuer & Witsch, 1972).

Dwork, D. and van Pelt, J., *Holocaust: A History* (John Murray, 2002).

Ebbinghaus, A. (ed.), *Opfer und Täterinnen: Frauenbiographien des Nationsozialismus* (Nördlingen, Delphi Politik, 1987).

Eley, G. (ed.), *The 'Goldhagen Effect': History, Memory, Nazism – Facing the German Past* (Ann Arbor, MI, University of Michigan Press, 2000).

Engelmann, B., *In Hitler's Germany: Daily Life in the Third Reich* (New York, Pantheon Books, 1986).

Evans, R.J. (ed.), *The German Underworld: Deviants and Outcasts in German History* (Oxford, Oxford University Press, 1988).

Evans, R.J., *In Defence of History* (Norton, 1999).

Evans, R.J., *Telling Lies about Hitler: The Holocaust, History and the David Irving Trial* (Verso, 2002).

Evans, R.J., *Rituals of Retribution: Capital Punishment in Germany 1600–1987* (Oxford, Oxford University Press,1996).

Evans, R.J., *The Third Reich*, 3 vols; Vol. 1: *The Coming of the Third Reich*; Vol. 2: *The Third Reich in Power*; Vol. 3: *The Third Reich* (Allen Lane, 2003–2008).

Evans, R.J., *The Third Reich in History and Memory* (Little, Brown, 2015).

Fahlbusch, M. and Haar, I. (eds), *German Scholars and Ethnic Cleansing, 1920–1945* (Berghahn, 2004).

Feldman, M. (ed.), *A Fascist Century: Essays by Roger Griffin* (Basingstoke, Palgrave Macmillan, 2008).

Fest, J., *Plotting Hitler's Death: The Story of the German Resistance* (New York, Metropolitan Books, 1996).

Finkelstein, N. and Birn, R. (eds), *A Nation on Trial: The Goldhagen Thesis and Historical Truth* (Holt and Co., 1998).

Fischer, C., *Stormtroopers: A Social, Economic and Ideological Analysis, 1929–1935* (Routledge, rev. edn, 2014).

Fischer, C. (ed.), *The Rise of National Socialism and the Working Classes in Weimar Germany* (Berghahn, 1996).

Fleming, G., *Hitler and the Final Solution* (Oxford, Oxford University Press, 1986).

Fraenkel, E., *The Dual State: A Contribution to the Theory of Dictatorship* (Clark, NJ: Lawbook Exchange, 2006 edn).

Frei, N., *National Socialist Rule in Germany* (Oxford, Blackwell, 1993).

Frei, N., *Adenauer's Germany and the Nazi Past: The Politics of Amnesty and Integration* (New York, Columbia University Press, 2002).

Friedlander, H., *The Origins of Nazi Genocide: From Euthanasia to the Final Solution* (Chapel Hill, NC, University of North Carolina Press, 1995).

Friedländer, S., *Memory, History and the Extermination of the Jews of Europe* (Bloomington, IN, Indiana University Press, 1993).

Friedländer, S., *Nazi Germany and the Jews – Volume 1: The Years of Persecution 1933–39* (HarperCollins, 1997).

Friedländer, S., *The Extermination of the Jews – Volume 2: Nazi Germany and the Jews* (HarperCollins, 2007).

Garbe, D., *Zwischen Widerstand und Martyrium: Die Zeugen Jehovahs in 'Dritten Reich'* (Munich, Oldenbourg, 1994).

Gebauer, T., *Das KPD-Dezernat der Gestapo Düsseldorf* (Hamburg, Disserta Verlag, 2011).

Gellately, R., *The Gestapo and German Society: Enforcing Racial Policy 1933–1945* (Oxford, Clarendon Press, 1990).

Gellately, R., *Backing Hitler: Consent and Coercion in Nazi Germany* (Oxford, Oxford University Press, 2001).

Gellately, R. and Fitzpatrick, S. (eds), *Accusatory Practices: Denunciations in Modern European History, 1789–1989* (Chicago, IL, University of Chicago Press, 1997).

Gellately, R. and Stolfus, N. (eds), *Social Outsiders in Nazi Germany* (Princeton, NJ, Princeton University Press, 2001).

Gerlach, W., *And the Witnesses were Silent: The Confessing Church and the Persecution of the Jews* (Lincoln, NE, University of Nebraska Press, 2000).

Gerwarth, R., *Reinhard Heydrich* (Munich, Siedler, 2011).

Gilbert, M., *Kristallnacht: Prelude to Destruction* (HarperCollins, 2006).

Gill, A., *The Journey Back from Hell: Conversations with Concentration Camp Survivors* (HarperCollins, 1989).

Glass, J., *Life Unworthy of Life: Racial Phobia and Murder in Hitler's Germany* (Basic Books, 1997).

Goldhagen, D., *Hitler's Willing Executioners: Ordinary Germans and the Holocaust* (Abacus, 1996).

Goldhagen, D., *A Moral Reckoning: The Role of the Catholic Church in the Holocaust and its Unfulfilled Duty of Repair* (Little Brown, 2002).

Gordon, S., *Hitler, Germans and the Jewish Question* (Princeton, NJ, Princeton University Press, 1984).

Graber, G., *History of the SS* (Robert Hale, 1978).

Graml, H., *Antisemitism in the Third Reich* (Oxford, Oxford University Press, 1992).

Grau, G. (ed.), *Homosexualität in der NS-Zeit: Dokumente einer Diskriminierung und Verfolgung* (Frankfurt am Main, S. Fischer Taschenbuch Verlag, 1993).

Grau, G. (ed.), *Hidden Holocaust? Gay and Lesbian Persecution in Germany 1933–45* (Continuum, 1995).

Gregor, N. (ed.), *Nazism, War and Genocide: Essays in Honour of Jeremy Noakes* (Exeter, University of Exeter Press, 2005).

Gross, L., *The Last Jews of Berlin* (Simon & Schuster, 1988).

Gross, M., *The War against Catholicism: Liberalism and the Anti-Catholic Imagination in Nineteenth-Century Germany* (Ann Arbor, Michigan, MI, University of Michigan Press, 2004).

Gruchmann, L., *Justiz im Dritten Reich* (Munich, Oldenbourg, 1988).

Grunberger, R., *A Social History of the Third Reich* (Penguin, 1971).

Gutermuth, F. and Netzbandt, A., *Die Gestapo* (Berlin, Nicolai, 2005).

Gutman, Y., Arad, Y. and Margaliot, A., *Documents on the Holocaust* (Jerusalem, Yad Vashem Publications, 1999).

Hamilton, R., *Who Voted for Hitler?* (Princeton, NJ, Princeton University Press, 1964).

Harris, W., *Tyranny on Trial: The Evidence at Nuremberg* (Dallas, TX, Southern Methodist University, 1999).

Heger, H., *The Men with the Pink Triangle: The True Life and Death Story of Homosexuals in the Nazi Death Camps* (Alyson Press, 1994).

Helmreich, E., *The German Churches under Hitler: Background, Struggle and Epilogue* (Detroit, MI, Wayne State University Press, 1979).

Henry, F., *Victims and Neighbours: A Small Town in Nazi Germany Remembered* (South Hadley, MA, Bergin & Garvey, 1984).

Herbert, U., *Best: Biographische Studien über Radikalismus, Weltanschauung und Vernunft, 1903–1989* (Bonn, Dietz, 1996).

Herbert, U., *Hitler's Foreign Workers* (Cambridge, Cambridge University Press, 1997).

Herbert, U. (ed.), *National Socialist Extermination Policies: Contemporary German Perspectives and Controversies* (Berghahn, 2000).

Herf, J., *Divided Memory: The Nazi Past in the Two Germanys* (Cambridge, MA, Harvard University Press, 1997).

Hett, B., *Burning the Reichstag: An Investigation into the Third Reich's Enduring Mystery* (Oxford, Oxford University Press, 2014).

Heydrich, L., *Leben mit einem Kriegsverbrecher* (Pfaffenhofen, Ludwig Verlag, 1976).

Hilberg, R., *The Destruction of the European Jews* (3 vols) (Holmes and Meier, 1985).

Hilberg, R., *Perpetrators, Victims, Bystanders: The Jewish Catastrophe 1933–1945* (Harper, 1992).

Hildebrand, K., *The Third Reich* (Allen & Unwin, 1984).

Höhne, H., *The Order of the Death's Head: The Story of Hitler's SS* (Penguin, 2000).

Hoffmann, P., *Stauffenberg: A Family History, 1905–1995* (Cambridge, Cambridge University Press, 1995).

Höss, R., *Death Dealer: Memoirs of the Kommandant at Auschwitz* (Washington, DC, Da Capo Press, 1992).

Housden, M., *Resistance and Conformity in the Third Reich* (Abingdon, Routledge, 1997).

IMT, *Trials of the Major War Criminals before the International Military Tribunal*, 42 vols (Washington, DC, Government Printing Press, 1947–1949).

Johannes, J., Pechel, P. and Showalter, D. (eds), *Voices from the Third Reich: An Oral History* (Washington, DC, Da Capo Press, 1994).

Johnson, E., *The Nazi Terror: The Gestapo, Jews and Ordinary Germans* (John Murray, 1999).

Johnson, E. and Reuband, K-H., *What We Knew: Terror, Mass Murder and Everyday Life in Nazi Germany* (John Murray, 2005).

Kaplan, M., *Between Dignity and Despair: Jewish Life in Nazi Germany* (Oxford, Oxford University Press, 1998).

Kater, M., *Doctors under Hitler* (Chapel Hill, NC, University of North Carolina Press, 1989).

Kater, M., *Different Drummers: Jazz in the Culture of Nazi Germany* (Oxford, Oxford University Press, 1991).

Kenrick, D. and Puxon, G., *The Destiny of Europe's Gypsies* (Basic Books, 1972).

Kershaw, I., *Popular Opinion and Political Dissent in the Third Reich: Bavaria 1933–1945* (Oxford, Oxford University Press, 1983).

Kershaw, I., *The Hitler Myth: Image and Reality in the Third Reich* (Oxford, Oxford University Press, 1987).

Kershaw, I., *Hitler – Volume 1: Hubris, 1889–1936* (Penguin, 1998).

Kershaw, I., *Hitler – Volume 2: Nemesis, 1936–1945* (Penguin, 2000).

Kershaw, I., *The Nazi Dictatorship: Problems and Perspectives of Interpretation* (4th edn, Arnold, 2000).

Kirkpatrick, C., *Women in Nazi Germany* (Jarrold Publishers, 1939).

Klee, E., *'Euthanasie' im NS-Staat: Die 'Vernichtung lebensunwerten Lebens'* (Frankfurt am Main, Fischer Taschenbuch Verlag, 1983).

Klemperer, V., *I Shall Bear Witness: The Diaries of Victor Klemperer – Volume 1: 1933–41* (Weidenfeld & Nicolson, 1998).

Klemperer, V., *To the Bitter End: The Diaries of Victor Klemperer – Volume 2: 1942–45* (Weidenfeld & Nicolson, 1999).

Koch, H., *In the Name of the Volk: Political Justice in Hitler's Germany* (I.B. Tauris, 1997).

Koehl, R., *The Black Corps: The Structure and Power Struggles of the Nazi SS* (Madison, WI, University of Wisconsin, 1983).

Kogon, E., *The Theory and Practice of Hell: The German Concentration Camps and the System Behind Them* (New York, Berkley Books, 1964).

Koonz, C., *Mothers in the Fatherland: Women, the Family and Nazi Politics* (Methuen, 1988).

Krausnick, H. and Broszat, M., *Anatomy of the SS State* (Paladin, 1973).

Lang, J. von, *Die Gestapo: Instrument des Terrors* (Hamburg, Rasch und Röhring, 1990).

Lang, J. von, and Sibyll, C. (eds), *Eichmann Interrogated: Transcripts from the Archives of the Israeli Police* (Washington, DC, Da Capo Press, 1999).

Laska, V. (ed.), *Women in the Resistance and in the Holocaust: The Voices of Eyewitnesses* (Westport, CT, Greenwood Press, 1983).

Levine, A., *The Strategic Bombing of Germany, 1940–1945* (Westport, CT, Greenwood Press, 1992).

Lewy, G., *The Catholic Church and Nazi Germany* (Washington, DC, Da Capo Press, 2000).

Lewy, G., *The Nazi Persecution of the Gypsies* (Oxford, Oxford University Press, 2000).

Lifton, R., *The Nazi Doctors: A Study of the Psychology of Evil* (Macmillan, 1986).

Lochner, P. (ed.), *The Goebbels Diaries 1942–1943* (New York, Doubleday, 1948).

Longerich, P., *Heinrich Himmler: A Life* (Oxford, Oxford University Press, 2012).

Lozowick, Y., *Hitler's Bureaucrats: The Nazi Security Police and the Banality of Evil* (Continuum, 2000).

MacDonogh, G., *Berlin: A Portrait of its History, Politics and Society* (St Martin's Press, 1999).

MacDonogh, G., *After the Reich: From the Liberation of Vienna to the Berlin Airlift* (John Murray, 2008).

Machtan, L., *The Hidden Hitler* (Oxford, Perseus Press, 2001).

Mallmann, K., *Die Gestapo im Zweiten Weltkrieg* (Darmstadt, Primus Verlag, 2000).

Mann, R., *Protest und Kontrolle im Dritten Reich: Nationalsozialistische Herrschaft im Alltag einer rheinischen Großsdadt* (Frankfurt am Main, Campus Verlag, 1987).

Marrus, M., *The Nuremberg War Crimes Trial of 1945–46: A Documentary History* (Bedford Books, 1997).

Marrus, M., *The Holocaust in History* (Key Porter, 2000).

Mason, T., *Social Policy in the Third Reich: The Working Class and the 'National Community'* (Oxford, Oxford University Press, 1993).

McDonough, F., *Hitler and the Rise of the Nazi Party* (Pearson, 2012).

McDonough, F., *Opposition and Resistance in Nazi Germany* (Cambridge, Cambridge University Press, 2001).

McDonough, F. with Cochrane, J., *The Holocaust* (Basingstoke, Palgrave Macmillan, 2008).

McDonough, F., *Sophie Scholl: The Real Story of the Woman Who Defied Hitler* (Stroud, The History Press, 2010).

McKale, D., *The Nazi Party Courts: Hitler's Management of Conflict in his Movement* (Lawrence, KS, University Press of Kansas, 1974).

Merson, A., *Communist Resistance in Nazi Germany* (Lawrence & Wishart, 1985).

Michelson, M., *City of Life, City of Death: Memories of Riga* (Boulder, CO, Colorado University Press, 2001).

Milgram, S., *Obedience to Authority: An Experimental View* (Pinter and Martin, 1995).

Moorhouse, R., *Killing Hitler: The Third Reich and Plots against the Führer* (Vintage, 2007).

Moorhouse, R., *Berlin at War: Life and Death in Hitler's Capital, 1939–1945* (Vintage, 2011).

Moorhouse, R., *The Devil's Alliance: Hitler's Pact with Stalin, 1939–1941* (The Bodley Head, 2014).

Moszkiewiez, H., *Inside the Gestapo: A Jewish Woman's Secret War* (Toronto, Macmillan, 1985).

Müller, I., *Hitler's Justice: The Courts of the Third Reich* (Cambridge, MA, Harvard University Press, 1991).

Müller-Hill, B., *Murderous Science: Elimination by Scientific Selection of Jews, Gypsies and Others in Germany 1933–45* (Oxford, Oxford University Press, 1997).

Neave, A., *Nuremberg: A Personal Record of the Trial of the Major Nazi War Criminals* (Hodder & Stoughton, 1978).

Noakes, J. and Pridham, G. (eds), *Nazism 1919–1945: A Documentary Reader*, 4 vols (Exeter, Exeter University Press, 1984–1998).

Oakshott, M. (ed.), *The Social and Political Doctrine of Contemporary Europe* (Cambridge, Cambridge University Press, 1953).

Overy, R., *Interrogations: Inside the Minds of the Nazi Elite* (Penguin, 2002).

Overy, R., *Göring: Hitler's Iron Knight* (I.B. Taurus, 2011).

Owings, A., *Frauen: German Women Recall the Third Reich* (Penguin, 1995).

Padfield, P., *Himmler: Reichsführer-SS* (New York, H. Holt, 1990).

Palmier, J.-M., *Weimar in Exile: The Anti-Fascist Emigration in Europe and America* (Verso, 2006).

Papen, F. von, *Memoirs* (New York, E.P. Dutton & Co., 1953).

Pätzold, K. and Schwartz, E., *Tagesordnung Judenmord: Die Wannsee-Konferenz am 20 Januar 1942* (Berlin, Metropol, 1992).

Paul, G. and Mallmann, K. (eds), *Die Gestapo: Mythos and Realität* (Darmstadt, Wissenschaftliche Buchgesellschaft, 1995).

Pehle, W. (ed.), *November 1938: From 'Kristallnacht' to Genocide* (Oxford, Oxford University Press, 1991).

Pendas, D., *The Frankfurt Auschwitz Trial, 1963–65: Genocide, History and the Limits of Law* (Cambridge, Cambridge University Press, 2006).

Penton, M., *Jehovah's Witnesses and the Third Reich: Sectarian Politics under Persecution* (Toronto, University of Toronto Press, 2004).

Peukert, D., *Die KPD im Widerstand: Verfolgung und Untergrundarbeit an Rhein und Ruhr, 1933–1945* (Wuppertal, Hammer, 1980).

Peukert, D., *Inside Nazi Germany: Conformity, Opposition and Racism in Everyday Life* (Batsford, 1987).

Pine, L., *Nazi Family Policy 1933–1945* (Berg, 1997).

Pine, L., *Hitler's 'National Community': Society and Culture in Nazi Germany* (Bloomsbury, 2011).

Plant, R., *The Pink Triangle: Nazi War Against Homosexuals* (Holt & Co., 1996).

Pohl, D., *Justiz in Brandenburg, 1945–1955* (Munich, Oldenbourg, 2001).

Pringle, H., *The Master Plan: Himmler's Scholars and the Holocaust* (Harper Perennial, 2006).

Proctor, R., *Racial Hygiene: Medicine under the Nazis* (Cambridge, MA, Harvard University Press, 1988).

Quinn, G., *Hidden Beneath the Thorns: Growing Up Under Nazi Rule, A Memoir of Ingeborg Tismor* (New York, iUniverse, 2009).

Reed, D., *The Burning of the Reichstag* (New York, Convici Friede, 1934).

Reynard, M. and Graffard, S. (eds), *The Jehovah's Witnesses and the Nazis: Persecution, Deportation and Murder, 1933–1945* (New York, Cooper Square Press, 2001).

Rittner, R. and Roth, J. (eds), *Different Voices: Women and the Holocaust* (New York, Paragon House, 1994).

Roseman, M., *The Villa, The Lake, The Meeting: Wannsee and the Final Solution* (Allen Lane, 2002).

Rosenhaft, E., *Beating the Fascists? The German Communists and Political Violence, 1929–1933* (Cambridge, Cambridge University Press 2008).

Roth, J. and Rittner, C. (eds), *Pope Pius XII and the Holocaust* (Continuum, 2002).

Rückerl, A., *The Investigation of Nazi Crimes, 1945–1978: A Documentation* (Hamden, CT, Archon Books, 1980).

Rürup, R. (ed.), *Topographie des Terrors: Gestapo, SS und Reichssicherheitshauptamt auf dem 'Prinz-Albrecht-Gelände': Eine Dokumentation* (Berlin, Willmuth Arenhövel Verlag, 2005).

Rüter, A. and Rüter, C. (eds), *Justiz und NS-Verbrechen: Sammlung West-deutscher Strafurteile wegen nationalsozialstischer Tötungsverbrechen*, 20 vols (Amsterdam, Amsterdam University Press, 1945–1979).

Sanford, G., *From Hitler to Ulbricht: The Communist Reconstruction of East Germany, 1945–1946* (Princeton, NJ, Princeton University Press, 1983).

Safrain, H., *Eichmann's Men* (Cambridge, Cambridge University Press, 2010).

Schellenberg, W., *The Schellenberg Memoirs* (André Deutsch, 1956).

Schleunes, K.A., *The Twisted Road to Auschwitz* (Champaign, IL, University of Illinois Press, 1970).

Schoppmann, C., *Days of Masquerade: Life Stories of Lesbians during the Third Reich* (New York, Columbia University Press, 1996).

Shirer, W., *Berlin Diary: The Journal of a Berlin Correspondent* (New York, Bonanza Books, 1941).

Shirer, W., *The Rise and Fall of the Third Reich* (Folio, 2004 edn).

Smith, H., *Last Train from Berlin: An Eye Witness Account of Germany at War* (New York, Alfred A.Knopf, 1941).

Smith, M., *Dachau: The Harrowing of Hell* (Albany, NY, State University of New York Press, 1995).

Sofsky, W., *The Order of Terror: The Concentration Camp* (Princeton, NJ, Princeton University Press, 1993).

Speer, A., *Inside the Third Reich* (Weidenfeld & Nicolson, 1970).

Stargardt, N., *Witnesses of War: Children's Lives under the Nazis* (Pimlico, 2006).

Steinacher, G., *Nazis on the Run: How Hitler's Henchmen Fled Justice* (Oxford, Oxford University Press, 2011).

Steinert, M., *Hitler's War and the German Public Mood during the Second World War* (Athens, OH, Ohio University Press, 1977).

Stollies, M., *Law under the Swastika* (Chicago, IL, Chicago University Press, 1998).

Stollies, M., *A History of Public Law in Germany 1914–45* (Oxford, Oxford University Press, 2004).

Stoltzfus, N., *Resistance of the Heart: Intermarriage and the Rosenstrasse Protest in Nazi Germany* (New York, W.W. Norton, 1996).

Stephenson, J., *Women in Nazi Society* (Croom Helm, 1975).

Stephenson, J., *Women in Nazi Germany* (Longman, 2001).

Stone, D. (ed.), *The Historiography of the Holocaust* (Basingstoke, Palgrave Macmillan, 2004).

Szanada, A., *Indirect Perpetrators: The Prosecution of Informers in Germany, 1945–1965* (Plymouth, Lexington Books, 2010).

Tarrant, V., *The Red Orchestra: The Soviet Spy Network inside Nazi Europe* (New York, Random House, 1995).

Tent, J., *Mission on the Rhine: Reeducation and Denazification in American-Occupied Germany* (Chicago, IL, Chicago University Press, 1982).

Tetens, T., *The New Germany and the Old Nazis* (Random House, 1962).

Thalmann, R. and Feinermann, E., *Crystal Night: 9–10 November 1938* (Thames & Hudson, 1974).

Theilen, F., *Edelweisspiraten* (Cologne, Emons H.J. 2003).

Tobias, F., *The Reichstag Fire* (New York, Enigma Books, 1964).

Todorov, T., *Facing the Extreme: Moral Life in the Concentration Camps* (Weidenfeld & Nicolson, 1999).

Vandana, J., *Gender and Power in the Third Reich: Female Denouncers and the Gestapo, 1933–1945* (Basingstoke, Palgrave Macmillan, 2003).

Wachsmann, N., *Hitler's Prisons: Legal Terror in Nazi Germany* (Yale University Press, 2004).

Wachsmann, N., *KL: A History of the Concentration Camps* (Little Brown, 2015).

Walton-Kerr, P., *Gestapo: The History of the German Secret Police* (Senate, 1996).

Weindling, P., *Health, Race and German Politics between National Unification and Nazism 1870–1945* (Cambridge, Cambridge University Press, 1993).

Weinreich, M., *Hitler's Professors: The Part of Scholarship in Germany's Crimes against the Jewish People* (New Haven, CT, Yale University Press, 1999).

Weitz, E., *Creating German Communism, 1890–1990: From Popular Protest to the Socialist State* (Princeton, NJ, Princeton University Press, 1997).

Whiting, C., *The Search for 'Gestapo' Müller: The Man Without a Shadow* (Barnsley, Leo Cooper, 2001).

Wildt, M., *An Uncompromising Generation: The Leadership of the Reich Security Main Office* (Madison, WI, The University of Wisconsin Press, 2009).

Articles and chapters

Abrams, L., 'Prostitutes in Imperial Germany, 1870–1918: Working Girls or Social Outcasts?' in Evans, R.J. (ed.), *The German Underworld*, pp. 189–209.

Adam, U., 'An Overall Plan for Anti-Jewish Legislation in the Third Reich', *Yad Vashem Studies*, Vol. 11 (1976), pp. 33–55.

Angress, T. and Smith, B., 'Diaries of Heinrich Himmler's Early Years', *Journal of Modern History*, Vol. 31 (1959), pp. 206–224.

Ayass, W., 'Vagrants and Beggars in Hitler's Reich', in Evans, R.J. (ed.), *The German Underworld*, pp. 210–237.

Barnett, V., 'The Role of the Churches: Compliance and Confrontation', *Dimensions*, Vol. 14 (2000), pp. 9–12.

Benedict, S., 'Nurses' Participation in the Nazi Euthanasia Programme', *Western Journal of Nursing*, Vol. 21 (1999), pp. 246–263.

Bergman, J., 'The Jehovah's Witnesses' Experience in the Nazi Concentration Camps: A History of their Conflicts with the Nazi State', *Journal of Church and State*, Vol. 38 (1996), pp. 87–113.

Best, W., '*Die Geheime Staatspolizei*', *Deutsches Recht*, Vol. 6 (1936), pp. 125–128.

Breitmann, R., 'Himmler and the "Terrible Secret" among the Executioners', *Journal of Contemporary History*, Vol. 26 (1991), pp. 431–451.

Conway, J., 'Coming to Terms with the Past: Interpreting the German Church Struggles, 1933–1990', *German History*, Vol. 16 (1998), pp. 377–396.

Czarnowski, G., 'Women's Crimes, State Crimes: Abortion in Nazi Germany', in Arnot, M. and Usborne, C. (eds), *Gender and Crime in Modern Europe* (UCL Press, 1999), pp. 238–256.

Frommer, B., 'Denunciations and Fraternisers: Gender Collaboration and Revolution in Bohemia and Moravia during World War II and After', in Wingfield, N. and Bucur, M. (eds), *Gender and War in Twentieth-Century Eastern Europe* (Indiana, IL, 2006), pp. 111–132.

Gellately, R., 'Rethinking the Nazi Terror System: A Historiographical Analysis', *German Studies Review*, Vol. 14 (1991), pp. 23–38.

Gellately, R., 'Situating the "SS-State" in a Social-Historical Context: Recent Histories of the SS, the Police and the Courts in the Third Reich', *Journal of Modern History*, Vol. 64 (1992), pp. 338–365.

Gellately, R., 'Denunciations in Twentieth-Century Germany', *Journal of Modern History*, Vol. 68 (1996), pp. 747–767.

Gellately, R., 'Denunciations and Nazi Germany: New Insights and Methodological Problems', *Historical Social Research*, Vol. 22 (1997), pp. 228–239.

Giles, G., '"The Unkindest Cut of All": Castration, Homosexuality and Nazi Justice', *Journal of Contemporary History*, Vol. 27 (1992), pp. 41–61.

Goeschel, C., 'Suicides of German Jews in the Third Reich', *German History*, Vol. 25 (2007), pp. 22–45.

Graf, C., 'The Genesis of the Gestapo', *Journal of Contemporary History*, Vol. 22 (1987), pp. 419–435.

Griech-Pollele, B., 'Image of a Churchman Resister: Bishop von Galen, the Euthanasia Project and the Sermons of Summer 1941', *Journal of Contemporary History*, Vol. 36 (2001), pp. 41–57.

Hall, C., 'An Army of Spies? The Gestapo Spy Network, 1933–1945', *Journal of Contemporary History*, Vol. 44 (2009), pp. 247–265.

Herbert, U., 'The Real Mystery in Germany: The Working Class During the Nazi Dictatorship', in Burleigh, M. (ed.), *Confronting the Nazi Past* (Collins and Brown, 1996), pp. 23–36.

Johnson, E., 'German Women and Nazi Justice: Their Role in

the Process from Denunciation to Death', *Historical Social Research*, Vol. 20 (1995), pp. 33–69.

Kater, M., 'Forbidden Fruit? Jazz in the Third Reich', *American Historical Review*, Vol. 94 (1989), pp. 11–43.

Kundras, B., 'Forbidden Company: Romantic Relationships between Germans and Foreigners, 1939–1945', in Herzog, D. (ed.), *Sexuality and German Fascism* (New York, 2005), pp. 67–94.

Lewy, G., 'Himmler and the "Racially Pure Gypsies"', *Journal of Contemporary History*, Vol. 34 (1999), pp. 201–214.

Mallmann, K. and Paul, G., 'Omniscient, Omnipotent, Omnipresent? Gestapo, Society and Resistance', in Crew, D. (ed), *Nazism and German Society* (Routledge, 1994), pp. 166–196.

Noakes, J., 'Leaders of the People? The Nazi Party and German Society', *Journal of Contemporary History*, Vol. 39 (2004), pp. 189–212.

Oosterhous, H., 'Medicine, Male Bonding and Homosexuality in Nazi Germany', *Journal of Contemporary History*, Vol. 32 (1999), pp. 187–205.

Peukert, D., 'Youth in the Third Reich', in Bessel, R. (ed.), *Life in the Third Reich* (Oxford, Oxford University Press, 1987), pp. 25–40.

Pine, L., 'Hashude: The Imprisonment of "Asocial" Families in the Third Reich', *German History*, Vol. 13 (1995), pp. 182–197.

Piper, F., 'Estimating the Number of Deportees to, and the Victims of Auschwitz-Birkenau Camp', *Yad Vashem Studies*, Vol. 21 (1991), pp. 49–103.

Reiche, E., 'From "Spontaneous" to Legal Terrorism: SA, Police and Judiciary in Nuremberg, 1933–1934', *European Studies Review*, Vol. 9 (1979), pp. 237–264.

Szobar, P., 'Telling Sexual Stories in Nazi Courts of Law: Race Defilement in Germany, 1933 to 1945', in Herzog, D. (ed.), *Sexuality and German Fascism* (Berghahn, 2004), pp. 133–163.

Time, A., 'The Ambivalent Outsider: Prostitutes, Promiscuity and VD in Nazi Berlin', in Gellately and Stolfus (eds), *Social Outsiders in Nazi Germany*, pp. 192–211.

Vandana, J., 'The "Private" becomes "Public": Wives as Denouncers in the Third Reich', *Journal of Contemporary History*, Vol. 37 (2002), pp. 419–435.

Wachsmann, N., 'From Indefinite Confinement to Extermination: Habitual Criminals and the Third Reich', in Gellately and Stolfus (eds), *Social Outsiders in Nazi Germany*, pp. 165–191.

Wachsmann, N., 'Annihilation through Labour: The Killing of State Prisoners in the Third Reich', *Journal of Modern History*, Vol. 71 (1999), pp. 624–659.

Welch, D., 'Nazi Propaganda and *Volksgemeinschaft*: Constructing a People's Community', *Journal of Contemporary History*, Vol. 39 (2004), pp. 213–238.

Weyrauch, W., 'Gestapo Informants: Facts and Theory of Undercover Operations', *Columbia Journal of Transnational Law*, Vol. 24 (1986), pp. 554–596.

List of Illustrations

Page 1
Top left: Bundesarchiv, Bild 183-K0108-0501-008
Top right: Private Collection
Bottom: Bundesarchiv, Bild 183-R97512 (1)

Page 2
Top left: Bundesarchiv, Bild 102-14367
Top right: Bundesarchiv, Bild, 183-R96954
Bottom: Bundesarchiv, Bild, 102-183-50

Page 3
Top left: Bundesarchiv, Bild 102-15282
Top right: Bundesarchiv, Bild 183-2002-0624-503
Bottom: Bundesarchiv, Bild 152-01-26

Page 4
Top: Bundesarchiv, Bild, 152-50-10
Bottom left: Bundesarchiv, Bild 194-5268-24
Bottom right: Bundesarchiv, Bild 121-0916

Page 5
Top left: Bundesarchiv, Bild, 183-B22627
Top right: Bundesarchiv, Bild 146-1991-014-09
Bottom: Bundesarchiv, Bild, 1788/ 004

Page 6
Top: Bundesarchiv, Bild 183-78612-0003
Bottom left: Bundesarchiv, Bild, R32484
Bottom right: Bundesarchiv, Bild, 183-308517

Page 7
Top: Bundesarchiv, Bild, 146-1970-083
Bottom: Bundesarchiv, Bild, 183-R986860

Page 8
Top: Landesarchiv Nordhein-Westphalen, RW 58/1959, Abb.3
Middle: Landesarchiv Nordhein-Westphalen, RW 58/288 Abb 44
Bottom: Landesarchiv Nordhein-Westphalen, RW 58/47309. Abb 4

Acknowledgements

Researching and writing this book has taken over four years of my life. I would like to thank a number of people who have helped along the way.

First and foremost I must thank my literary agent Georgina Capel. I'm really grateful for the faith she has placed in me. She pushed me to produce the detailed plan this book needed. Mark Booth at Coronet, part of Hodder & Stoughton, is one of the best editors in the publishing business. He has been a real joy to work with. His comments on the original manuscript really improved it. I would like to also thank Fiona Rose, the Editorial Assistant at Hodder, who has been a real no nonsense pleasure to work with. I'd like to thank Nick the copy editor for his eagle eye. To think my book is under the same imprint which produced all the James Bond novels, and so many other iconic books, is a great honour.

A special word of gratitude goes to Peter Bierl, who was invaluable in assisting me in researching the Gestapo files in Düsseldorf. He is also a top journalist with the *Süddeutsche Zeitung*, based in Munich. He is a very special person. I would also like to thank Christian Gropp, the archivist of the Gestapo files in Düsseldorf and Duisburg, who answered my numerous questions with charm and patience. A lovely man. The hospitality of Klaus and Magda Schlaier in hosting me in their home during research trips to Munich is greatly appreciated. Klaus had been a great help with my Sophie Scholl book and he is now a valued friend as is Magda. Little Sophie has a new uncle too. My great friend Jakob Knab has provided invaluable contacts for me throughout this project. His wife Steffi is a doctor, which means Jakob has his liver under firm control. He read the proofs too with his eagle eye. He has the greatest German contact book I've ever seen. He sure plays a mean guitar too. A giant in so many ways.

I would like to thank the History Department at Liverpool John Moores University, led by Dr Alex Miles, for providing the research funds which aided my trips to Germany and London during the course of this project. Dr Joe Yates, Director of the School of Humanities and Social Science, has been a source of constant support for my work.

I would like to thank the many students who have listened to my views on the Third Reich on my course at the university over many years.

The following have provided me with invaluable professional and personal support along the way: Dr Mike Benbough-Jackson, a great support to me, the mighty Sir Richard J. Evans, whose books inspire me, Professor John Charmley, whose work on appeasement also inspired me as did Andrew Roberts' book on Lord Halifax. I'd like to thank my friend Paul McGann, and all the amazing McGann family, including mum Clare for their support and friendship. I'm applying for honorary membership of the family. Professor Joe Moran provided me with very important advice on structure. Don Boyd provided useful advice on the development of narrative. I'd also like to thank the support of the following for providing either advice or fun evenings along the way: Dr Kate Williams, Dr Edward Harcourt, Phil Rothwell, Paul McDonough, Michael McDonough, my wonderful brother, Dr Lorie Charlesworth, Tom Webber, Stuart Maconie, Janet Suzman, Melanie Sykes, Clare Mulley, Professor Matt Feldman, Dr Emma Vickers, Dr Lucie Matthews-Jones, Professor Alan Sharp, Dr Sonny Kandola, Lord David Alton, Cat Lewis, Roger Moorhouse, Kate Haldane and Pete Wylie.

I have also enjoyed making the many new friends I have gained through my Twitter feed @FXMC1957 who tune in to my morning on this day in history tweets.

Above all, I'd like to thank my wonderful wife Ann, who has been the rock and foundation of my life ever since 1983. I love her body and soul. I'd finally like to thank my very lovely daughter Emily, to whom I've dedicated this book, and her brave husband James, and our lovely grand-daughter Martha. A new grandchild is on the way too.

Somebody up there likes me.

Index